SECOND EDITION

ESSAY DO'S AND DON'TS

A Practical Guide to Essay Writing

Lucia Engkent & Garry Engkent

OXFORD
UNIVERSITY PRESS

OXFORD
UNIVERSITY PRESS

Oxford University Press is a department of the University of Oxford.
It furthers the University's objective of excellence in research, scholarship,
and education by publishing worldwide. Oxford is a registered trade mark of
Oxford University Press in the UK and in certain other countries.

Published in Canada by
Oxford University Press
8 Sampson Mews, Suite 204,
Don Mills, Ontario M3C 0H5 Canada

www.oupcanada.com

Library and Archives Canada Cataloguing in Publication
Engkent, Lucia Pietrusiak, 1955-, author
Essay do's and don'ts : a practical guide to essay writing / Lucia
Engkent, Garry Engkent. – Second edition.

Includes index.
ISBN 978-0-19-902029-4 (softcover)

1. Essay–Authorship. 2. Report writing. 3. English language–
Rhetoric. I. Engkent, Garry, 1948-, author II. Title.

PE1408.E483 2017   808'.042   C2016-907797-7

Cover image: © iStock/frikota

Oxford University Press is committed to our environment.
This book is printed on Forest Stewardship Council® certified paper
and comes from responsible sources.

Printed and bound in the United States of America
1 2 3 4 — 20 19 18 17

Contents

ESSAY DO'S AND DON'TS

Preface

Essay Do's and Don'ts is a how-to guide to the academic essay. It is intended for students who are struggling with essay writing; therefore, it focuses on the basic skills and on areas where students generally have difficulty. It is not a text on creative writing or advanced rhetoric.

The book augments English courses where the main text is an anthology of readings or a selection of literature, especially courses for first-year college or university students.

Essay Do's and Don'ts can be used as a self-help book. The explanations are clear and concise. The points are illustrated with several examples. The answer key allows students to check their own answers to the exercises.

To make the material easily digestible and easy to find, the sections are short and have titles, and the paragraphs are kept short. Important terms and reminders are in boldface. Some of the advice appears in bulleted lists.

The essays in the book show a progression from simple to more complex forms. Chapter 2 goes over the essentials of essay structure; consequently, the essays are basic five-paragraph essays. In Chapter 3, different rhetorical styles are explored. Chapter 4 focuses on essays about literature. The next chapter, on research and documentation, contains two samples of complete, formatted research papers—one in MLA style and one in APA.

The three chapters on language use (Chapters 6–8) focus on areas where students are likely to need help. They are not meant, however, to be a comprehensive grammar of the English language. The exercises are short and are used mainly to give students examples to consider for each point.

There are three appendices. Appendix A consists of the full text of six readings: four newspaper articles and two short stories. These readings are used as the basis for Chapter 4, in which examples of paraphrasing, summarizing, and essay writing refer to these texts, as well as to other works of literature. Appendix B consists of four sample annotated essays. There are two topics—two versions of each, one of which is an unsatisfactory attempt at the essay. Appendix C is the answer key to the exercises. At the end is the glossary of grammatical and lexical terms, especially ones used in the text and ones that students are likely to need to understand.

The main changes in the second edition are the addition of two readings, assignment topics for each reading, and an expanded section on APA style.

Acknowledgements

We would like to thank the hard-working and talented staff at Oxford Canada, particularly Leah-Ann Lymer, Dave Ward, and Heather Macdougall, for their contribution to this book. Working with our colleagues and students at Seneca College and Ryerson University also helped to shape the material that went into this text.

We also wish to thank the peer reviewers, named and anonymous, whose thoughtful comments helped to shape this revised edition:

Kenneth Borris, McGill University
Jeoff Bull, Humber College
Kathryn Holland, MacEwan University
Stephen Schwartz, Seneca College
HelenJane Shawyer, Northern Lakes College
Scott J. Wilson, Luther College/University of Regina

The Basics

Writing is a skill that you develop with practice. The more you write, the easier it will get and the better your writing will become. Furthermore, reading and writing go hand in hand. While not all readers become good writers, all good writers are avid readers.

Essay writing is an art, not an exact science, and there are different kinds of essays, so you may get conflicting advice from different instructors. For example, an essay that you write for an English-assessment exam, such as the TOEFL test, will be slightly different from an essay that you write in an English-literature course. However, the essential skills remain the same: essay writing is all about organizing ideas and making points and supporting them.

This chapter introduces some basic principles that are important for your English course and your school work in general. These basics will set you on the way to developing the communication skills you need. These skills will be transferable to the workplace. For example, organizing your ideas is equally important in an essay and a business report.

Write clearly and concisely

Whether or not a piece of writing is successful depends primarily on how clear it is. If you are not communicating your ideas to your audience, your writing is not fulfilling its fundamental purpose.

Sometimes a piece of writing is clear to the writer but not to the reader. It may be that the writer has not explained the references, has not supported points with examples, has used terminology that the reader does not know, or perhaps has even misused words. Lack of clarity is harder to fix than basic grammatical mistakes or errors in structure. Sometimes the writer can recognize that the document is unclear when he or she rereads it, especially if some time has passed.

Here is an example of unclear writing by a student writing about why some people behave badly in times of crisis:

✗   As unpredictable events unfold, a person's true nature is revealed. Society follows ideas of ethics in daily human interaction. Human beings justify behaviour by logical reasoning. In early years of infancy, humans are educated to distinguish right from wrong. Human beings are products of their environment; disruption of peace will erupt survival instinct. A change within environment will cause emotional stress impairing rules of rationalizing.

While this paragraph is for the most part grammatically correct, it is unclear because some words (such as *erupt*) are misused and because the ideas are not explained and supported (for instance, the writer does not follow up on the "ideas of ethics"). Ultimately, unclear writing can be fixed only by the writer, but here is an attempt at explaining some of the same ideas more clearly:

✓ Human beings reveal their true natures in times of crisis. While people are expected to follow the rules of right and wrong that they were taught as children, these patterns of behaviour can change when the survival instinct kicks in. For example, when a boat is sinking, everyone may rush for the lifeboats, pushing aside the weak and infirm in their panic.

Note how the specific example of the lifeboat makes the point clearer in the rewritten paragraph.

A lack of clarity is frustrating for both the student and the reader. If the instructor writes "unclear" on the paper, the student often cannot understand why what he or she has written is not clear to the reader.

One part of clarity is **coherence**. The ideas should follow logically from one to the next. If a well-constructed paragraph is taken apart and the sentences mixed up, it is often possible to reassemble the paragraph like a jigsaw puzzle because each sentence has its logical place. Often the relationship between sentences is shown by transition signals (see p. 33). Note how the relationship between the following two sentences is made clear with the addition of a transition signal:

✗ Ian consulted the building code and double-checked his figures. He made a serious error in his calculations.
✓ Ian consulted the building code and double-checked his figures. Nevertheless, he made a serious error in his calculations.

Clarity is the fundamental test for every document. How serious a grammatical error is depends on how much it affects basic communication. Errors in spelling, grammar, and punctuation can be more easily forgiven if they do not lead to misunderstanding. However, they become grave errors if they confound the reader or even cause the reader to pause in momentary confusion. Note the difference in comprehensibility in these two sentences:

✗ Light rail transit can people efficiency provides that the trains do not have shared road in cars as streetcars doing. [Errors in parts of speech and verb forms make this sentence hard to understand.]
✗ Light rail transit can move peoples efficient provided that the train do not have to sharing road with cars like streetcars do. [There are minor

errors, such as singular and plural agreement, but the sentence remains relatively easy to follow.]

Both of these sentences are incorrect, but the first one is harder to follow—and therefore "more incorrect." Here is the corrected version:

✓ Light rail transit can move people efficiently provided that the trains do not have to share the road with cars as streetcars do.

To achieve clarity, you must ensure that your writing is suitable for your **audience and purpose**. You have to understand your readers to provide the information they will likely need and in words they know. For example, if you are writing a report for a manager who does not have the same technical background as you do, you would not use the **jargon** (technical language) of your field. A doctor would not tell a patient that he had a myocardial contusion, but she would use that term for bruising of the heart if she were talking to another medical professional.

Writing has different purposes. It can be for instruction, entertainment, or persuasion. The purpose determines what you say and how you say it. For instance, an account of an accident would read very differently in a comic novel, where the purpose is to entertain, than in an insurance report, where the purpose is to inform. Essay writing is different from most kinds of writing because you are not giving new information to your instructor. Instead, **the purpose of the essay is to demonstrate what you have learned, how you think, and how well you express your ideas**. For this reason, it is often necessary to include information to make your argument clear even if it is something that you think your instructor already knows.

In addition, unless you are writing an epic novel, your goal in writing should be **conciseness**. Being able to communicate ideas efficiently is a prized skill, especially in the business world. Wordiness is often the result of a weak vocabulary, unnecessary repetition, and an attempt to reach the required word count with padding. Writing concisely is a skill you develop with practice. As you edit your work, eliminate wordiness by looking for anything that can be said more succinctly. Make sure your essay sticks to the topic and you do not ramble. Wordy writing is also more likely to be unclear and frustrating to the reader.

Revise your sentences for conciseness, as in this example, which goes from 20 words to eight:

✗ A considerable number of these students who graduate need to pay the loans that they obtained during their study years.
✓ Many graduates need to pay off student loans.

Answer the question and follow instructions

English courses test your ability to communicate ideas. The primary communication is the instructor's question and your answer. If you do not answer the question that was asked, it makes the instructor doubt your ability to understand. Moreover, you do not fulfill the basic requirements of the assignment.

Always read the question several times. Look for key words.

Here are some examples:

1. In your own words, <u>describe the scene</u> the author uses at the beginning of the article. <u>Include</u> how the <u>participants felt</u>.

Describing a scene would include where it took place, the purpose of the action, the people involved, and what essentially happened. The main focus is not on the participants' feelings, but you are asked to mention them in the description of the action.

2. <u>Explain</u> the <u>role</u> of <u>setting</u> in the story.

Note that this topic does not ask you simply to describe the setting. You are asked to explain the role it plays—in other words, to show how the setting is important to the story. Setting includes the time and place that the story is set.

3. <u>Analyze</u> the <u>motivation</u> of the characters in the story.

Analysis requires you to explain why the characters do what they do and not just describe what they are doing.

Keep in mind that **the topic question is a prompt to elicit an essay**. Do not answer the question with a "yes" or "no" as if you were in conversation. Do not use the assignment question as the first sentence of your essay or paragraph. Instead, paraphrase and write your own opening statement.

As soon as you get an assignment, read the instructions carefully, highlighting important parts. Before you start doing the work, reread the instructions. If the instructions are complicated (as in a research assignment), you may want to revisit them several times. Do a final reading of the assignment directions before you finally hand in your paper to make sure you have not missed anything.

Answering the question may seem too obvious even to mention, but many students fail to get good grades simply because they were not paying attention to what was asked of them. When writing an essay, they may wander off topic and stray from the question that was asked. For instance, if the topic is on solutions for environmental problems, but most of the essay discusses the causes of these problems, the essay is unacceptable.

Follow the writing process

Essentially, writing is a three-step process: planning, drafting, and editing. These steps do not have to be distinct. Writers may go back and plan more or do editing on the fly, especially now that most writers work on computers. They are not producing separate documents, so they are more likely to go back and forth as an outline is fleshed out into a draft.

Planning involves both brainstorming and outlining. Brainstorming means coming up with ideas to include in the essay, whereas outlining involves organizing those ideas into a structure.

Drafting is the actual writing of the essay. It is a draft until the version is finalized and handed in to your instructor. You may write several drafts before you have a clean copy.

Editing is the step in which you revise and correct your essay to make it the best you can. You can eliminate repetition, reduce wordiness, and rephrase to vary wording. Most important, the editing process is where you correct your grammar, vocabulary, spelling, and punctuation. Even for in-class writing assignments, you should take the time to proofread your writing in order to fix your mistakes.

Have something to say

Content and ideas are a vital part of a good essay. Some students think they can bluff their way through an essay, but when they lack the background knowledge, they tend to repeat themselves, make gross generalizations, and wander off topic.

Choose a topic that you are comfortable with and know something about. Usually, your instructor will present you with a list of topics, based on the course readings, to choose from. You will generally have a chance to narrow the topic down and focus it on an area that is more interesting to you.

Brainstorming ideas will help you come up with enough material for your essay. Look at the topic from different angles. For instance, if you are asked to write about the disadvantages or advantages of something, brainstorm on both sides, because coming up with a disadvantage will often help you think of a corresponding advantage. Moreover, you can write about whichever side you have the better ideas for, and you can mention some of the counter-arguments in your essay (see "Opposing arguments" on page 67).

Here is an example of point-form brainstorming:

Table 1.1 What are the advantages or disadvantages of a traditional, strict style of parenting?

Advantages	Disadvantages
• children are more likely to succeed • children develop discipline • involvement of parents means love • sense of security • children know exactly where they stand and what is expected of them • togetherness	• children cannot develop at their own pace • children do not learn to make their own decisions or explore on their own • resentment in children at the time and later • children do not learn from mistakes • can foster rebellion, acting out

With these points, the writer can move forward, choose one side, and draft an essay outline. You can read more about brainstorming in Chapter 2 and see examples in the preliminary notes for both the MLA and the APA essays in Chapter 5.

Make your point and support it

Essay writing is all about making points and supporting them. Students often neglect to give sufficient explanation or clear examples. Sometimes they just repeat an idea and think this is sufficient support.

Here is an example of a paragraph where the student writer repeated his two ideas but did not support them:

> ✗   The most difficult technology to live without today is the cellphone. It has changed the way people communicate. Nowadays people cannot live without a cellphone if they want to be part of this society. The cellphone is the best invention of modern life. Because of the convenience of the mobile phone, people communicate differently. As a result, modern people cannot live without a cellphone. It plays an important role in our lives and brings us many benefits.

This paragraph would be improved if the student explained *why* people cannot live without cellphones and *how* they have changed communication. To prove how indispensable cellphones are, the writer could have mentioned specific uses for the cell that go beyond simple phone calls, such as information storage, GPS functions, and the ability to pay for goods and services. For the change in communication, the student could have talked about text messaging as the new form of conversation—even people in the same building exchange texts, and teenagers send an average of 60 messages a day.

The importance of supporting points is explored further in the discussion of body paragraph structure (beginning on p. 28).

Recognize the difference between spoken and written English

Spoken and written English are two different versions of the language. Everyday speech draws from a narrower range of vocabulary and uses shorter, less sophisticated sentences. To participate in casual conversation, a person needs only about two thousand words, but to read the newspaper and to write at a post-secondary education level, he or she needs a vocabulary ten times that size. For example, words like *plan* and *money* are more likely to appear in everyday speech than words like *schedule* and *currency*. (If you are interested in learning about word frequency, you can easily find lists such as the 2,000 most common English words and the "Academic Word List" on the Internet.)

Writers have to be more focused on clarity than speakers do. A speaker knows immediately whether the audience understands. If the listeners look puzzled or ask questions, a speaker can rephrase what he said. Moreover, a speaker can use tone of voice and gestures to get his meaning across. He also can take advantage of his physical surroundings, by pointing to objects, for instance. A writer, on the other hand, does not have these advantages. She must make her writing very clear; she cannot follow her documents around to make sure all the readers understand what is being said. She cannot refer to something as a "thingamajig"; she must use precise vocabulary. She must try to understand the needs of her audience. Written language demands more of the person communicating the message. On the other hand, writers can reflect on what they want to say and take the time to craft their document.

Use appropriate style

As a general rule, conversational English is not acceptable in essays. Sometimes you will be called upon to write a personal composition where your style can be more casual, but most essays have to be in academic style. (Although the word *academic* can also be used to refer to lofty, scholarly pursuits and abstract studies, the term can simply describe the style expected for university and college essays.)

Just as our style of dress has become more casual over the last few decades, our style of language is less formal, too. Business letters written in the 1950s had such formal phrases as "Yours of recent date received, and in reply to same . . ." and "I remain respectfully yours." Newspaper writing has also changed: columns today are often conversational. Likewise, the instructions in this textbook are less formal than the sample essays. You may be more comfortable with conversational language, but just as you are expected to wear a business suit and not blue jeans to a job interview, you are expected to be able to use more formal language when it is called for. We ask students to write in academic style precisely because they can write easily in conversational style. Writing more formally is a skill they need to develop in a college or university writing course.

Here is an example of conversational style, followed by the same ideas expressed in a more formal way:

> People today are, like, so rude. It's all those gadgets. People don't talk to each other, you know. They are too busy gabbing on the phone or texting and stuff. Like, yesterday, this guy just stops in the middle of the hall, and I bump right into him.

> Technological advancements in communication have led to a lack of civility in contemporary society. Instead of engaging with others face to face, people are so absorbed by their cellphones that they are not even aware of other people right next to them.

Note that academic style is impersonal. Even though you are expressing your opinions and talking about your experiences, you use general rather than personal statements. Moreover, you don't have to say "I think" or "in my opinion" in an essay, because what you are writing is clearly your opinion unless you state otherwise with statements such as "many people think" or "the author states."

To write in academic style:
- Don't use conversational expressions (such as "well, let's see now" and "right?").
- Avoid using *you* and *I*; use third person (*he, she, it, they*) instead.
- Limit your use of contractions (such as "don't").
- Don't use conversational reductions (such as "wanna" and "coulda").
- Don't use slang (such as "it sucks" and "ten bucks").
- Avoid vague and imprecise vocabulary (such as "things" and "stuff").
- Avoid starting sentences with coordinate conjunctions (*and, or, but, yet, so*).
- Use transition signals (such as "moreover" and "for example").
- Limit the use of questions (which can give a more conversational feel to the writing).

A note about you

In English, the word *you* can refer to both the audience (as in you, the reader of this book) and people in general (as in "you can climb Mount Everest more easily today"). This can sometimes be confusing, especially if *you* doesn't always refer to the same person and if the writer switches pronouns from *they* to *you*, as in this example:

✗   When those children grow up, they will be very surprised to see that life is hard, and you have to do things for yourself. If you don't baby your child, they will grow up to be adults who can think for themselves. [The first *you* refers to the children and the second one refers to the parents.]

Avoid using *you* in essays. It is conversational, rather than academic, and the meaning can be confusing.

Exercise 1.1 Conversational to academic English

Rewrite the following passages from conversational English to impersonal, academic style, correcting pronoun usage.

Example:
Conversational English: I get really bummed out when my prof asks me to put my cellphone away. Like, I can't live without it. It's got everything on it. And what if there's an emergency?

Rewritten in academic English: Students become anxious if they are asked to put their cellphones away during class. They depend on their phone and worry if someone cannot reach them.

1. College is better than university if you wanna learn practical stuff to get a job. If you're gonna be a chef, go to community college. And another thing is you can learn trades which pay way better than most jobs.
2. Even though professors tell us that attendance is the key to success, there's lots of reasons why students skip classes. Classes can be so boring especially if we've read or heard the stuff before. And some professors are so boring. And if there is a class at 8 a.m., or before a long weekend, or it's the only class on your schedule for the day—forget about it. We have better things to do.
3. Nowadays kids don't know any playground games like their parents played. Like, they don't know skipping chants and the chants are traditions that have been around forever. And so it's like we're losing something from our history and culture.

Read

The key to becoming a better writer is to read. Spoken language is different from written language. Reading is the best way to learn the conventions of the written form, that is, the words, structures, style, and tone that writers use. Moreover, reading more will help you build your vocabulary. Finally, the information and ideas in what you read will help you with your writing topics. With the general knowledge you will acquire, you won't be at a loss when you face your writing topic.

The more you read, the easier reading will become. Your comprehension and speed will increase.

Here are some general guidelines:

- Read a variety of materials—the newspaper, novels, your textbooks.
- Read at a level that is challenging to you but not so difficult that you are struggling to understand.
- Choose subjects that you are interested in. Expand into other areas as well.
- Pay attention to the language as you read—look for new words and expressions.
- Try keeping a reading journal, jotting down new words, ideas, and your thoughts about what you have read.

Where possible, practise using the words you have learned or the knowledge you have acquired so that you will remember it and become familiar with it.

Think critically

In addition to good communication skills, students are required to develop the ability to think critically—to evaluate, see relationships between ideas, and organize their thoughts.

Critical thinking includes

- recognizing the thesis in a non-fiction article
- understanding the relationship between main and supporting ideas
- organizing your essay structure so that ideas work together logically
- distinguishing general from specific statements
- evaluating what you read to determine the validity of the arguments
- appreciating other points of view
- recognizing themes and the use of symbols and figurative language

To develop your ability to think deeply, you must always ask the questions "why?" and "how?" In finding the answers, you may need to

- draw on previous knowledge (what you have read or learned from others)
- use personal experience (what you have seen and done)
- observe how others think or solve problems
- "talk" the problem or idea through by yourself or with fellow students
- spend more time researching a topic
- focus on the task at hand

In short, you develop a sense of curiosity and a desire to satisfy the urge. This piece of advice may sound as clichéd as "think outside the box" or "push the envelope," but such sayings do have a grain of truth. Everything begins with the willingness to do the work required—and to keep at it.

You will practise critical thinking in your coursework, especially as you discuss your readings with your instructor and classmates. It is important to have read the assigned articles or short stories before class—and not just a quick read five minutes before class begins. Give yourself enough time to read the article or story more than once, to look up words and references you do not understand, and to prepare questions and comments for the class discussion. Engage in the discussion; do not just sit back and listen. Active participation leads to better learning.

Each of the reading selections in Appendix A is followed by questions designed to get you thinking about what the author says and then relate it to broader questions on your own experience. For instance, after "We Should All Worry about Cellphone Searches," the discussion can start with basic questions such as "Do you agree with Kowalski's arguments?" and then go to broader implications for public privacy and safety. Answering these questions requires critical thinking.

Practise writing

With writing, as with any skill, practice is the key to success. The more you write, the easier it becomes.

Take advantage of any opportunity you get to practise writing essays. Some instructors will allow you to submit practice essays or rewrites. You can also write essays on your own. Try timed pieces for test essay questions, such as TOEFL topics, which you can search online. Even if you do not get these essays marked or graded, practising will make you more confident and skilled.

A common problem that writers face—even experienced writers—is **writer's block**. Sometimes you may stare at the blank screen or page and feel paralyzed. The more you know about your topic, the writing process, and standard essay requirements, the easier it will become to actually write your essay. One way to get your writing unstuck is to go to an easier section of the essay. For instance, you do not have to write the introduction of the essay first; you can write the body paragraphs and then come back to craft the introduction.

An exercise that can help you if you are having trouble committing your ideas to paper (or screen) is **journal writing**. You can write a journal for yourself without the pressure of knowing that someone else will read it (unless, of course, you are asked to do journal entries as part of your writing course). Writing is also cathartic—you can express your feelings about your boss or neighbour with impunity. Spending a few minutes at the end of a day recording your thoughts is also a good way to unwind for sleep. You can write about what you have experienced or read that day. Some people write their journal on a computer, while others prefer the tactile pleasure of pen and paper, perhaps in a beautiful notebook. Writing by hand fires up different parts of the brain than typing, so it is worthwhile to not do all your writing electronically.

Know your strengths and weaknesses

To improve as a writer, you have to know what you need to work on. When you get an assignment back, go over the instructor's corrections and comments. Instructors usually explain their marking system and give you a guide to the abbreviations they use. You can refer to your textbook and online resources to find explanations of some grammatical faults such as "run-on sentence" and "incorrect subject–verb agreement." Look up the misspelled words in the dictionary. If you do not understand something in the comments, ask your instructor for clarification.

Knowing what you are good at will let you concentrate on the areas that need improvement. Make a list of writing mistakes you make and consult this list before handing in an assignment. Check to see if you have made any of these errors. For example, if you mix up *their*, *there*, and *they're*, check each instance of these words to make sure you have used the correct one.

Learn from your mistakes. Consider them learning opportunities.

Edit and correct your work

Knowing your weaknesses is not enough. You have to apply this knowledge and take the time to edit and correct your work. Correcting involves fixing mistakes, but editing is on a larger scale. When you edit, you find ways to reword something, you may delete unnecessary words and sentences, and you may move entire sections around to find the best way to organize your ideas.

Students are often reluctant to make major changes to what they have written and may only make minor corrections. However, all writers need to be ruthless with their work. Even if they have spent an hour writing a single paragraph, they have to be prepared to delete it if it just doesn't work in their document.

In order to correct your writing, it is useful to understand the different types of errors. Some are careless slips or typographical errors—these can usually be corrected easily with careful proofreading. You can look out for common grammatical errors and punctuation mistakes; these are explained in Chapters 7 and 8. The feedback you get on your written assignments should help you identify which errors you tend to make. Some of these errors get fossilized, however. That means that they become a habit. If someone points out a fossilized error, you should be able to correct it easily. You understand the rule, but you keep making the same mistake. Like all habits, making fossilized errors is not easy to overcome. You have to be determined and work at eliminating these mistakes from your writing. Try concentrating on one at a time.

Students who speak English as a second language (ESL students) often make language interference errors where they apply rules and word meanings from their native language to English. Usually, they have learned where they should be careful, such as article use. Translation of vocabulary can be trickier because writers have to consider both meaning and usage. Two words can seem like synonyms but be used in totally different ways.

Catching errors before you hand in your work requires careful proofreading. For in-class assignments, you may only have a few minutes to read over your work. It helps if you have a mental checklist of the mistakes you tend to make. You may have several weeks to complete some writing assignments. If you have the time, use it wisely. It is best not to leave the work for the last minute. If you do it early, you can revisit it with fresh eyes to make corrections and revisions.

Use resources wisely

In order to effectively correct your writing errors, you need to use the tools and resources that are available. Use the **spelling and grammar checker** built in to your word-processing program when you have finished writing your work. But do not automatically accept the suggested changes; check them in the dictionary if you are not sure. In addition, do not assume that because a document passed a spell-check on the computer, it is perfect. The spell-check will tell you if a word is misspelled, but it won't tell you if you've used the right word. Proofread carefully.

Use a **dictionary** and **thesaurus** (a dictionary of synonyms and sometimes antonyms) to check your words and improve your vocabulary power. Use your dictionary judiciously, especially during timed writing assignments. Do not interrupt your creative flow while you are writing—just guess at the spelling and use the words you want to use, even if you are not sure of the spelling. When you finish your draft, you can check the words in your dictionary.

Some schools allow students to use print dictionaries (not electronic) for in-class writing tests and exams. If this is the case in your school, you should practise to get comfortable using a print dictionary so that you can use it effectively, especially if you are accustomed to using only electronic devices for looking up words.

Take advantage of your school's **tutorial services**, such as a writing centre. Although the tutors are not there to proofread or edit your work, they can point you to areas that need improvement.

Consult **usage guides** and **grammar books**. This textbook is just one brief guide to the basics of essay writing; hundreds of other books have been written on the subject. If you need more information, or even a different viewpoint, consult a usage guide such as *The Concise Canadian Writer's Handbook* or a grammar book such as *The Oxford Practice Grammar*.

The **Internet** is also a source of information about grammar and essay writing. Be careful with these resources, however, since, unlike books, most websites are not vetted by editors. Look for the resources posted by your school or links suggested by your instructor.

Communicate with your instructor

Establishing a good rapport with your instructor not only helps you improve as a writer, but also gives the instructor a sense of your ability and the effort you are putting into the course. Participate in class by asking and answering questions. Active learners retain more than passive learners, who just sit there and listen. (For this same reason, you should take notes during class.) Make use of your instructor's office hours to ask about anything you are unsure of. On the other hand, do not expect your instructor to correct your writing problems for you—you need to put in the effort to improve.

Send effective email messages

If you are sending an email to your instructor, be sure to use correct standard English. Here are some guidelines for writing a good email message:

1. Use a subject heading that says what the email message is about. For example, "Summary Assignment question" is a good subject heading; "Hi! It's me, Marwan" is not.
2. Write from a professional email address—preferably a school address that identifies you by name. Something like "sexyguy@hotmail.com" is not an appropriate email address.

3. Use standard written English. Capitalize correctly. Do not use the short forms common to text messaging, such as "U R" instead of "you are."
4. Be clear and concise. State precisely what you want or need. Keep explanations to a minimum. If the recipient needs more information, he or she will ask for it.

Becoming a better writer

- Read attentively and widely. All good writers are readers. As you read, you develop your vocabulary, gain background knowledge, and learn the conventions and forms of standard written English.
- Make sure you understand the demands of the writing task. Whether you are writing an essay assignment or a cover letter for a job, consider the audience and the purpose.
- Strive for clarity. Remember that writing, above all, is communication. Make your message clear to the reader.
- Always check your work for errors. You can catch many of your mistakes if you proofread diligently.
- Learn from your mistakes. Use the feedback from your writing to improve.
- Use tools such as dictionaries, spell checkers, and writing guides.
- Take full advantage of the opportunities afforded in your English course—attend class, do your homework, participate, and ask questions.
- Practise. Writing is a skill that you develop through practice.

Essay Structure

Structure is a very important part of the discipline of essay writing. You need to organize your ideas and develop them in the prescribed format. Academic essays are basically formulaic. If you follow the formula, you will write a stronger essay. Not all essays follow the academic structure, but using it will guide you as you hone your writing skills.

Like most formal documents, academic essays have three parts: an introduction, a body, and a conclusion. Sometimes this is described as a hamburger essay—the introduction and conclusion are the bun holding the meat of the essay (the body) together; this analogy can help you understand the importance of the body paragraphs. Generally, students work on five-paragraph essays when they are learning to write essays. These can easily be expanded with more body paragraphs.

Although some people find the five-paragraph essay restrictive, we find that it is a good learning tool. Beginner writers benefit from following a defined structure. Moreover, the structure is flexible enough to be adapted to other forms of writing. For instance, business reports also have introductions, body paragraphs where individual ideas are explained, and conclusions to summarize and wrap up. In a cover letter for a job application, ideas may be organized just as they would be in an essay with three body paragraphs to explain education, work experience, and skills.

Working with essay structure teaches you

- how to introduce and conclude a topic
- how to focus on one main argument (the thesis)
- how to divide your argument into supporting arguments (for each body paragraph)
- how to support arguments with examples and explanation

Generally, for a 500-word essay, you follow this breakdown:

- introduction: 50–75 words
- each body paragraph: 100–125 words
- conclusion: 40–60 words

For longer pieces, such as the 750- or 1,000-word paper, you increase the number of words proportionately for each supporting paragraph or add body paragraphs or both. Longer reports and essays may require more than one paragraph to introduce the topic and more than one paragraph as a conclusion.

The writing process consists of three stages—**planning**, **drafting**, and **editing**—but these may not be distinct stages. For example, writers may start revising before they finish their first draft, and they may adjust their plan in mid-project if they need to make adjustments. Working on a computer makes it easier to slide between the different stages as the essay evolves into its final form. The writer may also write the sections of an essay in any order. For instance, many essay writers feel that it is easier to draft the body of the essay before tackling the introduction.

This chapter follows the basic process of essay writing, but you can go to whichever sections you need. Planning includes choosing a topic, brainstorming, organizing ideas, and writing an outline and thesis statement. The drafting section follows the order of the essay: title, introduction, body, and conclusion. For editing, which includes major revisions and minor corrections, we have given you a handy essay checklist at the end of this chapter.

Choose your topic wisely

Generally, students are given a choice of topics related to readings that have been studied in class. Sometimes students are allowed to develop their own topic, usually in consultation with their instructor.

Make sure you understand the topic and what it demands of you. Ensure you have the background knowledge to do justice to the essay. Remember that you will spend a lot of time on the topic, so choose one you like and are comfortable with. If you are writing on a piece of literature, be prepared to study the work in depth to understand it thoroughly before writing about it.

Read the question very carefully—several times. Look for key words such as *compare*, *define*, *explain*, and *describe* in a command statement. If the topic question has more than one part, make sure you fulfill all the requirements of the assignment. Some essay topics begin with a general statement to start you thinking, and then ask you a question or make a command. Here are some examples of typical topics:

We have more ways to contact one another than ever before, yet many of us are choosing to live more insular lives. Agree or disagree with this statement, and discuss.

In "We All Should Worry about Cellphone Searches," William Kowalski makes the argument that the violation of civil rights by the police on cellphone searches is a slippery slope for citizens in losing their privacy. How can you protect yourself from further loss of liberty in a democratic country like Canada?

In "The Cask of Amontillado," Montresor has gotten away with the murder of Fortunato—a 50-year-old crime that Montresor is confessing to on his deathbed. In "The Moose and the Sparrow," Cecil most probably killed Maddon. Compare the two crimes.

Note that the first topic is based on a general observation, while the other two use readings in Appendix A as a point of departure. Sometimes an instructor gives topics based on readings or discussions you have had in class. You can see examples of reading-based topics after each selection in Appendix A. For these topics, the focus should be on your opinions and ideas; the instructor does not want a repetition of what the authors said.

Brainstorm to gather your ideas

Brainstorming is essentially thinking about the topic to collect your ideas together. It is a necessary preparatory function in all writing situations. Students who skip this step may wander off topic or run out of things to say. They may end up with shrinking paragraphs—a long introduction, followed by progressively shorter paragraphs and a practically non-existent conclusion. Even if you only have a short time for an in-class writing assignment, it is worth spending a few minutes brainstorming. Generating ideas and planning out your essay will save you time in the long run and will result in a stronger essay.

Brainstorming requires you to write down your thoughts on the topic. Otherwise, you may forget some of the points you want to make. Moreover, seeing the actual words in front of you helps you organize your ideas. When you brainstorm, you don't have to worry about sentence structure or proper style—you just want to get some ideas down. It is better to start with more points than you actually need for the essay so that you can pick what works best.

There are different brainstorming techniques. The method we usually recommend is simply jotting down **point-form notes**, as in this example:

Topic question: What role should parents play in helping their children in post-secondary education?

For this topic, the essay writer could start by thinking what parents could do and what some already do.

Brainstorming: What can parents do?

- help them with their application
- help them choose a college or university and a program
- pay their tuition
- pay their living expenses
- arrange accommodations

- help with registration problems
- make sure they are doing their work and getting good marks
- make sure they are healthy and happy
- confer with instructors and professors

At this point it is easier for the essay writer to go through the list and decide what he or she actually thinks parents should do.

Note that you do not have to use every idea that comes up in your brainstorming. After you have some ideas, examine your list and see what ideas can be grouped together in each body paragraph. If one idea is an outlier and does not fit your plan, leave it out. An essay does not have to include every argument for that topic.

If you have a topic where you are asked to choose one point of view, it is a good idea to brainstorm on both and then pick the one that you think will make for the more successful essay. Here is an example of point-form brainstorming on the topic of fame:

Table 2.1 What are the advantages or disadvantages of fame?

Advantages	Disadvantages
• instant recognition	• no privacy
• get special treatment and perks	• can experience public humiliation
• lots of attention	• can't be yourself
• sense of achievement	• get conceited and full of yourself
• feel special	• can't enjoy simple pleasures of life
	• paparazzi are very intrusive
	• people will think they know you
	• misrepresentation in the press
	• you get addicted to fame

Another example of brainstorming on both sides can be found in Chapter 1, on page 5, and for the sample APA essay (p. 136).

Asking questions about the topic can also work well as a brainstorming strategy:

Topic question: What do you think is the best way to handle the problem of plastic shopping bags?

- What is the problem? The bags are found everywhere—filling up garbage and as a source of litter.
- What about paper bags? Not as practical for some purposes, still take resources to produce.
- How much of a garbage problem are the bags? They make up a small amount of landfill.

- What about biodegradable bags? They get mixed in with regular plastic and cause messes when they break down. They pollute the recycling stream.
- How can plastic shopping bags be recycled? They can be reused for garbage and picking up dog poop—better than buying one-use bags for the purpose. They can also be recycled as part of a blue box program and made into other products
- What about charging for plastic shopping bags? It makes people use fewer bags and think more about reusing them.
- What about reusable shopping bags? They can cut down on the amount of plastic used, but people need to be careful to keep them relatively clean.
- What about banning plastic shopping bags? Banning something is not a good solution because the bags are useful. Instead, people can be encouraged to use fewer bags and to recycle them.

Some people, especially those who prefer visual representations, use **bubble diagrams** showing the relationship between ideas (see Figure 2.1).

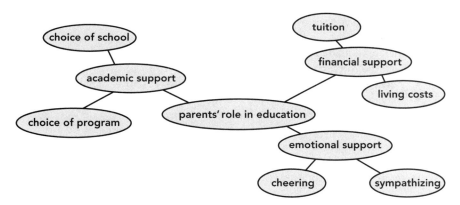

Figure 2.1 Sample Bubble Diagram

Some people like **free writing**—writing whatever comes to mind about the topic and then examining what they've written for usable ideas. We do not generally recommend free writing to our students because it is time-consuming for in-class writing and examinations. Moreover, students can find it difficult to identify workable ideas in their output. It can, however, help solve the problem of writer's block because it enables the essay writer to get some words down without worrying about the form they are in.

Although we generally recommend point-form brainstorming, if you have had success with any of these other methods, continue with whatever works for you.

Organize your ideas into body paragraphs

One of the hardest jobs in essay writing is figuring out what to say in each of the body paragraphs. Sometimes body paragraphs get weaker as the essay progresses and the writer runs out of ideas. Brainstorming and organizing the arguments before writing help to eliminate this problem. The points from your brainstorming can be arranged into body paragraphs according to the ideas that go together.

Here is an example of point-form brainstorming:

Explain the causes of failure in college or university.

Unsuccessful students

- lack basic literacy skills
- may not be truly interested in what they are studying
- lack defined goals
- lack financial support
- do not have the required background knowledge (math, science, whatever they need in their program)
- lack time management skills
- lack the required work ethic
- need to work to make money and thus have less time for school
- may not be comfortable with the teaching/learning styles
- do not have sufficient educational support
- have problems coping with work and family responsibilities
- get distracted socializing

Here are the same points, grouped together:

- lack basic literacy skills
- do not have the required background knowledge (math, science, whatever they need in their program)
- do not have sufficient educational support
- may not be comfortable with the teaching/learning styles

- may not be truly interested in what they are studying
- lack defined goals
- lack the required work ethic

- lack time management skills
- have problems coping with work and family responsibilities
- get distracted socializing

- lack financial support
- need to work to make money and thus have less time for school

With that grouping, you could write a thesis such as this:

> Students struggle in college if they do not have sufficient academic support, if they lack the motivation to do the work required, and if they cannot meet the other demands in their life.

Note that the idea of financial support has been left out. You do not have to use all the ideas of your brainstorming in your essay (in fact, it is better to start with more ideas than you need). Furthermore, you should not feel that your essay has to cover the whole topic. The idea of money could be included in the third body paragraph about balance because many students have to balance jobs and school because they need the money.

Each of your body paragraphs should give a main argument. **Avoid organizing your essay by example or situation.** For instance, in an essay on why people get tattoos, one paragraph could be about artistic pursuits, one about symbolic values, and one about social statements. Yet one student, at a loss as to how to handle this topic, wrote one paragraph about why children get tattoos, one about adolescents, and one about adults. Not only is this weak argumentation (children don't generally get tattoos), but it would have overlap—the same arguments would appear in different paragraphs.

Write an outline

An outline is a plan of the essay. It should contain a draft of the thesis statement, the main idea of each body paragraph, and point-form notes of the supporting points in each body paragraph. Once you have an idea of what you want to say in your thesis and what you want to cover in each body paragraph, you can formalize this in outline form.

Thesis: Parents should provide support for post-secondary students.

1. academic support, helping them choose school and program
   - parents know their children's talents and interests
   - parents have experience in and knowledge of work world
   - parents have more knowledge about schools

2. financial support
   - college or university is too expensive for students to handle on their own
   - parents usually support adult children in our society
   - students who have fewer money problems are less likely to fail
   - it can be an investment for the whole family

3. emotional support
   - children are used to getting support and encouragement from their parents
   - college and university is very hard and students need support to be successful

Thesis: Being famous can be a burden.

1. Celebrities experience a loss of privacy.
   - paparazzi and fanatics bothering them
   - inaccurate media representations of their life

2. Celebrities become different people.
   - start believing in the hype
   - change in personality
   - become conceited

3. Fame becomes an addiction.
   - become needy and want more spotlight
   - do things to keep being noticed
   - highs and lows, just like a drug

While outlines are usually in point form, it is sometimes helpful to draft the thesis statement and perhaps even the topic sentences for the outline. This makes it easier for the reader or evaluator to determine what shape your essay is taking.

Often instructors ask you to submit an outline before you write your essay. This allows them to see if you are on the right track and to give you feedback before you actually write your essay. Your instructor may require a specific format for the outline. If so, be sure to follow that format instead of the general format shown in the samples above. Some instructors give students charts or question sheets to fill out for their outline.

You can see other samples of essay outlines in Chapter 5 (p. 127 and p. 138).

Write an effective thesis statement

The thesis statement is the most important sentence of your essay. It answers the topic question and states your point of view. It should be a single sentence at the end of the introduction.

In a five-paragraph essay, the thesis often shows the organization of the essay by giving the main idea of each of the three body paragraphs. This type of detailed three-pronged thesis, however, does not work as well for longer essays because if you include the main point of each body paragraph, the thesis statement would become long and unwieldy.

Make sure your thesis statement answers the topic question or fulfills the task you have been set for your essay. Here are examples of topics and corresponding thesis statements:

What role should parents play when their children become college or university students?

- ✓ Although they must let their children live their own lives, parents can play a role in helping their children through post-secondary education. [General thesis.]
- ✓ When their children are in post-secondary school, parents can give academic, financial, and emotional support. [Detailed thesis.]
- ✗ Many parents have trouble letting go of their children when they go off to college or university. [Does not answer the question.]
- ✗ Students should let their parents help. [Incorrectly puts the focus on the students instead of the parents.]

What are the advantages or disadvantages of being famous?

- ✓ Celebrities have to deal with many problems their fame brings. [General thesis.]
- ✓ Famous people have to deal with a loss of privacy, a lack of balance, and the effects of addiction. [Detailed thesis.]
- ✗ Fame has many pros and cons. [Incorrect thesis because it deals with both sides.]
- ✗ What are the disadvantages of being famous? [Thesis should be a statement, not repeat the question.]

Do not write an announcement thesis (even though this style may be found in other disciplines and in business reports). Announcement theses are generally considered poor style in English essays.

- ✗ In this essay, I will explain how people can make simple lifestyle changes to follow environmentally friendly habits.
- ✓ People can make simple lifestyle changes to follow environmentally friendly habits.

- ✗ This essay will compare King Lear and Hamlet as tragic heroes.
- ✓ Although King Lear and Hamlet are both tragic heroes, they differ in temperament, intellect, and goals.

Make sure your thesis statement has parallel structure (see p. 189):

- ✗ At-risk students can be kept in school with arts programs to keep their interest, if they have mentors to inspire them, and by helping them succeed in their school work.
- ✓ At-risk students can be kept in school through arts programs, mentorships, and academic support.

Do not write four-sentence thesis statements:

- ✗ Being famous has many disadvantages. One disadvantage is the loss of privacy that famous people have to endure. Secondly, famous people lose balance in their lives. Fame can also become addictive like a drug.
- ✓ Famous people have to endure the loss of privacy, the lack of balance, and the addictiveness of celebrity.

Exercise 2.1 Writing thesis statements

Rewrite the following so that there is one concise, grammatical thesis statement. Remember that you do not have to include every bit of information that is given in these faulty thesis statements—much of the argument will be explained in the body paragraph instead. You can change the wording as much as you want, as long as you do not change the ideas. Be sure to use parallel structure.

1. There are three main stages to writing an essay: planning the essay, students have to write drafts, and then edit the final product.
2. Students graduate from high school without the reading and writing skills necessary for post-secondary education due to several reasons. First, reading for pleasure has declined because there are so many other distractions for leisure time—mainly technology. Second, literacy is not truly valued in society today. Third, students do not get as much practice in reading and writing in school today.
3. Overly strict parenting causes many problems. Children do not develop independence if their every move is controlled. They may rebel against the parents. They may not have the freedom to enjoy their lives.
4. In *Hamlet*, Shakespeare creates a complicated tragic hero. Hamlet cannot make up his mind about taking revenge against his uncle, he pretends to be mad so that he can find out the truth about his father's murder, and his unresolved mother issues.
5. Exercise can be easily incorporated into everyday life. People can use muscle power and walk, cycle, and climb stairs instead of using machine aids like cars and elevators. They can also do everyday household chores with more elbow grease instead of using chemical cleaners. They can choose leisure activities that promote movement, such as dancing.

Write a title

If you need to give your essay a title, you can do so at any time in the process—even leaving it to the very end. Some writers find a working title helps them to focus their essay, so they write one early in the process. Often the title comes out of the thesis statement.

Titles should be phrases rather than full sentences. Do not repeat the topic question as your title. Here are some examples of topics and possible titles:

Explain the advantages or disadvantages of being famous.
"The Downside of Fame"

Many people view citizenship as a matter of convenience and exploit their dual citizenship for work or travel. What are the obligations of citizenship?
"The Obligations of Citizenship"

What are the advantages or disadvantages of posting marks so students can see their ranking?
"Encouraging Competition in School"

Note that questions use inverted word order and question marks, while titles based on these questions use phrases with regular sentence order and no question marks. For example, for the question "Why can't my mother speak English?" the short story title is "Why My Mother Can't Speak English."

How a title is capitalized can be complicated. The two basic styles are title case (where the main words are capitalized) and sentence case (where the first word of the title is capitalized). Different style guides set out the rules for capitalization. For example, sentence case is used in APA-style citations and in newspaper articles (which have sentence-like headlines rather than titles). When main words are capitalized (as in MLA style), these words include the first and last word of the title and all the nouns and verbs, but not the prepositions and articles. Whichever style of capitalization is used, proper nouns (such as people's names and place names) are always capitalized. Follow the capitalization guidelines in the style guide your instructor recommends for your essays.

For more examples of titles, see the sample essays and readings in this book.

Exercise 2.2 Writing titles

Write a title for each of the five topics given in Exercise 2.1, on page 24.

Introduce your topic

Essays begin with an introductory paragraph. The introduction should provide background information, grab the reader's attention, and lead the reader to the thesis statement (the last sentence of the introduction). Essay writers often begin with more general statements, narrowing down to the thesis:

> Personal vehicles are an essential means of transportation in Canada. The distances are vast and the weather is harsh, and the only places well served by public transit are urban centres. However, cars are a major polluter, spewing toxic exhaust into the air. Without entirely giving up the convenience of their vehicles, Canadians can use them wisely by limiting trips, using fuel-efficient cars, and driving responsibly.

For a controversial issue, you can mention some of the main arguments of the other side:

> Many people point to the overcrowding of the prison system and the mounting costs of incarcerating criminals and wonder why we keep murderers in jail for so long. They argue that these criminals deserve to be executed for their crimes and that taxpayers should not have to foot the bill for their room and board in prison. Moreover, they claim that the threat of capital punishment would keep people from committing the most heinous crimes. However, the supporters of capital punishment are wrong. Capital punishment does not reduce crime rates, it may punish the innocent, and it is ultimately an uncivilized practice.

Note that the writer's opinion in this introduction is clear without the need to say "in my opinion" or "I think." The opening "many people" introduces a viewpoint that the essay writer probably does not agree with. Essay writers generally distance themselves from opposing opinions when they state what other people think; the reader expects this statement to be eventually followed by a "but" idea giving the author's own opinion.

Do not start your introduction with your thesis or by addressing the question directly. For example, if the essay topic asks "Are the fans ultimately responsible for violence in hockey?" and you begin your essay by saying "Yes, fans are responsible for hockey violence," you will end up either repeating that idea or launching into your reasons—and the reasons belong in the body of your essay. Furthermore, avoid repeating the exact words of the topic question.

Don't overload your introduction, throwing in everything you can think of. Remember that the meat of your essay is in the body and that the body paragraphs are therefore longer and more detailed. The introduction just introduces the topic. Many student essays have an over-long introduction, and the body paragraphs get progressively shorter. This happens when the writer does not plan the essay adequately.

Here are some other common ways you can introduce an essay:

- Begin with a quotation:

> "Those who cannot remember the past are condemned to repeat it," a statement by the philosopher George Santayana (1863–1952), is a well-known

quotation that reminds us how imperative it is to know our history. This is more important than ever as instruction in history seem to be reduced significantly as we move more to sciences and mathematics and away from traditional humanities courses. However, history should be learned at all levels of school, no matter what discipline is being studied. History courses are important because they give context to new learning, show us the mistakes of our past, and teach us critical thinking skills.

- Ask a rhetorical question:

Does the average voter really think about the long-term effects of reducing taxes? In almost every election, whether federal, provincial, or municipal, there is always one candidate who advocates cutting taxes. Unfortunately, enough voters buy into these political platforms to elect such right-wing politicians in order to save a few hundred dollars worth of taxes. To their regret, these same voters soon complain about the loss of public services. Cutting taxes is a bad idea. Realistically, voters should call for increased taxation because it helps sustain social-assistance programs, it reduces cutbacks to essential services, and it makes for a more dependable public service.

- Define a term, idea, or concept:

The term "boomerang children" refers to young adults who have moved back into their parents' home once they graduate from college or university. Like an Australian boomerang, they return once they are "thrown away." Whereas Canadian baby boomers sought to escape their childhood homes as soon as they reached legal adulthood, their own children are coming home, preventing the parents from becoming empty nesters. The boomerang generation is in no hurry to move out because they face economic hardship, they are too comfortable at home, and they have close relationships with their parents.

- Give a historical fact or statistic:

For more than one hundred years, Aboriginal children were taken away from their families and a familiar environment and sent to residential schools, often hundreds of kilometres from their homes. These government-sponsored church-run institutions were established to promote assimilation into "white Canadian society." To this end, students were not allowed to speak their native language or follow their own cultural practices. Many children were abused—physically, emotionally, and even sexually. Although custodial schools dated from early European settlement, the system thrived from 1880 to the 1960s, and the last residential school did not close until 1996. Many of the problems Aboriginal communities face today can be traced to the legacy of the residential school system.

- State a provocative or controversial point:

Tipping must be completely eliminated from the service industry. In the past, the purpose of tipping was to ensure prompt service from a reluctant server, to give the person some incentive to pay attention to a customer—in short, a bribe. Unfortunately, today, tipping is *de rigueur*—it is part of a service person's salary. It is expected, even demanded in many establishments. However, the practice of tipping is essentially unfair, forces the customer to supplement a meagre wage, and encourages money-grubbing practices.

- Relate a personal anecdote:

Yesterday, in Dundas Square, a young man of maybe 18 or 20 approached me. He wore the ubiquitous baseball cap, T-shirt with some design and logo, cut-off denims, and expensive Nike sneakers. He seemed well-fed, from a caring home, and educated. He then asked me if I could spare some change. My heart sank. This kid was a panhandler. Did he really need the money like the down-and-outs who smelled of cheap alcohol and stank from soiled clothing? He said he needed to get home and the money would pay for a bus ticket. Then his iPhone rang. As he answered his phone, I took the opportunity to walk away. There are better ways to support the poor than giving money to panhandlers directly.

Remember that, ultimately, the job of the introduction is to lead the reader to the thesis statement. **If you get stuck on what to say in the introduction, draft the body of your essay first.** Both the introduction and conclusion give ideas that do not belong in the body of the essay, so once you have the body of your essay in good shape, it is easier to see what needs to be said in the introduction.

Develop ideas in body paragraphs

The body paragraphs are the meat of your essay. You give your arguments and support them in these paragraphs.

Generally, in an academic essay, the body paragraph begins with a topic sentence and then makes two to four points, each supported with illustration, explanation, or examples. Note the development of ideas in these body paragraphs taken from different essays:

Tipping a restaurant server has become expected, even demanded. What was once a true gratuity, given by choice for good service, now becomes part of the business transaction. Customers are expected to supplement the low wages that servers receive. In some establishments, the tip has already been tallied into the check. Thus, the tip is not really something added, but now is part and parcel of payment for food. Often the service is mediocre, at times barely adequate, but the customer is pressured to tip. Sometimes servers hover near the table as the customers pay the bill.

In addition to helping financially, parents should support their children emotionally. They can show interest in their children's education by asking about their courses and professors even if they know little about the subject. If the students are living at home, their parents can provide a comfortable environment for them to study in and not burden them with other concerns. For students living away, parents can send them off with care packages of nourishing food and little gifts. Moreover, staying in contact with the students gives them emotional support. Today it is even easier to stay in touch with email, video calls on the Internet, and text messages.

Body paragraphs do not need concluding sentences. Do not just repeat your topic sentence idea at the end of the body paragraph—this becomes tedious, especially if the phrasing is the same. You can write a concluding sentence for the body paragraph if the sentence has a different focus or adds something to tie up the ideas of the paragraph. Note the difference between the topic sentence and the concluding sentence in this body paragraph:

> <u>Canadians can also be environmentally conscious by adopting smart driving habits.</u> Aggressive driving practices such as speeding, tailgating, and slamming on the brakes are hard on the vehicle and the gas gauge, as well as being unsafe. Idling the car in a parking lot or on the streets is not only wasteful but also illegal. Running the air conditioning can be more fuel-efficient than opening windows because it cuts drag when the car is moving fast on the highway. <u>Drivers have to educate themselves about the environmental impact of what they do behind the wheel.</u>

Sometimes you will be called upon to write single-paragraph passages—perhaps on a test. **Independent paragraphs** follow the same basic structure as body paragraphs, but they should end with a concluding sentence that echoes the idea of the topic sentence. The independent paragraphs are usually longer, 150–200 words. Here is an example of a single-paragraph personal writing assignment.

Prompt: Write a paragraph explaining why you are here (in this college, in your program).

> After a few years away from school, I decided to enroll in the Tourism and Hospitality program at Cabot College. One reason was purely practical—Cabot College is in my hometown. I can live with my parents while I study and save money on accommodations. Another reason is that Cabot College

has a program in the field I am interested in pursuing. After high-school graduation, I worked for a few years as a tour guide in Halifax and in a hotel in Yellowknife. I enjoyed the interaction with travellers and decided to make a career out of such work. Getting a diploma from Cabot will set me up to enter a range of jobs in tourism. I will have the business skills to start my own adventure touring company, or I could work in hotel management. The combination of a recognized diploma, co-op work assignments, and the work experience I have already garnered in the field will make me supremely employable and ready for an interesting future.

You can see other examples of independent paragraphs in Chapter 2. **Don't write one- or two-sentence paragraphs in your essays.** They are inadequate as carriers of ideas. You need to fully develop and explain your ideas, and this action requires more than a couple of sentences. One- or two-sentence paragraphs can, however, be used as transition paragraphs in long papers.

Start your paragraphs with topic sentences

The topic sentence gives the main idea of the paragraph. It is similar to the thesis statement. Although a topic sentence can appear anywhere in a paragraph, the best place is at the very beginning of the paragraph, especially in academic essays.

In an essay, the topic sentences should also relate to the thesis statement. Here are examples of thesis statements, each followed by three topic sentences:

Although they must let their children live their own lives, parents can play a role in helping their children through post-secondary education.

1. First, parents can help their children choose a school and a program of study.
2. Another way parents can assist their children is by giving financial support.
3. In addition to helping financially, parents should support their children emotionally.

Three main disadvantages of fame are loss of privacy, lack of balance in life, and addiction.

1. Instant recognition leads to life in a fishbowl.
2. Being famous makes a person lose perspective and balance.
3. Lastly, fame is a drug, and those who have had a taste of this drug soon become addicted.

As long as they do not give up what they truly value about themselves, people should be willing to improve their appearance, their behaviour,

<u>and even their attitudes in order to please a potential boyfriend or girlfriend.</u>

1. Appearance is often relatively easy to improve.
2. People can also change their behaviour to make themselves more attractive.
3. Attitudes may be harder to change deliberately, but as people grow and develop as persons, their attitudes can improve.

Don't overload your topic sentence by trying to say too much. It should be a relatively short, general statement that says what the paragraph is about. The ideas are developed with more detail in the body paragraph itself.

An important quality of a properly structured body paragraph is **unity**. In other words, all the sentences of the paragraph should fit under the umbrella of the topic sentence. Note the sentence that does not fit in this paragraph:

✗   Reading is one of the best ways to keep brains fit and exercised. Our minds have to work to decode the symbols into meaningful words. If we come across a word we don't know, we use mental strategies such as guessing the meaning from the context. Then we have to follow the ideas expressed—the arguments of an essay or the plot of a story. Some books are very heavy so we can keep our muscles strong as we carry them around. As we read a novel, we have to follow the action and use our imagination to picture the characters and the setting. All these skills require mental dexterity and become easier with practice.

The sentence about books being heavy talks about physical exercise, but the topic sentence is about mental exercise, so that sentence does not fit the paragraph.

Support your ideas

The most important principle of academic writing is that you must support your ideas. You do this with explanations or examples. Body paragraphs essentially move from the general to the specific. The topic sentence is general; the succeeding sentences give more detail.

Support is an important part of clarity. Here is an example of an overly general paragraph:

✗   In my country, there are things that people are permitted to do and not permitted to do. You have to be constantly there to know the situation and then do it. If you don't, then you may end up doing something not authorized. That may seem strange to people in this country. Here, people do not have strange rules whereas in my country it is different. A few years ago they changed the traffic rules and caused chaos because nobody really understood why. Some people tried to obey the new rules, and some stayed with the old.

Note the problem of referring to "my country" instead of identifying the country—this is actually something we see a lot in student essays.

Here is a revised, more specific version:

> ✓   In China, during the Cultural Revolution, the Maoists declared that it was counter to the revolutionary spirit to have vehicles stop on red and advance on green in intersections. So they instituted a change: drivers must proceed when the light is red and stop when the light turns green. Red, of course, is the symbolic communist colour of ongoing revolution. To stop on red is ideologically wrong. Unfortunately, not all drivers—especially foreign visitors who were familiar with the standard traffic rules—followed these changes, and there were a lot of accidents when some proceeded on the red light across the intersection and others on the green. This chaos went on for quite a while before the universal standards for traffic flow were restored.

Lack of specific support is one of the most common writing mistakes students make in essays. They write vague sentences and repeat ideas without actually explaining anything. You can see another example of this in the paragraph in Chapter 1 on page 1.

Exercise 2.3 Supporting statements

Give examples of possible supporting statements (explanation or examples) for each of these points.

1.   Finding a job is hard work.
2.   Video games allow students to develop practical skills.
3.   Cooking home-made meals serves more than a nutritional function; it also has social benefits.
4.   People can use different techniques to reduce their addiction to their smartphones.
5.   Extracurricular activities in high school help keep at-risk students from dropping out.
6.   Star professional athletes have various reasons for demanding multi-million-dollar contracts.
7.   People can learn a new language outside the classroom.

Don't change point of view

Just as you want to ensure that each body paragraph is unified as to the main idea, you want to avoid changing the point of view.

✗   Many young adults of the boomerang generation are forced to live at home because of financial difficulties. Companies have cut their work force to the bone, replacing full-time positions with contract workers. They pay the contractors less and do not offer them benefits or job security. In this way, the businesses save on labour costs. In such industries as television and journalism, where the demand for work experience is high, the companies exploit young people by making them work for nothing as interns. [This paragraph focuses on what companies do, instead of on the boomerang children.]

✗   Celebrities have to deal with a lot of responsibility. Young people are influenced by today's famous people. They try to model themselves after the people they look up to, whether this is good or bad. Young children become influenced by what they see and might believe everything a famous person they look up to does is right. [This paragraph does not work because the focus shifts to the fans.]

Use transition signals to show the relationship between ideas

Readers must be able to follow the argument in a paragraph. For instance, they need to see whether a sentence is an example of the point in the previous sentence, whether it is a new point, or whether it is an effect of what has been mentioned. Writers use transition signals to show these relationships and to give a logical flow to a paragraph. Here are the most commonly used transitions, listed by function:

Addition: also, finally, first, furthermore, in addition, moreover, next, second

Cause and effect: as a result, consequently, therefore, thus

Comparison: likewise, similarly

Contrast: however, in contrast, instead, nevertheless, on the contrary, on the other hand

Emphasis or clarity: in fact, indeed, in other words

Special features or examples: for example, for instance, in particular, mainly, specifically

Summary: in brief, in closing, in conclusion, in short, to conclude

Time relations: afterwards, at that time, earlier, in the meantime, lately, later, meanwhile, now, then

Note that the words and expressions in this list are adverbs—they cannot link sentences as conjunctions do (as explained in "Make adverb clauses with subordinating conjunctions" on p. 190). Sentence structure errors with the words **however** and **therefore** are very common:

> ✗ They had missed that crucial error in their initial work, however Andre caught it when he decided to check the figures again.
> ✓ They had missed that crucial error in their initial work. However, Andre caught it when he decided to check the figures again.

Working through the exercise below will show you how transition signals make your writing easier to follow.

Exercise 2.4 Using transition signals

Fill in the blanks with appropriate transition signals from the list above.

1. The team did not make a plan to divide up the work. _____, they got in each other's way and did not accomplish much.
2. First, gambling addicts must recognize that they have a problem. _____, they must seek help.
3. Schoolyard skipping games have many benefits beyond aerobic exercise. _____, they teach children the rhythm of traditional chants. _____, children play together co-operatively.
4. The students were supposed to do the project together in their study groups. _____, so many students dropped the course that the groups had to be reorganized before the work could proceed. _____, the instructor had to extend the time allotted for the group presentations.
5. Writing a shopping list helps someone remember the items even if the list is forgotten at home. _____, taking notes in class helps students remember the information given in the lecture even if they never read them again.
6. People demand lower taxes. _____, they complain about the lack of services and facilities, not seeing the connection between what they pay and what they get for the money. _____, politicians find it impossible to satisfy voters.

Make your paragraphs coherent

Every paragraph should have a logical flow from one idea to the next. *Coherence* refers to fitting or sticking together. If a well-constructed paragraph is taken apart and the sentences mixed up, it should be possible to put the paragraph back together like a jigsaw puzzle because every piece will fit into one spot. Coherence is achieved through the use of logical order (such as moving from general to specific), transition signals (explained above), and clear referencing with pronouns and articles.

In English, the definite article (*the*) shows that something has already been mentioned and thus can serve as a coherence device, as in this example:

> The design team came up with a new proposal. The proposal gave everyone a new perspective on the project, revitalizing the whole staff.

The indefinite article *a* is used for the first mention of the proposal while the definite article *the* shows that we know the proposal that is being discussed, that it has been mentioned before. Thus the two sentences are linked.

Combining two sentences into one can also improve coherence. Writing that contains many short, simple sentences is choppy and has no flow. Use of subordinate clauses (p. 190) also shows the reader the relationship between ideas. The subordinating conjunctions (words like *although*, *because*, and *if*) function like transition signals, but they work different grammatically, joining clauses to make one sentence. Note how conjunctions and transitions improve the following paragraph:

> ✗   Not meeting assignment deadlines has consequences. Students do not hand in the work on time. They will have marks deducted. The later the submission, the more severe the penalty. Students get extensions. Late assignments are returned later. Students do not benefit from the feedback. They can use the feedback for the next assignment.
>
> ✓   Not meeting assignment deadlines has consequences. If students do not hand in the work on time, they will have marks deducted. The later the submission, the more severe the penalty. Even if students get extensions, late assignments are returned later, so students do not benefit from the feedback they can use for the next assignment.

Clear referencing is important, as can be seen in this paragraph, which lacks coherence:

> ✗   The death penalty in Canada is another subject that has been debated heavily for decades. One reason is the cost of paying for people's lives in prisons as well as endless appeals and delays in carrying out the death penalty. This would allow Canada to spend that additional money on improving health care and other public services in Canada. Second, at least having the death penalty as an option would put fear in people not to commit heinous crimes. People will think twice before doing something illegal knowing that they could be sentenced to death. Thirdly, people who choose to kill another human for no reason at all should have to

pay for their consequences. The people's family and friends should be allowed to get some assurance that whoever took the life of their son or daughter should have to go through the grief of losing someone. Therefore, Canadians should think again about having the death penalty for the worst murders committed.

One reason this paragraph is hard to follow is that the reference to "people" changes. The first *people* refers to prisoners; the second is to people in general; the third and fourth is to criminals, or more specifically, murderers; and the last use of *people* refers to victims. The paragraph also lacks a clear point of view, so it is difficult to follow the writer's argument. Note, however, the good use of transition signals such as *second* and *therefore* to indicate the different points made.

Use transitions to link body paragraphs

Just as transitions improve the flow of ideas inside the body paragraphs, they can be used to create a bond between body paragraphs. You can start a paragraph with a reference to the idea in the previous paragraph in the essay. For example, after a body paragraph describing fuel-efficient car choices, the next paragraph could start with a topic sentence such as this one:

> In addition to changing the type of car they drive, responsible drivers can alter their driving habits to reduce pollution.

Don't overdo transitions. Use them when they seem appropriate, but do not begin every paragraph with a transition.

Don't end a paragraph with a reference to the idea in the next paragraph, especially if it repeats the same wording.

Write a satisfying conclusion

Every essay requires a conclusion, an ending to the discussion. Whereas the introduction leads the reader into the topic, the conclusion takes the discussion back out into the world, talking about results or implications. For example, in an essay about the solutions to a city's transportation problems, the introduction might give a background explanation so that the reader can understand exactly what the problem is; then the body paragraphs explain possible solutions; finally, the conclusion might discuss how the solutions could be implemented or what would happen in the future.

A concluding paragraph should start with a restatement of the thesis statement. (Don't repeat the exact phrasing of the thesis.) This restatement serves as a short summary of the essay.

Don't summarize too much in a short paper—it becomes repetitious. Although a summary is useful in a long paper where the reader needs to be reminded of the main arguments, in a short paper a summary can become boring and almost insulting to the reader. Restating the thesis is enough. You don't have to devote the whole conclusion paragraph to summarizing the essay.

Here is a conclusion that corresponds to the essay introduction on page 26. Note that the essay starts by restating the thesis statement (which was "Without entirely giving up the convenience of their vehicles, Canadians can use them wisely by limiting trips, using fuel-efficient cars, and driving responsibly"). After discussing how cars can be used more wisely in the body of the essay, the writer concludes by explaining results—what following these practices would mean:

> Sensible car use means driving less frequently, not buying gas guzzlers, and changing wasteful driving habits. If Canadians follow these practices, everyone can benefit. Having fewer cars on the road means less congestion. Burning less fuel conserves resources and reduces pollution. We do not have to be martyrs and give up the convenience of our cars entirely, but we cannot continue to drive them irresponsibly.

Another common type of conclusion is one that refers to what may happen in the future, as in these two examples:

> With all these benefits of taxation, it is not surprising that the tide may be turning. Instead of complaining about every single dollar taken in taxes, people are bemoaning the loss of services. They acknowledge the value of what the taxes paid for. Some of the wealthiest citizens are even publicly suggesting that they be taxed more heavily. This trend could mark a reversal in the anti-tax movement.

> Young adults are living with their parents for economic, social, and practical reasons. This trend is common in many countries. The boomerang generation will find no reason to leave their comfortable living arrangements any time soon, especially if the economic situation remains the same.

Do not add new information. You are wrapping up, and not trying to start another topic.

Do not throw in leftover ideas or thoughts that should have been in the body paragraphs.

Do not apologize for not having covered the whole topic. An essay is not meant to be an exhaustive treatment of an issue.

Examine the concluding paragraphs in the sample essays at the end of this chapter. Compare them to the introductory paragraphs to see how they differ.

Edit your draft

Once you have written a draft of your essay, it is important to go over it again to improve your writing. Editing includes making revisions in the content or organization. You can add, delete, or change sections or wording to improve clarity, coherence, and conciseness. Editing also includes correction. You can use tools such as spelling and grammar checkers, but you should also proofread your writing carefully to find mistakes.

Many writers revise as they work, but they also go over the whole paper after it has been written. It is always best to let a paper sit for a while so that you can revisit it with a fresh eye. Whether you can do that depends, of course, on the time constraints of the assignment. It is preferable to start work on an essay assignment as soon as you receive it so that you can leave enough time for this sitting period. In-class writing assignments, on the other hand, leave you less time for editing.

Proofreading is difficult. Readers often skip over mistakes, not really seeing them. Don't just rely on the spelling and grammar check of your word-processing software. Here are some tips:

- Give your work your full attention. Don't just do a quick read.
- Read your work out loud to see if it sounds right.
- Look for mistakes you commonly make.
- Double-check details such as the spelling of an author's name or a date.

In some writing courses, you have a chance to resubmit a paper. This gives you an opportunity to revise and edit your work, incorporating the corrections and suggestions made by your instructor. Unfortunately, many students do a superficial job in these situations, often just making grammar and spelling corrections. Make sure you read and consider all your instructor's comments. For instance, if the instructor considers your arguments weak or unsupported, think about what else you can use as a point.

You may also ask someone to read your paper over. For instance, you can get help from the tutors in your school's writing centre. It is important, however, that the other person does not edit the work for you, especially in an English course where the focus is on your writing skills—not someone else's.

As you revise and edit, consider the questions listed in the essay checklist at the end of this chapter. You should also compile your own individual checklist of mistakes that you often make. For instance, if you have a problem spelling *there/their/they're*, check every use of these words.

Study sample essays

Here are some sample five-paragraph essays for you to examine. They are basic expository essays—you can see other styles in Chapter 3. Annotated sample essays can be found in Appendix B. Look at the thesis statement and the three topic sentences—they should show the organization used. Study how the essay is introduced, developed, and concluded.

The essay prompt is given before the sample essay. Discuss how the essay fulfills the requirements of the essay assignment, and consider other possible approaches to the topic.

Essay prompt: Explain either the advantages or disadvantages of being famous. Focus on fame, not on wealth.

The Downside of Fame

Many people in this society want to be famous, to be known and talked about as the centre of worldwide attention. Some will even do strange things to be recognized, such as making fools of themselves on reality TV. They want fame so badly that they can taste it. However, this quest is not worth the prize. Three main disadvantages of celebrity status are the loss of privacy, lack of balance in life, and addiction to attention.

The most obvious price of fame is the loss of privacy. Attention from fans can make situations uncomfortable or even dangerous. As a result, simple pleasures such as a riding a bike or attending a concert become impossible. Some rabid fans become stalkers and have to be controlled with restraining orders. A few celebrities have been murdered by their fans. In addition paparazzi hound celebrities, competing to take sensational pictures to sell to the tabloids. Trying to escape this attention can lead to perilous situations such as car crashes. Even without the extremes, a famous person may need to have bodyguards about, also resulting in a loss of privacy.

Being famous makes people lose perspective as fame goes to their head. They are the privileged who get choice seats at special events and never have to make a reservation at the top restaurants. When celebrities get special treatment, they start to believe it is their due. They also acquire an entourage of sycophants. Sometimes their family and friends can help keep famous people grounded, but often they cannot compete with those who fawn and flatter. Celebrities often end up alienating their true friends as they turn to those who make them feel special.

Lastly, fame is a drug, and those who have had a taste of this drug soon become addicted. At first, a minor celebrity may show some restraint and modesty, even common sense, as the spotlight is on him or her. But if the attention is prolonged, then the celebrity needs the constant attention. Like a drug addict who craves a fix, the celebrity needs to feel watched, envied, loved, and worshipped. Without these things, he or she falls into a depression, becomes self-absorbed and morose, or may act in an extreme manner just to regain attention. Moreover, celebrities often get addicted to drugs and alcohol to maintain their high from fame.

The price of fame is high, and it is easy to see that many celebrities cannot handle it. There is a vicious circle as the pressures of fame drive many to drink, drugs, and divorce; these lifestyle choices fuel the tabloids and paparazzi, making the celebrities even more notorious.

Essay prompt: Helicopter parents are criticized for over-protecting their children, not even letting go when the students go off to post-secondary school. These children are now considered adults and should be responsible for their own lives. What is a reasonable role for parents to play when their children are in college or university?

Parental Contribution to Student Success

Baby boomer parents are more involved with their children's education than previous generations. They volunteer in schools, serve on parent committees, and help their children do their homework. After years of shepherding their children through elementary and secondary school, some parents find it difficult to let go when their grown children attend college or university. However, they can find a balance between hands-off parenting and the extreme cases of helicopter parents who hover over their adult children. Even though they must ultimately let their children live their own lives, parents can play a role in helping their children through post-secondary education.

First, parents can help their children make the primary academic choices—the college or university and program of study. This is a crucial decision. Students invest important years and thousands of dollars in their studies, so they need to make sure they are making a wise choice. Using their own academic and workplace experience, parents can give their children information about the various educational institutions and fields of study. Moreover, they know their children's talents and interests and can often predict what their children will find suitable. However, parents must realize this is guidance only; they should not push their children to follow the path the parents prefer.

Another way parents can assist their children is by giving financial support if they can afford it. Post-secondary education can be very expensive. Parents generally support students living at home by not asking them to pay rent or to contribute to household expenses. Parents can also support students who go away from their hometown to study. While students should be encouraged to work part-time and during the summer to earn money for tuition and living expenses, parents should also contribute to the education costs. Sometimes this can be just a loan. Whatever the arrangement, students will find their path to education much easier with a few extra dollars in their pocket.

In addition to helping financially, parents should support their children emotionally. They can show interest in their children's education by asking about their courses and professors even if they know little about the subject. If the students are living at home, their parents can provide a comfortable environment for them to study in and not burden them with other concerns. For students living away, parents can send them off with care packages of nourishing food and little gifts. Moreover, staying in contact with the students gives them emotional support. Today it is even easier to stay in touch with email, video calls on the Internet, and text messages. All students face times when they doubt their ability, and an encouraging message from their parents can help them stick with their studies.

In conclusion, parents can assist their children academically, financially, and emotionally—without being overly interfering. They can help them make a gradual transition from adolescence to adulthood, especially since the college years are too important to leave children totally on their own. With some support, the students can graduate and be on their way to fulfilling careers and satisfying lives as responsible adults. Then their parents can stand back and be satisfied with a job well done.

Practise essay writing

Here are some essay topics to try. Remember that, like all skills, essay writing takes practice. If you will be required to write an essay on an exam, give yourself a time limit corresponding to the time you will have on the exam and see what you can produce in that time.

Topics
1. Should high schools have later start times to accommodate teenagers' sleeping habits?
2. The fans are ultimately responsible for violence in hockey. Agree or disagree.
3. Explain why failure is a better teacher than success.
4. Explain why some students graduate from high school without the reading and writing skills they need for college or university.
5. Explain either causes or effects of people's obsession with checking their electronic messages.
6. Are the Olympic Games worth it (the time, effort, and expense)? (Focus on one group—the athletes competing, the host city and country, or the audience who gets so involved in watching.)

7. What are the advantages or disadvantages of posting marks so students can see their ranking in the class?
8. Tuition fees should be decreased. Agree or disagree, and support your answer.
9. What should high schools do to prepare students for college or university?
10. How should Remembrance Day be observed? For example, should it be a statutory holiday?
11. Explain what factors determine how much a second-generation immigrant (one that is born or raised in Canada) will maintain his or her native language.
12. Is a belief in the afterlife good for humanity?

Essay checklist

- Does the essay answer the topic question and follow the instructions given?
- Does the thesis statement address the question and clearly show the main argument?
- Is the thesis statement one sentence at the end of the introduction?
- Does the introduction lead the reader to the thesis, giving any necessary background information?
- Does each body paragraph have one main argument that supports the thesis?
- Does each body paragraph start with a topic sentence that gives the main idea of the paragraph and relates to the thesis?
- Is each body paragraph coherent, with transition signals showing the relationship of ideas?
- Is each point supported with examples or explanation?
- Does the conclusion begin with a restatement of the thesis?
- Does the conclusion lead the reader out of the essay by giving implications or referring to results?
- Do you stay on topic throughout your essay, not wandering off topic or changing the point of view?
- Are the ideas expressed clearly with correct use of words and expressions?
- Are the sentences correctly formed? Are a variety of sentence structures used, including complex sentences?
- Are spelling, punctuation, and format correct?
- Did you proofread everything carefully?

Types of Essays

All essays are, fundamentally, expository—that is, they try to explain something to the reader. (The word *essay* comes from the French verb *essayer*, which means "to try.") The two sample essays at the end of Chapter 2 are basic expository essays; they present arguments and support them.

Expository essays can also be divided into different types, depending on what kind of explanation you are giving. For instance, if you are explaining a scientific division, you are writing a classification essay. Essays can also be a mixture of types. For example, an illustrative essay can contain a definition or a descriptive paragraph.

Main types of essays

Narration: tells a story, relates an action or an incident

Description: gives information that conveys an image or picture to the reader

Illustration: clarifies an idea or concept by giving examples or analogies

Classification: separates the whole of something into parts or divisions for easier identification

Definition: explains what something is

Cause and effect: shows how something has come about and what it leads to or results in

Comparison: explains differences and/or similarities between two or more things or concepts (Sometimes these essays are called *compare/contrast*. Technically, *comparison* refers to similarities and *contrast* refers to differences, but in common use *comparison* is used for both.)

Process description: explains how things work or function

Instruction: explains how to do something

Persuasion or argumentation: offers reasons to make the reader accept a position, an idea, or a way of acting or thinking

Literary essay: analyzes literature (essays, short stories, poems, novels, plays)

This chapter explains the basic types of essays with sample paragraphs and essays. Examples of literary essays are in Chapters 4 and 5.

Distinguish between personal and impersonal essays

To some extent all writing is personal. While a news story is meant to be objective, it still reflects the thinking of the author in how the facts are presented. In contrast, newspaper columns are meant to be more personal and to present the arguments and opinions of the author. In other words, the news story may report the passing of a new law whereas a column may speculate on how the law will affect people.

In essays, students give their own opinions and points of view. A statement such as "High-school students need to learn more about Canadian history," for instance, is clearly the writer's opinion. It is unnecessary to say "I think" or "in my opinion" unless it is needed for emphasis.

We generally make a distinction between an academic essay and a personal essay that uses a lot of first-person references (*I, me, my*) and relates the writer's experiences directly. For instance, an essay called "What I Did on My Summer Vacation" would be a personal essay, whereas "The Importance of Summer Vacations" would be impersonal.

Personal essays are not common in college and university English-literature courses, or in history or social science essays. They are, however, assigned in general writing courses. You have probably written many personal compositions in school already, and you have probably read many personal journalistic essays. Some works show a mix of types. For instance, journalists may start their columns with a personal anecdote but then move to more general commentary.

In most of our English courses we ask students to write impersonal, academic essays. Writing impersonally is a skill that many students need to develop, especially for the work world.

Your instructor should make clear how personal an essay should be. Sometimes you may use personal examples to illustrate general points. At other times, you may use your experience but generalize it for the essay. Often the question will make it clear. For instance, "What are the benefits of studying abroad?" is impersonal, while "What did you learn studying abroad?" is personal.

In these two sample essays, the same points are made and the writer's personal experience is used, but the second essay uses generalizations, which make it more academic.

My Experience Studying Abroad

When I was a university student, I had the opportunity to take two separate trips to Europe, taking summer language courses. One was a six-week Polish Language and Culture course in Krakow, where I studied the language of my ancestors. The other was my third-year German course in Kassel. Although my family's financial resources were stretched to allow me to study abroad, these courses proved to be the most valuable educational experience of my university years.

My trips overseas strengthened my communication skills. In Krakow, I learned more than the "kitchen Polish" I spoke to my parents because I had to learn about history and geography in Polish. Moreover, my family used many English words at home, and now I had to learn the proper Polish words, such as *samochod* instead of *kara* for a car. My communication skills were tested when I visited my cousins because they knew no English at all, so I could not fall back on my first language. When my Polish failed me, I had to use gestures and even some words of German, which my cousins and I had studied in school. As for my experience in Kassel, it was the first opportunity I had to speak with native German-speakers after four years of studying the language. I boarded with a German family, along with a couple of students from Denmark. The paterfamilias was a retired school teacher, so he grilled us on our day's doings and school lessons, giving us a chance to practise our German.

My travels exposed me to different cultures. First, I had to get used to a mono-cultural society instead of the multiculturalism I was used to in Canada. I went to the one Chinese restaurant in all of Warsaw, which actually served Polish-style Chinese food. When I was in Europe, the faces were all white. The Poles and Germans I met were not as used to multiculturalism and acceptance of other ethnicities. Moreover, our group was actually criticized when we did not follow European etiquette—Canadians would note breaches in manners but not publicly deride someone. I had to get used to different styles of meals even though the food we ate at home was Western European. The main meal being served at midday, for example, is a tradition that does not fit the Canadian lifestyle. At my cousins' home, I was surprised when the vodka bottle came out before we headed to church on Sunday morning. Many of the everyday occurrences challenged my view of what was a proper lifestyle.

Finally, my studies overseas made me grow as a person. Although these trips were not my first time away from home, they were the first time I had been in another country. I was far away from my friends and family—my usual support network. I had to learn how to get around on my own, dealing with others in languages that I did not know very well. Moreover, my trips took place before the Internet made communication easier. When Germany proved more expensive than I expected, I learned how to make my money last. It was easier than contacting my parents and having them send more money—especially since I knew that the trip itself had been expensive for them. In addition, my surroundings made me aware of and humbled at the breadth of human achievement. I studied at the same university Copernicus had studied at and attended Mass in a medieval church among the tombs of kings.

Education is supposed to make students better communicators, more culturally aware, and more independent, and my studies abroad aided my growth in all three of those areas. Even though over the years I have lost touch with the friends I made, my photographs have faded, and my language skills have gotten rusty, I know that those two trips shaped the person I am today. More Canadian students should seek out opportunities to study abroad to add to their education.

The Benefits of Studying Abroad

University students are often given opportunities to do part of their studies abroad. They can take a course, a semester, or even a whole year overseas. They can study a foreign language or just continue their regular course of study in a different institution. Such programs, however, are often very expensive, and students' finances are already stretched thin. However, studying abroad is a priceless opportunity because students can develop communication skills, learn about different cultures, and grow as individuals.

A trip abroad can lead to improved conversation skills. Students learning foreign languages like Russian or Chinese can get the opportunity to speak with native speakers of the language. Sometimes students board with families, so they can communicate with different generations, from grandparents to young children. Students in residence may encounter other international students studying the same language. They may hear German spoken with a French, Italian, or Japanese accent. Even if the students are not abroad to learn another language, they have to learn to communicate with new people, in new cultural styles. For example, Australian slang can be like a foreign language to Canadians. Students might have to develop creative styles of communication if their language skills are not up to the task.

Exposure to other cultures is an important part of education. It broadens the mind to see how other people live, work, and study. For instance, university classrooms in Australia are more laid back and casual than in Canada, while European and Asian classrooms are run more strictly. Students who have homestays learn about family life in another country. While every family has its own style, this is determined by ethnicity. Meals, for instance, can be quite different—both the type of food eaten and when, where, and how it is served. There is a saying that a fish cannot really understand water (because it is the only world the fish knows), and in the same way, a person who never leaves his or her culture cannot really understand it. When students study abroad, they can see another way of life. As a result, they can question and understand their own culture and not just take it for granted.

Studying overseas can also make someone grow as a person. Students are far away from their friends and family—their usual support network. They have to learn how to get around on their own, often in a language they are not entirely comfortable with. They may also have to live with other international students, dealing with the day-to-day problems that all close living arrangements produce and that are exacerbated when the people have different cultures. The sense of place also expands the students' world and, by extension, themselves. Seeing cathedrals, monuments, and ancient structures makes students understand the vastness of civilization. In more natural settings, they can experience the wonder of the rainforest or the stillness of the desert. Travel changes people and the way they view the world.

At its best, education makes students better communicators, cultural ambassadors, and confident, independent people. Adding a touch of travel to schooling helps students achieve their education goals. Schools need to offer students more opportunities to study abroad and sponsor fundraising and scholarships to allow the students to take those opportunities.

Exercise 3.1 Personal vs. impersonal essay

With a partner or in a small group, discuss the following essay topics. Determine whether they are asking for a personal or an impersonal essay. Rewrite the personal topics so they are impersonal, and vice versa.

1.   How have you benefitted from the volunteer work you have done?

2. Why are horror movies so popular among young people?
3. Discuss the popularity of veganism. Is this a legitimate food movement or a bizarre fad?
4. How could your high-school education have prepared you better for post-secondary studies?
5. Would you eat meat from animals such as dogs, cats, horses, or rabbits? Explain why or why not.

Narrate

Narration is basically telling a story—relating what happened. It is not used frequently in academic essays. It is more common in personal compositions and creative writing. However, some narration may be included in an essay even if the whole essay is not a narrative.

To know what the style and format of the narration should be, it is necessary to know the function of the story. For instance, a story meant to entertain an audience has more detail and a different structure (building to a climax, for instance) than a story that is simply a summary of events used for a report.

A brief story is called an anecdote. Often this kind of story is an opener for a long essay. It captures the reader's interest, sets the tone, and establishes a basis for the main content of the piece. Journalistic writing and popular magazines frequently use this strategy; academic papers less so.

When the story takes over the entire paper, it is no longer an anecdote. It becomes the main part of the paper. Sometimes the narrative can be used in more personal academic essays. (A personal academic essay balances the subjectivity of the writer's private life with objectivity in analysis.)

In storytelling, the common method of writing is to use the past tense. After all, usually the incident has already occurred, whether in the distant or recent past. Therefore, the natural tendency is to tell the story with the simple past tense verb form. However, in English, the simple present tense can also be used for narration. The present tense gives immediacy to the story. Moreover, in an essay analyzing a story, it is better to relate the story's events in the present tense.

Narratives can also be used to explain something, as in this example:

The Fox and the Grapes

The expression "sour grapes" comes from Aesop's fable about the fox and the grapes. The story begins with a hungry fox that sees a bunch of grapes on a trellis. It is a hot day, and he is thirsty and hungry. His stomach growls. He thinks how delicious the grapes look. He smacks his lips. He can taste the sweetness of them already. "I can snatch those grapes in one leap," he boasts. As he jumps up, a gust of wind catches the grapes and lifts the vine out of reach. So close! Not deterred, the fox leaps, and again he is foiled. He howls in disappointment. He tries this a number of times without success. Finally, tired, he trots away, saying, "These grapes are probably sour anyway." Now whenever we hear people denigrate something they could not obtain, we call it a case of sour grapes.

Writing Topics 3.1

1. Write a brief narrative account of an accident that you witnessed or were a part of—an account that could be used in an official report.
2. Write a narrative summary of one of your favourite movies or television episodes.
3. Write a narrative account of something you experienced while travelling.

Describe

Description is often combined with narrative, because telling a story and describing go hand in hand. On its own, description works well when information needs to be detailed, accurate, and precise. Without pictures and with only words, a description can give the reader a visual image of an object, person, place, or concept.

Description is not used only for physical objects, but also for non-physical, such as emotional states in a psychology essay. Physical descriptions may be as simple as relaying information about shapes and forms. For example, in science, you can reveal details of an organism with exact measurements; in literature, you describe the setting or a character's appearance; in psychology, you may show the change of mental states or give an account of the stages of grief.

There are some general principles to follow when you write descriptions:

- Begin with the simple and then move to the complex or intricate.
- Start from general and go to specific (the overview before the details).
- Organize and categorize into manageable units.
- Use techniques such as analogy and comparison to help clarify.
- Establish consistency in the direction of your description (for example, clockwise, counter-clockwise, going upwards or downwards).

Descriptive essays are rarely assigned, but you may have to describe something in another kind of essay. In literature, the description of imagery may include all five senses rather than just a visual description. Here is an example of a literary description:

The Ideal Lady in the Courtly Love Tradition

In the courtly love tradition, the description of the lady or mistress is formulaic: she is described from head to toe. The courtly lady's hair is almost always long and blond; its length is associated with fertility, and its colour is associated with gold, suggesting both worth and beauty. Next, her eyes are compared to stars for their brightness and clarity, and her cheeks are as rosy as apples. Her teeth are pearly white while the lips are well formed, not too thin and not overly full. The lady's neck is always as graceful as a swan's. Her breasts are perfect orbs, milky or alabaster in their voluptuousness. Her figure, while not hourglass, may be compared fairly to any Olympian nymph's or to Aphrodite's. Although her legs are not given special mention in a physical description, they are associated with the way she floats gracefully as she walks. Finally, to complete the adoration of the lady's physical attributes, her feet are like those of Thetis, dainty and sensuous.

Writing Topics 3.2

1. Write a description of your home. It can be a room, a house, a town, or a country. Do not try to include everything in your description; focus on aspects that convey the essence of the place.
2. Describe your favourite artwork.
3. Write a description of a person you admire.

Illustrate

The illustrative essay explains by giving examples. It is a basic expository essay.

Examples support your general statements and assumptions. They are part of the proof that college and university professors expect in an essay. An example is just one specific thing, and in supporting an idea, you may not need more than one example per paragraph. That having been said, your example must be relevant to the topic. At times, you may need to explain the example as well.

To explain something, you may have to draw on other rhetorical devices, such as classification, description, and comparison.

In an academic essay, use *for example* and *for instance* at the beginning of sentences; use *such as* and *include* when you want to give examples within a sentence. Don't use abbreviations such as *e.g.* and *etc.* or the conversational expression *and so on*. Here are example sentences:

- ✓ In high school she played many sports, such as basketball, rugby, and volleyball.
- ✓ The sports she played included basketball, rugby, and volleyball.
- ✗ She played many sports in high school, e.g., basketball, rugby, and volleyball.
- ✗ The sports she played were basketball, rugby, volleyball, and so on.
- ✗ The sports she played included basketball, rugby, and volleyball, etc.

Note the uses of *for example* and *for instance* in the following essay. The two expressions are synonyms. They are both adverbials, so they can appear in the middle or at the end of the sentence though their most common placement is at the beginning.

House Guest Etiquette

With today's mobile society, it is inevitable that people end up staying with family or friends when they travel. Whether it is casual couch surfing or extended stays in designated guest rooms, visitors need to follow the rules of etiquette to ensure that the stay is pleasant for both guest and host. Above all, house guests must be considerate, entertaining, and appreciative.

Primarily, guests need to consider the host's needs and lifestyle. First, they must make sure that their visit comes at a convenient time. They must also not stay too long and wear out their welcome. They should clean up after themselves and not make a lot of extra work for their host. For example, they should not leave their dirty dishes on the kitchen table. Finally, they should not expect the host to be their personal tour guide. The guests can go out sightseeing on their own, especially since it is likely that the host has already seen the local tourist attractions many times. In return for not having to go up the CN Tower again, for instance, the host might take the guests on a scenic bike ride along the river.

To minimize the trouble even well-behaved guests create, it is better if they are entertaining. After a day of sightseeing, guests can make amusing and insightful observations about what they saw and how the streets of Montreal, for example, compare to those of their hometown. They should try their best not to be grouchy in the morning before their coffee. Above all, they should not criticize the host or the accommodations. Guests need to be charming and fun to be around at all times.

Showing proper appreciation is important in the etiquette of staying over. The guests should thank the host for the hospitality, both verbally and with small presents such as flowers and wine. A larger gift may be called for, depending on how big a favour the host is granting. This gift could be bought later in the visit, or even sent afterwards, once the guests figure out what the host would truly like. Treating the host to a dinner out is a good way to show thanks. After the visit, the guests should send a thank-you note.

A thoughtful, amusing, and grateful guest is a true treasure, sure to be welcomed back. Unfortunately, many house guests do not fit that description. They are high-maintenance, requiring hosts to spend time and money on their accommodation and entertainment. It is not surprising that many people avoid having house guests as much as they can, pulling the welcome mat away from the door when friends or family members hint that they need a place to stay.

Writing Topics 3.3

1. Explain the life of a student. Focus on one kind of student—at a certain level, at a specific kind of school, or in a particular education system. For example, you could explain what students do to study English in a typical Chinese high-school class. Be sure to illustrate your points with examples.
2. Explain a specific strategy for surviving modern life. For instance, you could talk about the importance of challenging yourself with new activities or of taking rest and relaxation.

Classify and define

Classification and definition are common in social sciences and technical courses. A classification essay defines the different categories of something, while a definition essay explains the meaning of words, ideas, and concepts.

For a classification essay, you might be asked to describe kinds of drivers, travellers, shoppers, restaurant diners, or students. In a history essay, you might consider three types of governments; in a psychology paper, three causes of depression.

Classification is methodical in its description of kinds. The standard strategy begins with an overview and then moves to in-depth details. In short, as you progress in your explanation, you move from general to more detailed and specific statements.

In a definition essay, you might write about abstract qualities—what is success, truth, or beauty? Definition essays may include dictionary meanings, common understanding of a term, etymology and history, and examples.

You may also include definition in other essays, establishing what something means before you talk about it. For instance, you might include a definition of a baby boomer in your introduction to an essay on the effects of this segment of the population.

What Is a Baby Boomer?

Put simply, a baby boomer is a person born during the Baby Boom, which in Canada is generally considered to be 1946–1965. Compared to typical birth rates, 18% more babies were born during this prosperous post-war period. This resulted in a bulge in the population distribution, which made boomers a dominant generation with economic clout and cultural impact. As the first television generation, they drove technological advancements. For instance, both Bill Gates and Steve Jobs were born in the middle of this era. Boomers were hippies and revolutionaries in their youth, galvanizing social change such as feminism, civil rights, and the sexual revolution. Their sheer numbers necessitated the construction of schools and houses, and their power as consumers fuelled economic boom times. Now their presence is creating a demand for services for seniors and retirees, such as health care and travel. Their strength in numbers has also made it difficult for subsequent generations, who faced such problems as job shortages and higher housing prices as a result of pressure from the Baby Boom. The boomers' influence on Canada will remain long after they themselves are gone.

Different Ways to Learn

We learn throughout our lives. As children, we do not even realize we are doing it, but as we grow older, we become more cognizant of the process and how well we succeed at acquiring new knowledge and skills. Learning extends beyond the classroom and beyond the control of the teacher. While teachers can facilitate the acquisition of knowledge and development of skills, ultimately it is the learner's responsibility. Learning can be categorized into different types: book learning, demonstration, and trial and error.

Book learning is an academic style of learning. It involves theory and interpretation of facts. History, for instance, is generally learned through books since we cannot experience it. With so much knowledge packed into documents, both printed and electronic, we can get a very good education just from reading. It takes the ability to follow what is written, understand it, and internalize it. As we read, we have to imagine scenes and people. We have to recognize the arguments and evaluate their soundness. While there is a wealth of information in books, some people do not learn well from reading.

Demonstration leads to hands-on learning. Someone shows us, whether in person or on a video, how to do something, and we do it. This method works best for manual skills, such as cooking, changing a tire, or wiring a lamp. New avenues for this type of learning have appeared with the proliferation of how-to videos on YouTube. Now we do not have to sign up for a class or search out an expert personally; we can find whatever we want demonstrated on the Internet. Of course, as is the case with all Internet-based information, we have to make sure we are getting sound information.

Trial and error often does not involve formal instruction. People who refuse to read the manual and just start pushing buttons on their new digital camera are learning by trial and error. Hands-on learning can involve trial and error if we have not mastered the skill when it was first demonstrated. Making mistakes has to be viewed as part of the learning process, as learning opportunities. While some people enjoy figuring things out for themselves, others find trial and error frustrating.

While these are three different ways in which we learn, we usually combine them as we master anything. A scientist, for example, will read about what other scientists have discovered and will learn to use the lab equipment in a demonstration, but then will ultimately work with trial and error in his own experimentation. What is important is that we keep learning and take advantage of all learning opportunities presented to us.

Writing Topics 3.4

1. Write a paragraph defining an abstract term, such as *success*, *leadership*, or *freedom*.
2. Write a classification essay on three kinds of drivers, bosses, or friends.

Describe process

Process description explains how something works or how an action is performed. It requires careful organization of the steps in the process to make it clear. Process description is common in technical writing.

The process can be explained in a list of instructions, as in a recipe. Alternatively, the instructions can be given in paragraph form, still in second person. The process can also be described without expectation that the reader will perform the actions. In this case, the third person and passive voice are generally used. Biological and geological processes, which describe actions people cannot actually perform, are another form of process description. For instance, how to plant and maintain a garden is process instruction, and how the plants grow is also process description.

The process of getting exempted from paying American taxes on income earned from an American company is explained below in three different formats and styles.

Instructions:

In order to be exempt from paying US taxes on monetary compensation in the United States, you must be a non-resident alien, student, professor, or researcher. You must first apply for an Individual Tax Identification Number (ITIN) from the Internal Revenue Service. Please follow these instructions.

1. Go to the United States Government website.
2. Find the IRS (Internal Revenue Service) site.
3. Search through the menu for the specific site for ITIN.
4. Look for the form W-7.
5. Download the application.
6. Print out the application and fill in the form completely.
7. Provide a valid Canadian passport or photo ID driver's licence with the application. In lieu of the original, submit a photocopy, authenticated by a notary public or lawyer.
8. Mail in both the application and proof of identification to the Department of the Treasury.
9. Wait for about 6–8 weeks to receive the ITIN from the IRS.

Instructional process paragraph:

If you are a non-resident alien, student, professor, or researcher who wishes to claim a tax exemption for income earned from an American company, you need an ITIN (individual tax identification number) from the IRS (Internal Revenue Service). First, go to the Internet and find the IRS site and, using the menu, locate the W-7 form for the ITIN. Next, download the form and print it out. Fill out the application completely. You will note that the form requires you to provide proof of identification, either a current Canadian passport or a valid driver's licence. You may submit one of the originals with your application, or you may include just a photocopy of one of these documents. However, you must have this photocopied document notarized by a lawyer or a notary public. Then mail the form and document to the United States Department of the Treasury, IRS. Within 6–8 weeks, you should be receiving your ITIN, and with it you can apply for a US tax exemption.

Process description paragraph:

In order to be exempt from the one-third withholding tax for income earned from American institutions, Canadians can apply for an Individual Tax Identification Number (ITIN). Applying for the ITIN is free, and application information and documents are available on the Internet at the Internal Revenue Service website. The W-7 form required can be downloaded from this website. Then the form can be printed, completed, and mailed to the IRS. Along with the form itself, applicants must send proof of identity—either a valid passport or a driver's licence with photo ID. Because mailing and processing original documents would take several weeks, notarized photocopies can be sent instead. Once a Canadian citizen receives an ITIN, he or she can use this number to apply for a US tax exemption.

Writing Topics 3.5

1. Write a process description for a task you perform at work, such as closing a store or restaurant for the day.
2. Write instructions for a task performed with some sort of technology or equipment. Tailor your instructions for someone not adept with this kind of task. For example, you could write computer log-in instructions for your grandparents.
3. Explain how to prepare one of your favourite dishes.

Explain causes and effects

One of the most common essays that students are called upon to write is a cause-or-effect essay. A cause paper explores the reasons that something happens, answering the questions why or how; an effect paper explains the results—what happens afterwards. Essays explaining problems and solutions are often cause-or-effect essays.

Sometimes you can talk about both causes and effects in an essay—especially to explain a domino effect where one event causes another, which causes another. For example, in an essay about the situation after the surrender of Germany in 1918, you can focus on the punitive monetary reparations imposed by the Allies and explain the destructive effects on the defeated nation, which in turn led to the Second World War.

Sometimes causes and effects become a vicious circle. For instance, incarceration of young offenders can lead to hardened criminals who commit more crimes and end up in jail again.

Don't get causes and effects mixed up. If you are explaining the effects of an event, don't drift off to explore the causes. You can give causes in the introduction to set the background, but the body paragraphs should explore the effects.

Signal words for causes: reason (for), cause (of), why, because (of), since, result (from), due to, consequence (of)

Signal words for reasons: so, therefore, thus, consequently, to cause, affect, result (in)

Watch out for the spelling of *affect* (a verb) and *effect* (usually a noun).

The two following sample essays show the difference between cause and effect on the same topic:

The Causes of Rudeness in Modern Society

Once upon a time, people all behaved responsibly and properly from birth to death. Perhaps there were a few incidents of rudeness, bad behaviour, and incivility during a lifetime, but these were not so serious as to tar society and the individual. That is the piece of fiction handed down to us—that previous generations were all conducting themselves appropriately and that today we are lost in a wilderness of impropriety, misconduct, and indecency. The truth is that every generation sees the past as perfect and the present as degeneration. However, although people have always been seen behaving badly, there are strong influences that can be identified as contributing to modern incivility. These include the influence of the media, relaxation of social rules, and the failure of role models.

Everyone blames the media for the unruliness in the world, and this accusation is essentially valid. People are influenced and manipulated directly and indirectly by what they see and hear on television, in the movies, and on the Internet. For example, coarse language—swearing and profanity—populates dialogue in television interviews, in action movies, and now even in romantic comedies. Most movies seem to be made to appeal to the vulgar sense of humour common to teenaged boys. YouTube glorifies outrageous acts as they are captured by cellphone cameras, uploaded, and viewed by millions. When people see all this day in and day out, they may at first remark about the loss of civility, but they soon adapt to it as the new norm. Then they no longer see it as bad and may start to engage in it themselves.

Unruly behaviour comes with a society that has relaxed its standards. Formal dress and language has given way to the casual, which has in turn led to the vulgar. Showing underwear was once viewed as shocking; now it is commonplace. People are naturally more polite when they are dressed in suits and less so when they are dressed in sweats. While the clock cannot be turned back to the time when manners and deportment were taught in charm school, it must be recognized that casualness breeds rudeness as standards become lax. In addition, social niceties, such as thank-you notes, have fallen by the wayside because people feel they no longer have the time to attend to such matters.

Thirdly, people no longer have the same role models and icons to look up to. Parliamentarians behave like kindergartners in Question Period, politicians get caught in sex scandals, and business leaders cheat and con investors. Political attack ads bring down the level of discourse in elections. While this type of behaviour has always existed, it has now become more public thanks to the media. As a result, people's trust has been eroded, and they lack heroes to emulate. People then behave badly, thinking that if so-and-so can do something, so can they. Furthermore, teenagers look to their peers instead of their parents, and parents have no power to bring their children's behaviour in line. Children lack respect for their parents, and students lack respect for their teachers, and so bad behaviour spreads.

It is not surprising that people's behaviour today reflects the poor influences of the modern lifestyle. While it can be argued that people are more honest today now that they do not feel the need to pretend to be polite, this incivility also makes urban life more uncomfortable. However, perhaps that does not really matter. People are too busy looking at their cellphone screens to interact with others anyway.

The Effects of Rudeness in Society

Incivility and rudeness are ingrained in modern life. People are too rushed to hold the door for someone, too busy to wait patiently for the trainee cashier to fumble through a transaction, and too engrossed in their cellphone to look up and communicate with their neighbours. People are short with others when they become impatient. Sometimes they even berate and yell at the poor souls who cross their paths when they are in a hurry. Such uncivil behaviour takes a toll, not only on society as a whole but also on the individual.

Rudeness can escalate to aggressive acts. If one person swears at another, more than likely the offended one will respond in kind. From merely having a shouting match, the two may end up pushing and shoving each other. Then both individuals suffer the consequences. Some instances of road rage have even led to vehicular manslaughter. Often people do not think of consequences when they start a sequence of events that gets out of control. Even if one person has enough sense to stop, he or she may still carry the experience of pain and anguish far beyond the momentary incident. Harbouring a grudge may eat at the psyche for a long time. Then suddenly such suppressed feeling may explode, and the person takes it out on an individual totally unconnected to the actual distant event. This action may in turn cause a vicious cycle.

Secondly, rudeness changes a person spiritually and psychologically. Feeling victimized and bullied, the individual may get depressed. His or her outlook on life alters. One person may suffer in silence and take it all in. Another may have the attitude that if that is how a person is treated in this society, then "when in Rome, do as the Romans" and act boorishly himself. All sorts of defence mechanisms come into play to rationalize this change in the self. Very few will take rudeness in stride and let it flow off their backs like water off a duck. This change comes so gradually that the individual may not even be aware of it.

Individual acts of rudeness affect the whole of society. Incivility spreads like a cancer, slowly but surely. People become untrusting and cynical. They are suspicious of random acts of kindness since they cannot imagine people behaving altruistically. People find it hard to live together as selfishness breeds more selfishness. Cities become cold and hard as everyone looks out for number one and ignores others' needs. Vicious attack ads colour people's view of politics, and so they withdraw from civic life—not even voting—thus affecting the political balance and encouraging callousness in government.

The effects of rudeness are grim and pervasive. Fortunately, there is enough goodness in the world to counter the effects of incivility. Polite and cheery people can banish the gloominess of others, and just as impoliteness spreads, so does politeness.

Other examples of cause-or-effect writing can be seen in the definition paragraph about baby boomers (p. 52) and in the non-fiction articles in Appendix A.

Writing Topics 3.6

1. Write about the effects of the widespread use of a particular technology such as cameras (in cellphones, in smart TVs, or in public spaces), driving assist features in cars, and home security.
2. Discuss the causes or effects of Internet addiction.
3. Explain the causes or effects of unemployment, either for an individual or on a larger scale such as a main industry in a region.

Compare

A common essay directive is to compare two things, in other words, to point out both the similarities and the differences. These could be two pieces of literature, two versions of the same story, two cultures—almost anything. In a comparison essay, you can write about similarities, differences, or both. The topic question might limit your scope by specifying only differences or similarities, so read the question carefully.

Comparison should have some sort of logic behind it—a reason to compare the two things. For instance, you would not compare a desk and an apple, but you could compare two kinds of desks or two kinds of apples, often with a recommendation as to which is preferable. You might compare two cities, two cars, two characters in a play, or a novel and the movie based on it.

Comparison essays are considered difficult to write. One reason is that they need to be carefully structured so the reader does not get confused between the two things being compared. Moreover, it is important that the essay writer do the work for the reader, explaining the differences or similarities and not just describing two different things.

Don't write a four-paragraph comparison essay, with one body paragraph on each item being compared. The danger here is that the writer does not actually make the comparison. Usually, the thesis announces, "I will compare A and B." Then, one body paragraph describes A and the other body paragraph describes B. The conclusion then states, "As you can see, A and B are very different." But two separate descriptions do not make a comparison essay. It is the writer's job to explain the points of comparison.

Start each body paragraph with **a topic sentence relating the point of comparison** and mentioning both items to be compared. For instance, a paragraph beginning "A crucial difference between soccer and hockey lies in the pace of the game" would then go on to compare the pace of soccer and the pace of hockey.

Brainstorm your comparison essay by identifying **different points of comparison**. For some of these categories, there will be similarities; for others, differences. Using a chart is helpful (see, for example, Table 3.1).

Table 3.1 Points of comparison—outline for an essay

Point of Comparison	Hockey	Soccer
where it is played	ice rink	a field, or any open, flat surface
number of players	5 on the ice + goaltender	10 on the field + goalkeeper
time of game	3 periods of 20 minutes each; clock is stopped when play pauses	2 halves of 45 minutes each, continuously, with some stoppage time added at the end
equipment needed	skates, hockey stick, puck, safety equipment (padding, jock straps, helmets, visors)	cleated soccer shoes, soccer ball, limited safety equipment (shin pads, jock straps)
physicality	short bursts of intense play, followed by time on the bench; body checking frequent; fighting can break out	continuous running over the field; can go after the ball but not the player; fighting not allowed
fans	rabid fans in Canada and some northern countries	rabid fans all over the world
scoring	can be many goals; goalie has relatively small area to protect	limited scoring in games; keeper protects huge net

This kind of brainstorming makes it easier to organize the essay. You don't have to cover everything in your chart—you can choose the more interesting similarities and differences. Note that two perspectives are presented here—the two sports from the point of view of both players and fans. Make sure not to confuse the two perspectives in your essay.

Avoid generalities. For example, if you are comparing two works of literature, don't use the characters and plots in general as points of comparison. Instead, be specific. Use the protagonist, the heroine, and the minor characters instead of just the characters. Plot can be defined as plot twists or surprise endings.

Your body paragraphs can follow either the block or the point-by-point method of comparison (see Table 3.2). In the block method, you talk about item A first and then go to item B, following the same order of points. In the point-by-point method, you go through each point, talking about A first and then B. This is illustrated in the chart below and the two sample paragraphs that follow.

Table 3.2 Two methods of comparison

Block		Point-by-point	
A:	Point 1	Point 1:	A
	Point 2		B
	Point 3	Point 2:	A
B:	Point 1		B
	Point 2	Point 3:	A
	Point 3		B

Block method

There are four main differences between the Canadian and the American dollar. First, the Canadian dollar is minted as an alloy coin, which was quickly dubbed a "loonie" after the image of the waterfowl, the loon, appearing on its face. According to the Canadian Mint, a loonie can last in public exchange for twenty years or more before it is taken out of circulation. After two decades since the loonie made its debut, Canadians have become used to the heavy coins clinking in their purses or pockets and sharing the same space with the toonie, the two-dollar coin. On the other hand, the American dollar is still printed paper currency. The America bill is nicknamed either a "buck"—a slang term for a dollar—or "greenback" because of the greenish colour that distinguishes all US paper money. The greenback has a short life expectancy: it has a circulation life of about eighteen months before the bill, having become ragged and frayed, is withdrawn by the Treasury Department and disposed of. The Americans have resisted the change to coinage and still prefer "folding money." Moreover, they do not have a two-dollar bill in common circulation. Whatever the form the money takes, the value of the American and Canadian dollar is usually close to equal.

Point-by-point

There are four main differences between the Canadian and the American dollar. First, the Canadian dollar is minted as an alloy coin whereas the American dollar is still printed as paper currency. Second, the Canadian currency is called a "loonie," after the imprint of the waterfowl, the loon, on the coin. The American bill is nicknamed a "buck"—a slang term for a dollar—or "greenback" because of the greenish colour that distinguishes all US paper money. Another difference is how long the currency lasts. A one-dollar Canadian coin can last in public exchange for twenty years or more before it is taken out of circulation. A greenback has a much shorter life expectancy: it has a circulation life of about eighteen months at best before the bill, having become ragged and frayed, is withdrawn by the Treasury Department and disposed of. Finally, after two decades of use, Canadians have grown used to the heavy coins clinking in their purses or pockets and sharing the same space with the toonie, the two-dollar coin. The Americans, however, have resisted the change to coinage and still prefer "folding money." They do not have a two-dollar bill in common circulation. Whatever the form the money takes, the value of the American and Canadian dollar is usually close to equal.

In a comparison paper explaining similarities, since you are dealing with things alike, you can economize by using the word "both" to save needless repetition.

Comparison: only similarities

Although Canadian and American currencies have many differences, they share commonality in three areas. First, both currencies are legal tender, issued by their respective governments for public and private transactions. What this means is that anyone can use the bill or coin legally to buy goods and to pay for services. Second, both currencies are backed by the federal government: the Canadian and American governments guarantee the value of the currency. They can print more bills and circulate them, and if need be, withdraw the currencies from circulation. Finally, the almighty dollar is the backbone of the health of the nation. Canadians and Americans put their trust in their monetary system. It is the bellwether of economic and financial health.

In a comparison essay, you may use both organizational patterns. You are not restricted, say, to using the block method throughout. What you need to decide is which method is best for expressing the relationships between the two items.

Comparing Text Messaging and Face-to-Face Conversation

Cellphones have brought about a revolution in the way we communicate. Young people, especially, are addicted to their smartphones, which offer not only instant communication, but also access to social networking sites. Text messaging has displaced voice calls and even, in some instances, face-to-face conversation. It is not unusual to find people living in the same house texting each other. The most notable differences between face-to-face talk and text messaging are found in physical presence, privacy, and convenience.

The most obvious difference is in the lack of physical presence in electronic communication. Much of what we communicate is in body language. We watch and gauge each other's facial expressions, stance, and gestures. Sarcasm and joking are often transmitted by tone of voice. In speech, we can use our surroundings as part of our message. For instance, we can point to what we are talking about. When we send a text message, however, we lack these visual cues. We can only imagine how the recipient looks as he or she reads our message. Without tone of voice, we run the risk of being misunderstood. Surroundings can be described, but they cannot be seen.

Keeping a conversation private is different with speech and texting. In a spoken conversation, the speakers must find a private place to talk or keep their voices low if they are in public. Their conversation is unlikely to be secretly recorded—unless they are the subjects of an investigation. Although they could be caught on security cameras, what they were saying would be hard to figure out unless the resolution is very good and a proficient lip-reader is available. On the other hand, people sending text messages cannot expect their messages to remain secret. They do have a certain privacy as they are communicating because no one observing them would know who they are corresponding with or even that they are actually sending messages. Perhaps the silly grin is from watching a YouTube video instead of sharing a joke in a conversation. Text messages, however, are stored electronically and thus can easily be retrieved by hackers or someone just picking up a person's phone and scrolling through the stored messages. Crime and scandal have been unearthed by digging through text messages.

Face-to-face communication lacks some of the convenience of text messages. The former is limited in that we have to be in the same place. Text messages can be sent around the world. Voice conversation is immediate, while text messages can wait until we can retrieve them. We have to arrange a mutually convenient time to talk, but we can send a text message whenever we think of something we want to say. However, speaking is generally faster than typing, but reading is faster than listening. In addition, facing the person we are talking to can sometimes be uncomfortable, while sending a text message can become a cowardly act, as in the case of someone breaking up with his or her significant other with a text message. Another difference is that it is more difficult to get away from a determined conversationalist, yet relatively easy to check out of a texted conversation.

While it is true that text messaging has certain advantages over actually talking to someone, depending on that form of communication has some dangers. Studies have already shown that young adults lack some skill in reading faces. Moreover, their addiction to text messages leads them to rudeness as they ignore the people who are actually present so they can answer the siren call of a message received. As text messages become even more prevalent, we will have to establish rules of etiquette for their use.

Writing Topics 3.7

Compare two ways of learning something or two systems of education. For example, you could compare two ways of learning a foreign language, or you could compare coaching for a sport in Canada and in another country.

Persuade

The mainstay of English courses is the persuasive essay (also called **argument essay**). Instructors want to know how well you can define and defend a position on a controversial subject. For the most part, you will be presenting your own viewpoint, but keep in mind that sometimes, as an academic exercise, you may be asked to argue something you do not personally agree with. This is a similar exercise to debates conducted in class where students may find themselves supporting the opposite side of a position they do not take themselves.

In everyday use, the word *argument* refers to a fight or dispute. In academic use, it refers to a reason given to show that something is true or correct. While all academic essays offer arguments, the term *persuasive essay* is usually used to refer to an essay on a controversial topic, where there are two distinct sides to the issue. The goal of this type of essay is to convince the reader that the point of view presented is the correct one to take.

It is important to present a view with impersonal, objective viewpoints that can be argued. For example, "I like horror movies" is a personal opinion. You can explain why you like them, but no one can argue against the fact of your liking them. However, in order to support your own personal attraction, you could use some sociological, physiological, or psychological studies showing why people enjoy a good scare.

Your argument is stronger if you use verifiable facts and relevant statements from trustworthy authorities. See "Find suitable sources of information" in Chapter 5 (p. 110) to read more about finding useful information.

Deductive and inductive reasoning

In classic argument, a distinction is made between deductive and inductive reasoning even though you will generally find deductive reasoning in essays.

In logic, the deductive method begins with a general observation or statement. Thereafter, the proof, evidence or support comes in the form of specific information, relevant to the subject. For example, a person can claim that tomatoes with green skin are not ripe. To prove or support that general statement, the person can pick some green tomatoes, cut them open, show how immature the seeds are in each, and perhaps even taste a few slices. Secondly, the gardener may introduce expert opinion, from scientists and agriculturalists, as added evidence. In short, the deductive method moves from general to specific.

The inductive method in argumentation starts with the specific. An adequate sampling of the subject is introduced before coming to the conclusion, or the making of a general statement. For example, in the tomato illustration, the person picks, say, twenty-five tomatoes with green skin. She tastes every one of those green tomatoes or observes the immature seeds in each. They all are deemed unripe. This gardener can now draw the conclusion or state general consensus that tomatoes with green skin are not ripe. In short, the inductive method begins with the particular, the exact, the definite, and finding the commonality then states the general result.

The deductive method in argument and basic exposition is used more often than the inductive. Setting up the condition in a general statement immediately establishes position. The audience or reader knows at once and exactly the person's stand on the topic. From there on, the reader merely follows the support or evidence to be presented. The deductive method is clear and upfront. It is the preferred strategy. On the other hand, the inductive method creates suspense. It is climactic, as each support is delivered and the reader can draw on the commonality of, perhaps seemingly disparate, evidence. When the conclusion or general statement is made, it is tried, tested, and indisputable.

The deductive method works well in the writing of paragraphs and essays. In most cases, the organization begins with the overview and then moves into details and specific information. We have advocated this strategy in our text. The classic essay structure has body paragraphs which begin with general topic sentences and then move to specific support of those statements—this is deductive reasoning in a nutshell.

Moving from general statement to specific support is found in most writings. For example, in "We All Should Worry about Cellphone Searches," William Kowalski starts his second paragraph with a general statement: "First, cellphones are the sites of our digital lives, and they contain an ever-increasing portion of our personal lives, making them much more than simply telephones in our pockets" (p. 217). He then goes on to give specifics: "Cellphones are portals into every aspect of our existence: What we've written to whom, what pictures we have taken, who's in our contact list, which websites we have viewed" (p. 217). The examples of what kind of information we store on our cellphones serves to prove his point that they are more than simple telephones. You can see more examples of this style in the four non-fiction readings in Appendix A.

Logical fallacies

The art of rhetoric also distinguishes between different kinds of logical fallacies, or errors in reasoning. Here are examples of common **logical fallacies** to avoid:

- Argument against the person (e.g., Hans has shifty eyes. You can't trust him to tell the truth.)
- Ambiguity (e.g., No vote is good.)
- Hasty generalization (stereotyping) (e.g., Fat people are lazy.)
- Begging the question (e.g., A good cause is good because it is good.)
- Appeal to pity (e.g., I'll be deported if you don't raise my grades.)
- Appeal to popularity (e.g., Four out of five dentists recommend this toothpaste.)
- Appeal to (false) authority (e.g., John has played a lawyer in a TV show; let's ask him about this point of law.)
- Appeal to fear (e.g., If you don't buy this product, you will get cancer.)
- Appeal to force (e.g., If you don't accept my argument, we can settle it outside.)

An astute reader will recognize these common fallacies and may dismiss your entire argument.

Overstating the argument

Another weakness common in essay writing is overstating the argument. Students may think that they must present serious problems to make a strong argument. For example, several students writing about the problems caused by cellphone addiction focused on dire health consequences such as brain cancer and eventual blindness instead of writing about simple, observable problems such as neck cramps and repetitive stress injuries. None of the students in the group wrote about the most likely route to injury from cellphone use—accidents caused by distraction (walking or driving while texting). Readers were unconvinced by their arguments and wondered why the writers were still using cellphones themselves with the threat of such calamity. You do not have to overstate the case—write about what you can observe and understand.

Other ways to avoid exaggeration include the use of modal verbs (such as *may* and *can*) and qualifiers like *many* and *some* instead of *all*. In addition, the simple present tense expresses general tendencies and does not need to be intensified with *always*.

- ✗ The older generation is not computer literate.
- ✓ Some older people struggle with computer technology.

- ✗ Students always hate morning classes.
- ✓ Morning classes are less popular.

- ✗ Students who skip classes fail their exams.
- ✓ Students who skip classes may fail their exams.

If you overstate an argument, your readers will be skeptical and will not accept your point of view.

Opposing arguments

In a spoken argument, you have the back-and-forth volley of opposing viewpoints being expressed. A persuasive essay, on the other hand, is essentially one point of view. However, it is useful to mention some arguments against your position—especially strong ones that readers will automatically think of. It's like dealing with the elephant in the room. By mentioning these points, you can defuse them and strengthen your own argument. Often this becomes a "yes, but" argument. You acknowledge the validity of an opposing viewpoint, but then offer something else that must be considered.

It is important, however, to make a clear distinction between your arguments and the opposing ones so that readers do not get confused. You can do this with sentence structure, presenting the opposing viewpoint is in a subordinate clause while the main idea is in the main clause, as in this example:

> Although people have a right to do what they want to their bodies, they do not have the right to force others to breathe in second-hand smoke. [for an anti-smoking essay]

> Although second-hand smoke can be annoying to other people, smokers can still enjoy their cigarettes if they do not indulge their habit in small, crowded spaces. [for an essay that argues for smokers' rights]

Transition signals, such as *however*, can also be used to distinguish opposing viewpoints from the writer's argument:

> Signatures are becoming less necessary as more institutions are moving towards biometric identification. However, it is still good to have a distinct and attractive signature. [for an essay about the usefulness of learning cursive writing]

In a short essay, do not give too much space to the opposing viewpoints—a sentence or two is often sufficient. You want to keep the focus on your point of view.

> Car manufacturers are racing to develop workable self-driving cars since so many collisions are caused by human error. While driver error is a problem, we must also acknowledge that computer systems are far from perfect—they can be hacked, they often behave in unintended ways, and they can break down.

As you read academic articles and journalistic essays, note how opposing viewpoints are given, and study the different techniques used so that you can incorporate them in your writing. Note, for example, that the two sample essays below use the opposing arguments in the introduction.

Exercise 3.2 Good argument or bad?

Determine whether the following statements work well as arguments. If not, identify the problem—whether it is a logical fallacy (and which one) or an overstatement, for instance.

1. Transportation in Toronto would be improved if we built more highways and roads. In addition, we should stop having so much construction in the city.
2. These must be the best athletic shoes on the market. All the celebrities are wearing them.
3. Women need male protectors because they are not competent enough to live on their own.
4. The assisted dying legislation allows doctors to help terminally ill patients end their lives. If doctors get that power, they will kill patients they don't like.
5. Skydiving is like scuba diving. Both sports require the athlete to jump into another element. In the former, the participant swims in the air; in the latter, the person is immersed in water. Both need specialized equipment such as a parachute or an air-tank. Both are dangerous activities where the failure of the equipment can cause death. Therefore, skydivers can scuba dive without much training.

6. People no longer need to know how to cook for themselves. They have many options for mealtime—restaurants, delivered packaged meals, and prepared foods in the grocery stores.
7. Students today have trouble writing essays because of text messaging. They are too used to relying on spell checkers, predictive text, and abbreviations.
8. Children who play violent video games grow up to be violent in real life.
9. Before modern technology, people could not communicate with each other over long distances.
10. I don't have to study for that test because I got an A on the last one.

Read the two sample essays that follow and the four non-fiction articles in Appendix A, examining the way the writers make their arguments. What techniques do they use and how effective are these techniques? Do you find the arguments convincing? You can compare your answers to your classmates' opinions in a discussion.

The World on a Screen

Much of computer technology is essentially communication-based. Cellphones have become essential tools of modern life, and teenagers send hundreds of text messages each day. The Internet allows us to have video chats with people all over the world. We can get tweets and see videos from political revolutions and natural disasters as they happen. With all these ways to communicate at our fingertips, our knowledge base should be expanding. However, instead of actually making our world wider, this technology is shrinking our world.

Today, people spend more time looking at screens than looking at the world around them. They are not in the here and now. They are glued to their smartphone screens at restaurants instead of talking to each other. Tourists view the scenery through their cameras instead of appreciating the grandeur of the sights. First-year university students spend their free time in their rooms communicating with their high-school buddies on Facebook rather than making new friends in the floor lounge. Even international students, whose parents spend thousands of dollars for them to learn English and a new culture, skip class to play video games in their rooms.

Not only are we glued to screens, but what we choose to watch is actually quite limited. Instead of broadcast media, we consume media that is narrowcast. We cannot gather around the water cooler to talk about the cliff-hanger ending of our favourite show—because we do not share a favourite show. When there were only a dozen channels, we had more shows in common. Even the popular TV shows are watched at different times. For example, some people may binge-watch a show on a streaming service months after it was initially broadcast. Our music is also individualized, as we make playlists for our personal music players, which we listen to on the bus, shutting out the world around us. As a result, we have no shared language of cultural events.

Even when we do use modern technology to communicate, we do it to exchange trivialities, not to have real conversation. Thousands of text messages are sent asking, "What are you doing?" with the inevitable answer, "Nothing much." Even people living in the same house text each other rather than going to the trouble of actually talking to each other. Text messages and Facebook updates take up so much time that teenagers have little time to expand their knowledge through reading and discourse. Students are addicted to their phones and focus on their messages rather than their lectures.

With all the promise computer technology offers, we are using it to help us retreat into our own comfortable little worlds. We need to take more time to explore those functions that help us create new art forms and reach out to others. We can start blogs and make our own websites. We need to travel and seek new experiences, taking advantage of all opportunities to interact with people face to face.

Why We Need Violence

Today, people argue that violence has no place in the world. Politicians, preachers, and the general public all buy into the mantra that violence is unacceptable, bad, and evil. Many use sports as the whipping boy to illustrate their point. This is especially true in hockey, where they say violence has gone amok. However, we need violent sports, like hockey, because we are hardwired to violence, because we require the vicarious experience, and because we would be hypocrites to deny its place in society.

Violence is part of being human. It's only recently that we try to act civilized and rein in our tendency to spank an unruly child or react physically to a slight. Hunting is still a popular sport despite the easy access to meat in our supermarkets. A police officer with a nightstick stops a fight among young toughs on the mean streets of Toronto. In the Air Canada Centre, a hockey enforcer slams an opponent against the Plexiglass, hard enough to drop the man onto the ice for several minutes. These are all acceptable levels of violence in our society. In each case, we are attracted to the natural kill, the righteous arrest, and the body check that may have stopped a goal from being scored. Sometimes we even act out violently, perhaps not on a person but in frustration, on an innocent chair or mess at the desk. Given the right conditions, we may even hit someone to protect ourselves or loved ones. Being human is to acknowledge our violent tendencies.

Violence needs an outlet. It cannot be totally suppressed or repressed. People have to blow off steam, and what better way to do so than at a hockey game. Instead of participating in the fisticuffs or the upper body check, we as spectators can experience the violence vicariously. We can let someone else do it for us. We need the cathartic moment, the purging of aggressive desires, pent-up frustrations, and unsanctioned urges that we dare not even admit to ourselves. Hockey is the proper release and relief valve. In an arena of twenty thousand fans, we can have a collective outburst. We cheer on the fight and revel in the violence. While it may seem improper to wish pain and suffering on someone else, it is better to relieve our desire for violence where it does not hurt someone else.

Finally, we are hypocrites if we do not acknowledge that we love violence. In the movie theatres, we have films that show people being blown up, dismembered, beaten to a pulp—all in the name of entertainment. Similarly at home, parents purchase video games for their adolescent children with CGI carnage. Killing becomes a measure of skill in hand–eye coordination. As a matter of fact, the fastest-selling and most popular video games are those that illuminate the most gore and mayhem in minute detail. In short, violence pays, and violence is fun. Implicitly we have accepted this, although in public we pay lip service to peace, order, and good government. So long as we ourselves are not victims but rather the perpetrators, violence is quite acceptable.

There is no sense keeping our collective heads in the sand when it comes to the subject of violence. Hockey is just one manifestation of it in society. Clearly hockey violence is an acceptable outlet as its fans attest. If there is any blame, the fault is not in hockey but in ourselves. Violence in hockey should not be the whipping boy to our societal ills.

Writing Topics 3.8

1. Take a controversial issue currently in the news, and write a persuasive essay on your point of view. This could be about a new law (such as assisted dying), the results of a court case, the actions of a politician, the plans for a new civic development—anything people are arguing about.
2. Write a persuasive email asking someone to do something for you. For example, you could be asking a professor for an extension on your assignment or asking your supervisor for a raise.

Answering essay questions on tests

Writing within the time limits of tests and exams is different from writing when you have weeks to complete an assignment. Doing an essay for an assignment affords you plenty of time for all three steps of the writing process (planning, drafting, and editing). For an essay test, however, you have to work quickly. You may have to rush your planning, but it is important not to neglect it entirely. Taking a few minutes to brainstorm and outline your essay can save you time once you start writing and can lead to a better essay.

In-class essays are often handwritten. This in itself can cause problems for students used to typing, not wielding a pen. You can minimize the amount of writing you have to do by doing only a point-form outline. Do not write a rough first draft; go straight to your good copy, writing as neatly as possible. Ensure there is lots of space on the page by double-spacing and leaving sufficient margins—you can use this space to make changes and corrections. Don't, however, use a pencil unless your professor approves. Most test instructions ask that you write in ink.

Know what you are expected to do and what your instructor will be looking for. Read the instructions carefully. If the instructions specify that you must write a five-paragraph essay, make sure that you have five paragraphs. You may be given an approximate word count—this is a guideline, so don't worry about counting all your words. (As a rule, however, you should know how many words you get to a typical page in your usual handwriting, so that you have a rough estimate of how much you need to write.) If you are asked for a 500-word essay, don't settle for half that number or write three times what the instructor wants.

Sometimes students are allowed to prepare for in-class writing. They may be given the topics beforehand and asked to bring in an outline. More often, however, an essay question on a test or exam is testing the students' ability to think and perform quickly.

If you know that you will be writing an essay based on works of literature you have studied in class, make sure you know those works thoroughly. Take notes, and highlight important sentences. (Always use highlighters judiciously—if you have transformed most of the text into brilliant colours, you know that you have gone too far and that your highlighting is ineffective.)

Be aware of your time constraints. You will usually be told in advance how much time you have for your exam. If you have other questions to answer in addition to the essay question, manage your time well. You should have an idea of how long it generally takes you to write a 500-word essay, for instance.

Try to save time for proofreading and correcting your essay. As you are writing, it is best not to interrupt your flow to figure out how to spell a word or to puzzle out a sentence structure. Keep going, get the words on paper, and then come back to fix the mistakes.

You may be allowed to use a dictionary for your test. Usually, this is restricted to a paper-based dictionary. Use it wisely, and don't waste time looking up every word you are unfamiliar with. Try to guess the meaning of some words from the context, and figure out which are the important words that need checking in the dictionary. Look up any words in the question that you may not be sure of, including those in any reading or passage that the essay is based on. Use the dictionary to check the spellings and meanings of words in your essay—but do this once you have finished writing the essay.

Remember that in a final-exam essay, you are showing your instructor what you have learned, what you have synthesized, and what you can do. Follow the style of essay you have been taught in class. Your instructor has probably made clear what criteria he or she will be primarily using for marking the essays.

Note that if you are writing a standardized exam such as TOEFL or IELTS, you should get specific training in writing essays for those tests. The goal is to score as many marks as possible on the test, so it is important to know exactly what criteria are being used. Examine the model essays provided in the study materials, and follow the guidelines carefully.

Approaching essay assignments

Each essay assignment is different, and each instructor has different expectations. Make sure you know what kind of essay you are supposed to write. The topic question should tell you, for example, whether you are writing a comparison or an argumentative essay. If the instructions are not clear to you, ask your instructor for clarification. Consider these questions for the different kinds of essays usually assigned in post-secondary English courses:

- Are you writing a personal, informal essay, or an impersonal, formal academic essay? Have you used the appropriate style?
- Have you supported your points adequately in expository essays?

- For cause and effect essays, have you made the distinction between causes and effects clear?
- For comparison essays, have you followed the recommended structure so that the reader can easily follow the points of comparison?
- For persuasive essays, is your position clear? Are your arguments logical and clear?

Writing about Readings

4

Reading and writing go hand in hand. All good writers are avid readers because from their reading they learn the vocabulary and structures common to the written language, which is not the same as the spoken variety. Reading not only teaches the language, it gives people something to write about as they build on other writers' works.

English courses are, therefore, built around the writings of other people—journalists, researchers, and literary writers. In other courses, you have textbooks and journal articles to read, but you are mainly reading these for content and information and less for analysis of the writing itself. Students are often tested on their reading comprehension, whether they are asked to paraphrase on specific reading tests, to write summaries, to respond to what the writers have said (either by agreeing with, disagreeing with, or extending the argument), or to analyze the reading itself.

Professors expect you to come to class having read the assigned article or story. This requires more than a quick skimming—you need to be prepared to discuss the work in class and ask questions about what you did not understand. You must engage in the conversation. Then you can write competently about the material.

In English composition courses (those generally taught in first-year college and university programs), the focus is on developing writing skills, but these courses include reading selections such as newspaper articles and short stories. In literature courses, there is less emphasis on writing skills; instead, students read and analyze poetry, plays, novels, and short stories. Although the term *literature* refers most broadly to anything that is written, it usually focuses on works that are considered to have literary value—that is works that are considered high quality because of the use of language and emotional effect.

The essays students are asked to write generally respond to the readings that have been assigned or to ones the students have found in their research. The reading is a point of departure, and the essays should be the students' ideas but should include references to the article or story. In this chapter and the next, you will see how readings are used in essays. The six reading selections in Appendix A are followed by sample questions to prompt discussion and essay writing.

Essays about literature require you to read carefully, to know about life and human behaviour, to understand the culture and traditions of the writer, and to comprehend the use of language and literary technique.

Literature reflects reality; art imitates life. The accumulation and understanding of experience will help you explain ideas in literature. For example, if you have ever been rejected in love or affection, you can understand both the hurt Hamlet feels when Ophelia returns his love letters to him and the reason that he lashes out at her.

Literature is more than understanding the words. It requires you to have a grasp of history, culture, and tradition. Writers write in, for, and about their time. They make assumptions about their readers' background knowledge. Generally speaking, the stories in an introductory literature course have a Western bent. From *Beowulf* to Virginia Woolf, the writings are based on Judeo-Christian teachings and European mythology and history. This means that writers will commonly use elements from Bible stories, fairy tales, Greek myths, and historical events. A standard Western education covers these areas, but you may find that you need to read more to supplement your background knowledge. This does not mean, however, that you need very specific information. For example, you do not have to understand the logging terms in the short story "The Moose and the Sparrow" (p. 222) to follow the plot, but some knowledge of the demands of a lumberjack's job will help you appreciate the story.

Information is given literally and figuratively, explicitly and implicitly. Knowing the literal and explicit is easy. A rose is a flower; a dog is an animal. There is little need for interpretation. However, understanding the figurative and implicit may not be so easy. The rose may be a symbol of passion, and the dog may represent wretchedness. Idioms are examples of figurative language; "letting the cat out of the bag" has nothing to do with cats and bags—it means revealing a secret. Interpreting meaning in real life helps in interpreting meaning in literature.

Read diligently. Reading for academic purposes requires you to spend more time than you would in reading for pleasure. You are absorbing and digesting information, and you are correlating what you are reading with what you already know. In short, you are thinking critically.

Take notes on what you read. The act of writing something down helps you to remember the particular reading. While you do not have to memorize what you read, you are expected to know the material well enough for class discussion, tests, and essay writing.

Look up words or concepts that you do not know. Use a reliable dictionary for words and phrases; use reference books or the Internet to search for information such as names and historical events. For example, if a story or article refers to the Montreal Massacre and you do not know what it is, look it up.

Don't just ignore references you don't understand. Develop a sense of curiosity, a desire to know more about something and everything. For example, if you are interested in the latest vampire fad in literature, you may want to learn the reason why vampires don't go out in daylight and cannot stand the smell of garlic. With a little research, you can discover that the disease called porphyria has these very symptoms. With this piece of information, you can understand how one aspect of vampire lore originated. While it is impossible (and time-consuming) to pursue every thread of interest, the Internet makes such searches relatively easy.

Think about what you have read. This serves not only as a review of materials but also as a way of making connections with what you already know. For example, as you read about Moose's bullying of Cecil in Garner's short story (p. 222), you can relate it to your own experiences with bullying in school.

When you write an essay about literature, the topic question may ask you to do one or more of the following:

- **analyze:** to examine critically details and ideas, to make judgments and to draw conclusions
- **argue for or against:** to persuade the readers that they should accept your opinion or point of view on a topic
- **examine or investigate:** to look into a topic objectively and closely, and report findings
- **develop or expand upon:** to take an idea and extend it with related and relevant information; flesh out
- **discuss:** to talk about or to explore generally one or more ideas
- **explain:** to make a concept, idea, or thing clear and comprehensible to people who know little of that subject
- **compare (and contrast):** to reveal similarities and/or differences in two or more works or readings on common elements
- **show:** to illustrate or demonstrate how something works
- **take a stand:** to have a firm opinion on the topic and explain your reasons for it

Distinguish between fiction and non-fiction

In libraries and bookstores, the primary division of books is between fiction (made-up stories) and non-fiction (verifiable, real stories). Even though works are often labelled as to which group they belong to, it can be confusing to distinguish between them, especially since the dividing line is not always distinct.

Works of fiction can be novels, short stories, or plays. In this book, there are two short stories in Appendix A: "The Moose and the Sparrow" by Hugh Garner and "The Cask of Amontillado" by Edgar Allan Poe.

Appendix A also contains four works of non-fiction, generally referred to as articles or essays. All four were first published in newspapers. When we are dealing with newspaper articles, we need to distinguish between news stories (which report the news) and columns or editorials (which give opinions). The latter category is similar to the essays that you are expected to write in your English course, except that you must follow a more academic style, not a journalistic style.

It is important to understand the distinction between fiction and non-fiction when you write about the works you read. You need to keep the terminology correct ("article" versus "short story," for example), and not refer to the author of an article as if he or she were a character. **Note that the word** *story* **has a general meaning.** A story can be any narrative, from a person's account of what happened to her when she encountered a shark on a vacation to a back story explaining a crime. Stories can include personal anecdotes and novels. That is why the term *short story* is used for a work of fiction.

Recognize that the line between fiction and non-fiction can blur. All fiction writers use their own experiences in their works, but when they tell a story very close to their own life, the work is described as **autobiographical fiction**. They may take the events, use actual people as characters, and make up dialogue. For example, D.H. Lawrence's *Sons and Lovers* is considered autobiographical fiction. In addition, **historical novels** are based on real characters and events, but they are fictionalized. **Non-fiction includes biographies and memoirs,** which are supposed to be true life stories, but they are based on imperfect memories and can become works of fiction. Non-fiction writers sometimes alter reality by using pseudonyms and changing personal details to hide the identity of informants. They may even create composite characters who are based on the experiences of different people. They do this to shelter identities but still maintain a certain truth in journalistic and investigative reports.

The blurred line between fiction and non-fiction extends to the movies you watch. Most movies are essentially fiction, even those "based on a true story"—they can veer widely from the accounts of actual events. Documentaries are non-fiction, but **docudramas** such as *United 93* use whatever information is available to recreate historical events, so they are a hybrid variety.

Although it may sometimes be difficult to distinguish between fiction and non-fiction, most of the time you will know by how the work is presented. Works of fiction, for instance, are often labelled as fiction when they are printed in anthologies, newspapers, and magazines. You can also get a feel for the differences as you read more of both. For example, works of fiction use more narration and dialogue than non-fiction.

Understand the use of first person ("I")

Part of distinguishing between fiction and non-fiction is to know who the first person in the work refers to. Generally speaking, you may assume that in non-fiction pieces whenever *I* is used, it is the author of the article. For instance, in "Why Are We So Scared of Eye Contact" Katrina Onstad uses the first person (as in "I'm constitutionally shy," on p. 215) to refer to herself. Similarly, in your essays, you use *I* to refer to yourself. This may sound obvious, but sometimes students copy the *I* from a quotation to a paraphrase or summary.

The use of first person gets tricky when you see it in works of fiction. Many short stories and novels are written in the first person. Both short stories in this book have first-person narration. As is often the case, the narrators' names are revealed in the dialogue. We learn that the narrator of "The Moose and the

Sparrow" is Pop Anderson: "'Oh! Oh, it's you, Mr Anderson!' He was the only person in camp who ever called me anything but 'Pop'" (p. 224). In "The Cask of Amontillado," Fortunato cries out "For the love of God, Montresor!" identifying the narrator as Montresor (p. 233).

If the narrator's name is not thus revealed, you cannot call the character by the author's name. Instead, you can say *the narrator* or refer to the character by whatever you know about him or her. For example, you can use expressions such as *the mother* or *the architect*.

Calling the character by the author's name sounds especially odd when the author is nothing like the narrator. For example, the novel *Memoirs of a Geisha* is written in the first person. The narrator is an elderly Japanese woman looking back at her life as a geisha; in contrast, the author, Arthur Golden, is a middle-aged American man. Another example is *Fugitive Pieces* by Anne Michaels, which has two male narrators.

In poetry, the use of the first person is generally considered to indicate the poet himself or herself—but not always. The *I* could be a persona, that is, the poet may be speaking through his character and the sentiments expressed may or may not be fully the poet's. For example, in Sonnet 73 (p. 97), the speaker may or may not be Shakespeare himself.

Refer to the author and characters correctly

Once you have determined who the *I* is, you must ensure that you use names correctly when you refer to both authors and characters. Note that in academic writing, the convention is that authors are referred to by family name.

Don't use the author's first, or given, name without the surname because that implies that you know the author personally:

> ✗ In "What if Dostoyevsky Had Been an Online Gambler?" John speculates whether the great Russian writer who wrote *Crime and Punishment* would have been so creative if he had not been a compulsive gambler in casinos.

The way of identifying the author of a piece generally follows a sequence. The first time you mention the name it should be in full. Later references to the person by name will be the family name alone. You can cut down on the number of times you use the author's name by sometimes saying *the writer, the author,* or *he* or *she*:

> ✓ In "What if Dostoyevsky Had Been an Online Gambler?" **John Sainsbury** speculates whether the great Russian writer who wrote *Crime and Punishment* would have been so creative if he had not been a compulsive gambler in casinos. **Sainsbury** then ponders whether the Russian author would have gained insight into human behaviour if he had gambled

electronically on online gambling sites. Finally, **the author of the article** questions Ontario's plan to expand into online gambling.

Note that the referencing in this summary could get tricky because both Sainsbury and Dostoyevsky can be referred to as "the author" or "he." With the use of the phrase "the author of the article," it is clear that this means Sainsbury and not Dostoyevsky.

Paraphrase

Paraphrasing essentially means expressing something in your own words instead of copying the phrasing of the author. If you repeat what the author says word for word, you need to use quotation marks and be sure to make no copying errors—a quotation has to be verbatim, exactly what the original said, including the punctuation. A paraphrase, on the other hand, expresses the same ideas, often summarizing them to make them somewhat shorter and perhaps even easier to understand.

> *Original passage*: "I must not only punish but punish with impunity." (Poe, paragraph 1, p. 229)
> *Paraphrase*: Montresor wants to hurt his victim but does not want himself to be hurt in the process.
> *Paraphrase*: Montresor wants to get away with committing murder.

Note that in a paraphrase you **don't repeat the *I* of the original**.

Paraphrasing is an important skill to develop, and so you are often tested on it in English courses. Not only does essay writing require the rephrasing of ideas, but on reading comprehension tests you are generally required to write short answers paraphrasing the original. On such tests, copying sentences from the passage will likely not net you any marks because copying shows no comprehension—someone who knows very little English can come into the test and get lucky and choose the right sentences to copy without understanding what he or she is copying. Paraphrasing, therefore, is a common test of comprehension.

> *Original quotation*: "Eye contact is vanishing and even I miss it—and I'm constitutionally shy, prone to ducking people by hiding behind pillars and shrubs in a cowardly Scooby Doo fashion. It's harder to catch a gaze these days; the mass focus is inward, toward the electronically curated self." (Onstad, paragraph 2, p. 215)

> ✗ *Poor paraphrase*: Eye contact is disappearing. Although I am shy, like Scooby Doo, I miss it. Catching a look today is difficult. People focus inward, and there is a digital self in the museum. [incorrectly uses *I*; uses many of the same words with some synonyms; shows poor understanding of the word *curated*]

✓ *Good paraphrase*: Onstad is complaining about the loss of eye contact in social interactions even though she is not very outgoing herself. Instead of looking at each other, people look at their devices, focusing on their own online world.

Paraphrase includes **indirect speech**. Direct speech is a quotation; indirect speech (also called reported speech) follows certain rules that require you to shift word order, pronouns, verb tense, and time markers. You can see the rules at work in these examples of direct speech, followed by versions in indirect speech:

John said, "Do you want to go to the movies after dinner?"
John asked whether we wanted to go to the movies after dinner.

Elena said, "Don't buy that cellphone. It's got bad reviews."
Elena warned me against buying that cellphone.

Melissa said, "I'd like to go to the mall with you."
Melissa said she would like to go to the mall with us.

When you **restate ideas in your essays**, you are also paraphrasing—but paraphrasing your own words instead of someone else's. An essay becomes tedious when the same phrase is repeated over and over again—especially when that phrase originates in the topic question. For example, if the question asks, "What is the key to successful learning in the classroom?" instead of repeating "The key to successful learning in the classroom" dozens of times, you can reword it in many different ways:

Attendance is the key to successful learning in the classroom. [Statement to be paraphrased—uses the wording from the topic question.]
Students who attend class regularly will be more successful.
Attending class is important.
Students who attend class regularly ultimately learn more.
Coming to class is the most important step in passing a course.
Achieving success in the classroom depends on regular attendance.

Note that knowing the derivative forms of words can help you paraphrase. For instance, instead of repeating the adjective *successful*, you can use the noun *success* and the verb *succeed*.

In order to paraphrase well:
- Make sure you understand the original passage. Use a dictionary for words you are not sure of.
- Make sure you understand the context. For instance, if you are asked to paraphrase a sentence from a reading, go over the sentences before and

after that sentence to understand what is being referred to, such as a pronoun reference.

- Use your own words—words you "own" that are in your active vocabulary, not words you understand from the reading but are not comfortable using.
- Don't quote or copy phrases from the original passage.
- Correct pronoun reference. (For instance, switch the pronoun *I* to whomever it refers to—the author or a character.)
- Don't just paraphrase by thesaurus. In other words, don't just merely substitute synonyms for some of the words in the original.
- Don't just manipulate the structure, moving phrases around.

Exercise 4.1 Paraphrasing

Paraphrase these quotations from the readings in Appendix A:

1. "All the evidence suggests that online gaming will prove an irresistible temptation to those who already have the gambling bug (while probably making some new recruits)." (Sainsbury, paragraph 8, p. 221)
2. "We should not be made complacent by the fact that only 'criminals' will have their digital lives laid bare." (Kowalski, paragraph 4, p. 218)
3. "And even when safeguards are put in place to ensure the devices are used for learning, they are often no match for students' ingenuity." (Maharaj, paragraph 5, p. 213)
4. "You could almost say he was carrying out a personal vendetta against the kid for refusing to knuckle under or cry 'Uncle.' From then on everybody but Moose let the kid alone." (Garner, paragraph 7, p. 223)
5. "The socially networked self arrives tidily edited; Facebook is an exercise in selective broadcasting." (Onstad, paragraph 7, p. 216)
6. "There were no attendants at home; they had absconded to make merry in honour of the time. I had told them that I should not return until the morning and had given them explicit orders not to stir from the house. These orders were sufficient, I well knew, to insure their immediate disappearance, one and all, as soon as my back was turned." (Poe, paragraph 24, p. 230)

Summarize

Being able to summarize well is not only an important skill for students; it is also an essential communication skill. For example, in the workplace, you may be asked to summarize an incident report or a business proposal. Those who can do the task well will rise in the ranks of the company because clear, concise communication is valued. We have all had to endure long-winded explanations—both oral and written—wishing that the person would just get to the point.

In school, summarizing lectures and reading material is a useful study tool. Summarizing forces you to understand and think about what you have read. It requires more thought than simply highlighting sentences in your reading.

Don't confuse summary and analysis. A summary should accurately and dispassionately convey what the author said and not include the summary writer's opinion. On the other hand, an essay is an analysis—don't just summarize what the author said or what happened in the story.

Write a summary

Although the subject of this book is essay writing, you may be called upon to write a summary in your English course. A summary is a brief version of a piece of writing. It can be as short as one sentence for an annotated bibliography in research work. It can also be as long as one-third the length of the original work, but more commonly it is about 10 per cent of the original length.

We often give summary tests to our students. We ask them to write a one-paragraph summary of an article, limiting them to 100 words for articles of 800–1,000 words. Conciseness is vital in this test, and students must rework their summaries until they have met the word limit but have still covered all the key points. For such a summary, the topic sentence should identify the work by title and author and should give the main idea of the original article. The summary should be a paraphrase, with no quotations.

Writing a summary involves several steps:

- Read the material thoroughly, looking up words and references you do not understand.
- Write down the main points in your own words.
- Follow the sequence of the original as much as possible.
- Write a draft from your notes.
- Make sure you identify the work in the first sentence (thus showing the reader that this is a summary and not your own ideas).
- Revise to make the summary meet the length requirements.
- Proofread and correct errors in grammar, spelling, punctuation, and word choice.

To avoid copying the author's phrasing, it is often a good idea to put the article aside after you are sure you have read it and understood it. Then write the first draft of your summary without looking at the article. Look back through the article to make sure your draft covers all the main points.

Ensure that you

- don't quote or use the wording of the original
- don't include your own comments or ideas
- don't use unnecessary examples or details from the original
- don't go over the word count for the assignment

The test of a good summary is in its clarity—it should be able to stand alone and be clear to someone who has not read the original work.

Sample summaries

Here is an example of a summary for a reading from this book, including the steps taken—the notes taken from the reading, the first draft, and the final draft. Consider each of the steps to understand what has been done:

1. How does the indenting in the notes show the relationship of the ideas?
2. Compare the article with the notes to see how the original wording has been paraphrased.
3. Look at what phrases and sentences have been dropped from the first draft for the final version. Why were these unnecessary?
4. Examine how some of the first draft sentences have been combined and reworded to retain the ideas but to express them more concisely in the final version.

Assignment prompt: Write a one-paragraph summary of "Beware the Risks of Smartphones and Tablets in Schools" by Sachin Maharaj (pp. 213–14). Do not exceed 100 words.

Preliminary notes:
"Beware the Risks of Smartphones and Tablets in Schools" by Sachin Maharaj
- schools are allowing and encouraging the use of smartphones and tablets in class
- digital devices can have educational benefits
- but problems with their use include:
  - distraction of games and social media
  - devices overused already, addiction
  - affects brain development, leading to
    - lack of empathy → cyberbullying
    - warped values (such as a desire for recognition)
    - reduction in intelligence, attention span
    - desire for instant gratification

First draft [needs to be edited and reduced to meet assignment requirements]:
In the article "Beware the Risks of Smartphones and Tablets in Schools" by Sachin Maharaj, the author draws attention to the negative effects of the use of cellphones and tablets in the classroom. Currently, Canadian school boards are encouraging the use of digital devices as a learning tool. However, as teachers can attest, students tend to use these devices for game play and social media and get distracted from their schoolwork. Even when

students are given locked devices, they manage to get into forbidden applications. Moreover, many students are addicted to cellphone use. Other research reveals problems in brain development. Young people do not get the opportunity to gain the benefits of deep thinking, do not learn empathy, and do not develop their attention spans and patience. Social media emphasizes instant approbation, which people get addicted to. According to Maharaj, school boards should rethink the implementation of technology in the classroom. [151 words]

Final draft:

In "Beware the Risks of Smartphones and Tablets in Schools," Sachin Maharaj argues against the move towards using digital devices in the classroom. Students are distracted from their schoolwork by games and social media, and using these devices just fuels their addiction. Overuse of digital devices can affect intellectual and emotional intelligence. Students may have weaker attention spans and less empathy for people. They depend on the gratification of acquiring social media "likes." They need to unplug, so Maharaj advocates reconsidering introducing smartphones and tablets into classrooms. [87 words]

For fiction, you can write a plot summary:

In "The Cask of Amontillado," Edgar Allan Poe tells of an aristocrat planning and executing a horrific scheme of revenge for a slight. Montresor lures Fortunato, his victim, by playing on the man's greed, pride, and gullibility. Moreover, the perpetrator has dismissed his servants from his palace so there will not be any witnesses. As Montresor leads Fortunato down to the catacombs, he plies his victim with alcohol to dull the man's wits. Finally, Montresor chains Fortunato and commences to wall him in alive. In the end, we learn that Montresor has got away with murder for over fifty years. [100 words]

Exercise 4.2 Editing for conciseness

Edit this 189-word summary to bring it under 100 words. Eliminate unnecessary phrases, choose more concise wording, and make any other corrections necessary.

In the fascinating cautionary article "We All Should Worry about Cellphone Searches," by William Kowalski, the author warns us about the problem of unwarranted digital invasions committed by the police, telling us that we should all worry about cellphone searches. On

December 11, 2014, the Supreme Court of Canada ruled that the police have the right to go through the information on people's cellphones. Kowalski says this ruling is wrong. He says that cellphones today contain a lot of private information about us and a search can reveal sensitive facts about a person's life that could be misused by the police. It's not only criminals that will have to worry about this invasion of privacy because innocent people are often caught up in police actions. If the police think someone is suspicious, they can go through that person's phone. We do not know what the police will do with such information in the long run. Kowalski offers some suggestions that people can take measures to limit such intrusions into their private lives, but it would be better if Canada did not allow such invasive laws in the first place.

Analyze non-fiction

You may be called upon to read and analyze works of non-fiction in your class. These works are commonly essays and newspaper articles. The first task is to **identify the thesis**—the main idea or argument.

Journalistic essays are similar to academic essays in that they have a thesis, but the thesis will not be as easy to locate as in the structured essay you write for school. It might be at the end of the introduction, but the introduction may be more than one paragraph, especially in newspaper and magazine articles where paragraphs are only one or two sentences (mainly because the text appears in narrow columns, and paragraph breaks serve to make the text more readable). Or the thesis might not appear until the end of the article, or it might be implied and not appear directly stated at all.

Use the title to guide you in determining the author's thesis, especially in newspaper articles, where the headline is often a summary of the main idea. Here are some sample titles that show you clearly what the article is about:

We All Should Worry about Cellphone Searches
Beware the Risks of Smartphones and Tablets in School
What If Dostoyevsky Had Been an Online Gambler?
Why Are We So Scared of Eye Contact?
The Case against Bottled Water
Fighting Hockey Violence Will Give You a Concussion
Disconnecting Hard to Do, Cellphone Generation Finds
No Point Fearing Terror Attacks We Can't Stop

Remember that **the thesis is not the topic**. If you say, "Maharaj's article is about the use of cellphones and laptops in school," you are relating the topic.

If you say, "Maharaj explains why personal computing devices should not be used in the classroom," you are giving the thesis. You give the topic in an *about* phrase; you give the thesis in a full statement. The thesis expresses an opinion—a position about the topic.

The rules that govern the thesis statement in essay writing (see Chapter 2) can guide you in finding the thesis in an article. The thesis statement is a supportable idea, not a fact. It is an argument. It is an opinion that might be related as a *should* idea. For example, "fighting should not be allowed in hockey" is a thesis; "hockey has a lot of fighting" is a fact.

Once you have determined the thesis, you can **identify supporting arguments and details**. For instance, Kowalski mentions the G20 protests in Toronto as an example of innocent people being arrested to support his thesis that everyone should be concerned about police searches.

When you study a non-fiction piece in class, you may be called upon to identify arguments in reading comprehension tests. You may be asked to paraphrase parts of the article or summarize the whole. You may be asked to write a personal response or a review giving your opinion of the article itself. When you write an essay based on a non-fiction article, you may simply use that article for a jumping-off point for your own essay, or you may be called upon to analyze the article.

After studying the article "Why Are We So Scared of Eye Contact?" you could be asked to explain the importance of eye contact. This is mentioned in the article, but your essay has to expand on that. You give your own ideas, but you can include a point or a quote from the reading. The article gives you a starting point, but you do not focus on the article itself. On the other hand, for the topic "How effective is the integration of personal and impersonal information in Katrina Onstad's article?" your essay should analyze the reading, so you will need more direct references to the article.

Whether your essay is analysis of the work or opinion of the ideas presented, **do not let the quotations do your work**. Quoting is not analyzing. (See "Quote effectively," p. 118.) When there is excessive quotation in a paragraph or an essay, you are padding the assignment. Instead, analyze by using your own words, and use quotation sparingly to support your points.

As an example, let's say you were writing an essay on William Kowalski's essay "We All Should Worry about Cellphone Searches" (p. 217) with the topic question "How effective are Kowalski's solutions to the problem of police searches?" Here are two versions of a body paragraph that could fit in this essay. This first example uses too much quotation and not enough argument:

✗　　Kowalski's suggestions are impractical. He says, "A simple step is to password-protect your phone. For now, the police cannot compel you to give up your password, although they may use other means to access your data." However, passwords are difficult to make and remember. In addition, he suggests, "It would also be wise to create a video or audio record of your encounters with police, and to connect your smart phone to a cloud storage service, so that pictures and audio are immediately uploaded." Cloud storage can also be accessed by the police and hackers. Kowalski cautions that ". . . this does not necessarily protect your files from 'accidental' deletion during a search, and it may allow police to access your other documents online." [123 words, of which 90 words are Kowalski's, not the student's]

This body paragraph paraphrases and explains more, rather than just quoting:

✓ Kowalski's suggestions for dealing with police searches are impractical. First, he suggests using passwords to lock the phone. While this is a logical first step, many people find passwords difficult to remember and awkward to use. Consequently, they use simple sequences such as "1234" which are easy to crack. He also suggests that people record their encounters with police on their phone. This can be useful if done surreptitiously, but the police have learned from their mistakes and will be on the lookout for this strategy. Uploading files to cloud storage can protect them but, as Kowalski points out, it does not "protect your files from 'accidental' deletion during a search." They can also be accessed by others once they are online. Kowalski's advice can be useful as primary measures, but may not be practical or fully protective. [135 words]

In an essay, body paragraphs should begin with a topic clearly stating your main idea—your argument. Don't begin body paragraphs with quotations. This may lead to explaining the quote rather than analyzing a point or idea. Here is an example for the topic "In 'What If Dostoyevsky Had Been an Online Gambler?' John Sainsbury argues that gambling online is worse than in casinos. Do you agree? Explain why or why not."

✗ "The most terrifying outcome of Internet gambling is isolation, estrangement from friends and family, estrangement even from the company of strangers in traditional casinos." What Sainsbury states is quite true. Internet gambling isolates gamblers. They cannot be with family members, like their spouse and children, or even with friends. It is very lonely. Furthermore, Sainsbury says that Internet gambling is worse than the kind of gambling in casinos where people can at least rub shoulders with fellow gamblers.

Instead, begin with a specific topic sentence that is relevant to the assignment:

✓ Internet gambling erodes the gambler's soul. In traditional gambling, the gambler must at least associate with like-minded individuals and thus have some form of social activity. Internet gambling destroys the gambler's social nature. His companion is the screen and his "friend" is computer-generated visuals. In the casinos, the gambler can share the cheer of winning a hand or howl at a losing one. In front of a monitor, no one can hear him laugh or cry. This is what Sainsbury means when he says: "The most terrifying outcome of Internet gambling is isolation, estrangement from friends and family, estrangement even from the company of strangers."

Here is an example of a full essay comparing the writing techniques of two of the articles in Appendix A. The topic is "Compare the writing techniques used in 'What If Dostoyevsky Had Been an Online Gambler?' and 'Why Are We So Scared of Eye Contact?'"

Writing Techniques Used by Sainsbury and Onstad

"What If Dostoyevsky Had Been an Online Gambler?" by John Sainsbury and "Why Are We So Scared of Eye Contact?" by Katrina Onstad both focus on human behaviour. Sainsbury writes about gambling addiction, while Onstad bemoans the loss of eye contact in today's digitally focused world. Although their topics are different, the writers use similar writing techniques, ones that are common to journalistic essays. Sainsbury and Onstad both use anecdotal openings, conversational style, and touches of humour.

Sainsbury and Onstad each open with a story of a specific person. Sainsbury paints a picture of Feodor Dostoyevsky, the roulette tables he was addicted to, the wife he wronged, and the exile from his Russian homeland. Sainsbury moves from the problems of a nineteenth-century Russian writer to the modern problems of online gambling. Onstad draws us in with a scene in which a conversation is interrupted by a woman using a cellphone. Because we have all experienced (and probably committed) this breach of etiquette, we can relate to the situation. Onstad then goes on to discuss lack of eye contact in general. While Sainsbury uses a historical personage and Onstad talks about an anonymous woman, both personal examples help the reader understand the broader issues.

Both articles are scholarly musings with touches of conversational style. The titles in the form of rhetorical questions—"What If Dostoyevsky Had Been an Online Gambler?" and "Why Are We So Scared of Eye Contact?"—not only underscore the topic but also pique the reader's curiosity. Both

Sainsbury and Onstad mix formal and informal registers. For example, Sainsbury uses academic analysis: "Dostoyevsky lays bare his own gambling compulsion…so convincingly that even prosaic behavioural psychologists remain in awe" (220) but also includes phrases such as a nanny's "money-grubbing purposes" (221) and addresses Dostoyevsky with "Feodor, you've got to switch off the computer and come out of the basement. Right now" (221). Onstad uses academic language when she refers to studies that conclude "eye contact came to be the cornerstone of communication because of the 'cooperative eye hypothesis,' which suggests that collaboration and cooperation are optimized when our eyes are locked" (215-16) but she also uses conversational phrases such as "Surely there's a word for this" and "Let's call" (215).

Both Sainsbury and Onstad pepper their article with touches of humour. The levity makes the serious arguments easier to digest. Sainsbury's amusing picture of Dostoyevsky in a modern setting calls to mind the stereotypical nerd, hunkered down in a basement with his computer, reinforcing the idea that online gambling is lonely and joyless. His call to "Feodor" to get out of the basement ends the article on a humorous note. Onstad draws on her own awkward experiences with eye contact and compares her actions to a cartoon Great Dane, calling herself "constitutionally shy, prone to ducking people by hiding behind pillars and shrubs in a cowardly Scooby Doo fashion" (215). Her description of proper eye contact "neither staring like a stalker, nor flitting like a butterfly" (216) is also funny.

Both John Sainsbury and Katrina Onstad use time-honoured journalistic techniques to interest readers in their subject matter. They take serious social issues and use light touches with academic analysis to make the arguments accessible to newspaper readers.

Analyze fiction

In English courses, you study literature, and in general, literature means fiction, or made-up stories, that are not real but have relevance to life, society, and you. While these stories entertain, they express certain truths—some obvious and some subtle. Works of fiction may be in the form of short stories, novels, plays, or poetry. In a literature class, you are expected to examine various elements in the works to appreciate the skill of the author, the ideas expressed, and the way the ideas are conveyed.

Remember that real life is messy and chaotic; made-up stories are orderly and disciplined. Because fiction is art, and art follows well-defined rules so that we can make judgments, you will find after a while that analyzing fiction is merely applying the rules and conventions that govern fiction.

Pay close attention to the reading

Know it well so you can write confidently about it. When you don't know enough, you show this weakness in the essay. Often this comes in the form of generalities instead of specific information and mistakes in naming characters and explaining concepts.

Start to analyze by following these steps:

- Identify the theme or subject of the piece of literature. Knowing what it is about will help you see how other elements of literature are incorporated and used.
- Focus on one aspect you are going to analyze in the essay. All other elements will be subordinate to this prime goal.
- Search for and interpret patterns. For example, the writer may use repetition of words or motifs to emphasize something important.
- Find supporting evidence. To do so, you may have to use sources other than the piece of literature itself, such as critical studies of the work.

The paragraph below illustrates how literary analysis works. The topic sentence gives the main idea of the paragraph. In this case, it states that bullying is the theme of the story. The rest of the sentences support this main idea by explaining how the theme of bullying is developed throughout the story.

> In Hugh Garner's "The Moose and the Sparrow," the theme of bullying in the workplace is evident. Throughout the summer in the lumber camp, Moose Maddon, the seasoned lumberjack, made Cecil, called the Sparrow, miserable. What started as customary hazing turned dangerous: Maddon tosses the young man into a freezing river, deliberately steps on his glasses, and burns his hand. This kind of bullying is often exhibited in the workplace, and because Moose Maddon's skills are needed, the company ignores his actions to the detriment of the victim. What this means is that Maddon is implicitly given permission to continue his cruel actions against a vulnerable young man. Without adequate protection from the company, Cecil effects his own defence and plots to kill his tormentor. Garner makes the case then that when pushed to the breaking point, the victim will react violently. The consequences of bullying are bad for both instigator and victim.

Learn to extrapolate

Extrapolation is the expanding of knowledge or information from limited facts or known qualities. You make **inferences**. It is a useful skill to acquire in any discipline. By using what is known, you can confidently make educated, accurate guesses or projections relevant to the topic. For example, in Poe's "The Cask of Amontillado" Fortunato is described as wearing motley. You realize immediately that Fortunato is a fool. Motley is multi-coloured clothing—the typical dress of a clown or a fool. As the story progresses, you learn that Fortunato is a fool to be lured to his doom by Montresor. It is with the word *motley* that Poe defines his character trait and foreshadows Fortunato's fall.

Analyze, don't retell

Do not merely retell the story. The most common problem in literary essays is that students relate what happens in the story without analyzing it. They assume that by summarizing the story they have examined and explained the idea. Plot summary is inadequate in analytical essays.

Here is an example of retelling the story:

✗　In "The Cask of Amontillado," Montresor vows vengeance on Fortunato for an unspecified insult. The avenger, disguised, seeks out Fortunato during high carnival in which everyone is in costume and inebriated. He baits his victim with the promise of an expensive and rare wine, and at the same time wounds the man's pride by suggesting that he would seek out another connoisseur. Next, Montresor takes Fortunato to his palazzo where he has earlier "dismissed" the servants and thus any possible witnesses to his crime. To keep Fortunato off guard, he continually plies the man with other brands of wine. Finally, down in the depths of the catacombs of his palace, Montresor binds Fortunato in chains and bricks the victim alive in the wall to die. We learn in his confession that Montresor has gotten away with murder for fifty years.

Instead of summarizing, explain ideas with incidents from the story to support your point. First, however, you need to have a topic sentence that makes a point. Then, use the incidents in the story to support that point:

✓　In "The Cask of Amontillado," Montresor uses his knowledge of human behaviour to further his vengeance on Fortunato. First, the avenger works on Fortunato's weaknesses, which ironically the victim believes to be his strengths. He uses a cask of rare wine as bait. By asking the victim to verify the Amontillado, Montresor flatters Fortunato for his connoisseurship of vintages. Moreover, he waylays any suspicion of treachery when he ingratiates himself into Fortunato's vanity: Montresor has doubts about the vintage; only an expert like Fortunato can assuage his doubts. Next, the avenger wounds Fortunato's pride by suggesting he would seek another connoisseur. (Montresor has no intention of calling upon Luchresi but by suggesting it Montresor tightens his trap.) This action makes the victim want to prove himself. At the same time, he triggers

Fortunato's greedy nature. The man cannot resist a free drink or two or three. Knowing Fortunato's nature, Montresor uses it to his advantage in order to effect his revenge for an insult by walling in the victim alive.

In analysis, you must use parts of the plot to support your interpretation. Somewhere in the paragraph, you have to explain why, how, or what to secure your point.

Here is another example of analysis:

In H.G. Wells's *The Time Machine*, the earth of A.D. 802701 is shown as a nightmare world to the time traveller in three distinct ways. First, although the traveller is initially impressed with the pristine vegetation and the carefree humanoids, called the Eloi, he quickly learns that these child-like people in this world lack certain human traits. Their hedonistic ways hide their lack of responsibility and moral obligation to one another. For example, when a female Eloi, Weena, nearly drowns, none of her companions tries to help her; none of them cares whether she lives or dies. It takes the time traveller to save her life. This incident is the first among many other disillusionments about a utopian world for him. Second, at the decaying and dust-filled Palace of Green Porcelain, to his sorrow, the traveller discovers that the Eloi have abandoned the glory of past civilizations, the achievements of humanity, and the desire to progress. The Eloi prefer sloth over preserving the best traits of being human. Third, the traveller's misconception that this world is an earthly paradise comes to an end when at night the cannibalistic Morlocks rise from their underground caverns to harvest the Eloi. Later, to his horror, the Morlocks snatch Weena from the campfire and kill her. At each new discovery, the time traveller grows more disenchanted with the far future.

Here is a sample analytical essay on the topic "Did the Sparrow kill the Moose?"

Solving the Mystery in "The Moose and the Sparrow"

In "The Moose and the Sparrow," Hugh Garner offers the reader an ambiguous ending, a mystery as to whether a 19-year-old university student murdered a lumberjack. Throughout the story, Garner provides evidence that can be interpreted either way. I believe the Sparrow did do away with the Moose. Cecil had motive, opportunity, and means.

Cecil had motives for murder. The first reason is revenge. Throughout the summer, Cecil was harassed by Moose Maddon. At the beginning, it was ritual hazing of a greenhorn by all the lumberjacks. However, Maddon went beyond what was acceptable: he tarred Cecil's face; he dumped Cecil into the cold river at night; he broke the young man's glasses; and he burned Cecil's hand with a heated saw blade. Cecil could not get back at Moose through physical strength as the lumberjack was stronger and more skilled in fighting, so he concocted a way to dispose of Moose using intelligence and skill. Second, Cecil feared for his life. He told Pop Anderson that Moose was going to hurt him seriously or kill him before the summer was over. In doing away with Moose, he was protecting himself from serious harm or even death.

The Sparrow had the time and the chance to commit premeditated murder. As a bright university student, Cecil could identify and exploit Moose's weaknesses, such as his habit of drinking heavily during off hours. Although he was guarded in the bunkhouse on the night of the murder, Cecil could have sneaked out. The good-hearted loggers were looking out for Moose coming into the bunkhouse, not Cecil leaving. That would have made it easy for Cecil to go to the ravine unnoticed, set the trap, wait until Moose returned from the other camp, taunt the lumberjack, and then watch Moose trip and fall into the ravine.

Cecil also had the means to kill Moose. During the summer, he showed his dexterity in fashioning trinkets with copper wires. Even Pop Anderson received a braided watchband as a going-away present. As a matter of fact, Cecil almost told the older man his intentions when he cryptically said he had enough wiring "for what [he had] in mind" (p. 226). In short, he was smart enough to hide the murder weapon in plain sight. Although Cecil had a burned hand, he could still braid the wire, so his injury would not have prevented him from wrapping the copper wires around two saplings—if, as Pop Anderson speculated, that is what caused Moose to fall to his death.

Cecil the Sparrow killed Moose Maddon. He had the motive—revenge and self-preservation—he had the opportunity when others did not expect him to go out to lay a trap, and he had the equipment to do it. As a matter of fact, he committed his crime so well that the district coroner announced that Moose Maddon, a sure-footed, champion logger, died in an accident.

This essay is a comparison of the two short stories in Appendix A:

Death in "The Moose and the Sparrow" and "The Cask of Amontillado"

The taking of a human life is both morally and legally wrong, but some people go to the extreme of doing just that. In "The Moose and the Sparrow" and "The Cask of Amontillado," Hugh Garner and Edgar Allan Poe show us two killers—Cecil "the Sparrow" and Montresor respectively. In the former story, the killing is done as self-protection and revenge; in the latter, walling in the victim is sheer vengeance for a slight. The two stories show how the murders were set up, the motives behind the acts, and the surprising conclusions.

In both stories, the killings are premeditated and planned carefully. Garner's Sparrow plots the death of his nemesis, Moose Maddon, at the lumber camp. Having observed Maddon's traits and habits over the course of the summer, Cecil knows when and where his victim is most vulnerable. He sets a trap at a ravine where Maddon would return after a night of partying, and then provokes Maddon to rush at him to make him fall to his death. In a similar fashion, Poe's Montresor plans the death of Fortunato, his enemy. The murderer knows the weaknesses of his victim and uses them to his advantage: Fortunato is greedy, vain, and gullible. Montresor strikes at high carnival where everyone is drunk and disguised in costume and he dismisses his servants so there will be no witnesses. He uses the lure of the Amontillado to lead Fortunato into the catacombs, where he traps him and leaves him to die. In both cases, the killers succeed in ending the lives of their victims, exactly in the manner of their schemes.

Both Cecil and Montresor have motive to justify their acts. From the moment that Cecil starts working at the lumber camp, Moose Maddon bullies him. At first it is the standard hazing of a new recruit, but then Maddon's attacks become life-threatening. Cecil gets dumped into the freezing river and has his hand deliberately burned. Thus, self-preservation and revenge are Cecil's motives. In comparison, Montresor seems to have less reason for hating Fortunato. The insult Montresor refers to is not revealed in the story, but he says that Fortunato has caused Montresor a thousand injuries in the past. Moreover, Montresor himself admits to losing aristocratic status while Fortunato's star rises: "'The Montresors . . . *were* a great numerous family [italics mine]'" (p. 231). Finally, Montresor is both envious and contemptuous of Fortunato. He wishes to vindicate his family's honour in his fashion. Thus, both men believe they have cause to commit murder.

Finally, Garner and Poe break the rule that in crime good triumphs over evil by having both Cecil and Montresor get away with murder. After his tour of work at the lumber camp, the Sparrow flew back to Vancouver. At that time, no one suspected him of foul play. A district coroner already pronounced Moose's death as accidental. All Pop Anderson has are some suspicious burn marks on two saplings and what was possibly the murder weapon transformed into a wrist band. Cecil has covered up his crime well. Similarly, Montresor lives fifty years after the walling in of his nemesis, Fortunato. He too lives to enjoy a long life. Only his confession to a priest reveals him to be a cold-blooded murderer. Both Cecil and Montresor escape detection and legal punishment. Both murderers are calculating, remorseless, vengeful. Both men know that premeditated murder is illegal and immoral in society's eyes, but they are cocky enough to do it and to get away with it without any repercussion or suspicion falling back on them.

In "The Moose and the Sparrow" and "The Cask of Amontillado," Hugh Garner and Edgar Allan Poe each present a study in revenge and murder. Whether set in nineteenth-century Italy or contemporary British Columbia, these stories show people driven to plot and kill—and get away with it. The reader can admire the cleverness of the crime, sympathize with either victim or murderer, and determine whether getting away with murder is justified.

Analyze poetry

Analyzing poetry is similar to analyzing a story, a play, or a novel. You work with the same literary elements, such as theme and point of view. Greater focus is placed on imagery, symbols, metaphors, and similes. (If you are not familiar with these terms, see the list starting on page 104.) You also have to consider poetic techniques—alliteration, rhyme schemes, rhythm and metre, and versification. Some poems are narrative and so have a plot, characters, and setting. Poets use different kinds of poetic forms, such as the ode, sonnet, and haiku. Poems can stretch to book-length works such as Tennyson's *Idylls of a King* or Chaucer's *Canterbury Tales*.

Poetry is concentrated—mainly because most poems are relatively short and have to pack a lot into a small package. Poems have been compared to the layers of an onion, so as you peel one layer off there is another whose meaning has to be unravelled. Poetry is probably more difficult to examine and explain than prose because of the suggestiveness that forces you to see a lot more than the literal meaning of a word or image. For example, in Shakespeare's sonnet, the ending of life is given in three images: a season, a day, and an ember. Each image is reduced significantly to almost nothing as the man is dying. However, the sonnet is not about the brevity of life but rather the loss of love. The poem ends with some ambiguity as to who is affected more: the lover who lives or the lover who dies.

William Shakespeare's Sonnet 73

That time of year thou mayst in me behold
When yellow leaves, or none, or few, do hang
Upon those boughs which shake against the cold,
Bare ruined choirs where late the sweet birds sang.
In me thou see'st the twilight of such day
As after sunset fadeth in the west,
Which by and by black night doth take away,
Death's second self, that seals up all the rest.
In me thou see'st the glowing of such fire,
That on the ashes of his youth doth lie
As the deathbed whereon it must expire,
Consumed with that which it was nourished by.
    This thou perceivest, which makes thy love more strong,
    To love that well which thou must leave ere long.

Analysis of Shakespeare's Sonnet 73

When the writing of sonnets was in fashion, William Shakespeare wrote about 156 of them. He did not follow the Petrarchan structure as many of his contemporaries did. He changed a number of features. Instead of the octave and sestet divisions, he introduced three quatrains and a rhyming couplet, and an easier rhyme scheme. These innovations became not only the hallmark of a Shakespearean sonnet but also a pattern of creativity. Sonnet 73 "That time of year thou mayst in me behold" is typical of his method. Here, Shakespeare uses analogy, imagery complementing the speaker's state of mind, and reversal of perspective in the couplet to develop the eternal theme of death and love.

In expressing the concept of the end of life, Shakespeare compares old age or dying to the closing of a season, to the closing of a day, and to the embers of a fire. The first quatrain develops the death theme by comparing the aged speaker to autumn, a season that inevitably leads to winter or death. The speaker himself draws attention to this comparison: "thou mayst in me behold / When yellow leaves, or none, or few, do hang/ Upon those boughs . . ." (ll. 1–3). In the second quatrain, the analogy shows the narrator as twilight or a short moment between light and darkness, with of course darkness meaning death. Here Shakespeare reduces the length of a season to twilight, suggesting the brevity of life. Death is closer; life is shorter. In the third and final quatrain, the reduction of time and life is represented by the embers of a fire in the hearth or fireplace. The comparison is clear: a season or even twilight has some length, but the last glow of a spent log cannot last more than a few hours or minutes. Like a season, an evening, and an ember, the narrator's life too follows ultimately to an end.

The images that accompany the theme do more than just compare the speaker to three natural pictures. These pictures reveal a sense of self-pity and manipulation in the speaker. Even as the narrator draws relationships of dying nature, such as fallen leaves, the end of day, and a spent fire log, he wants to elicit an emotional response from the silent lover. First, the repetition of "in me" three times (ll. 1, 5, and 9)—once in each quatrain—forces the listener (and the reader) to focus on the speaker. Season, day, or embers are merely trappings or illustrations of the speaker's state, and it is his own dying to which he wants attention paid. With these images, the speaker mourns his lost youth ("on the ashes of his youth doth lie" l. 10) and needs validation that his listener/lover has feelings for him. There is a strong resonance of "you should pity me because I am going to die." In addition, he hints at a past in which both he and his lover shared the summer season, a full day, and a glowing fire. But even here, the speaker is manipulating emotions in the listener.

In the rhyming couplet, Shakespeare shifts focus but the conceit remains the same. Whereas for twelve lines the attention is on the speaker, now in the thirteenth and fourteenth lines, Shakespeare, through the narrator, emphasizes "thou," the silent lover. This person now must be aware of the speaker's condition, and because of his relationship the listener must surely feel the pain of separation. Knowing that death will sever the ties between these two, the listener must increase his affection: "thy love more strong, / To love that well which thou must leave ere long" (ll. 13–14). This may be a natural response, but it is nonetheless sheer manipulation of emotion. The power of the couplet is its ability to put a guilt trip on the survivor. It is not merely a gentle reminder; it is emotional blackmail.

Shakespeare's sonnets all follow a consistent pattern in form and content. Sonnet 73 is representative of the poet's method in his sonnet sequence. The first twelve lines or verses, divided into three quatrains, has one perspective, and in the rhyming couplet (conclusion), he almost always switches to another. It is the couplet then that delights or surprises the reader with its dramatic twist.

Understand literary terms

When you are asked to write an essay about a work of literature, you may have to examine theme, compare characters, or explore symbols. To do this, you must understand the basics of literary terminology. Here's a primer. You can consult books on literary analysis for more detailed explanations if you need to go into more depth.

Plot

Plot is essentially the action or events that occur in a story. The most basic plots are categorized as man versus nature, man versus man, and man versus himself. The first category includes stories of disasters and survival, such as *Lost in the Barrens*; the second includes war stories such as *All Quiet on the Western Front*; and the third includes psychological drama such as *Dr. Jekyll and Mr. Hyde*. All plots require some sort of **conflict**.

Stories rely on basic dramatic situations that make up classic plots, such as these:

- boy (or girl) meets girl (or boy)
- love lost then found again
- the protagonist is confronted with a problem and solves it
- the protagonist succumbs to temptation but is redeemed
- a person is forced to choose between duty and personal desire
- the protagonist overcomes a failing of some sort
- an aged person comes to terms with the past
- lovers, friends, or family members quarrel and then reconcile
- the protagonist sets out on a quest or performs an impossible feat
- a doubt about a protagonist is laid to rest
- a good or bad person comes to an unexpected end
- a bully becomes a victim (or vice versa)
- a person solves a mystery or foils a plot

A plot needs cause and effect. Something must have happened to make the protagonist act or react. This is the **inciting incident**. For example, Hamlet merely mopes about his father's death until he discovers from his father's ghost that Claudius murdered him. This discovery pushes him into action.

Plot twists keep the story going. Something unexpected happens—and although it is prepared for by the writer, the reader does not suspect until it occurs. For example, detective mysteries often have many twists and turns before the exposing of the true criminal or murderer. The introduction of a new character or of a new piece of information may turn the plot 180 degrees.

In short stories, there is usually a single plot; however, in novels and longer pieces, such as Tolkien's *Lord of the Rings*, writers include multiple plots. This requires the interweaving of characters and actions.

Subplots generally bolster the main plot. The writer uses a subplot to underscore by repetition or variation the action of the main plot. Some subplots are short, whereas others carry on to the end of the tale. For example, in Shakespeare's *King Lear*, the main story is that of Lear and his three daughters; the secondary plot is that of Gloucester and his two sons.

Finally, **plots require a conclusion, or an ending**. In fairy tales, the prince marries the princess and they live happily ever after. In adventure tales, the hero has in his quest achieved his goal. In mysteries, Sherlock Holmes has uncovered the murderer and explained how he did it. In short, the conclusion wraps up the loose ends. However, some writers give the reader a surprise ending. The reader is caught totally unprepared. This kind of ending demands that the writer play fair by providing enough clues in the story.

As a final comment on plot, the writer has the right to decide when and where to end the story. The reader may wish the story to continue or may imagine alternative endings or may debate with other readers about the conclusion, but the writer ultimately chooses how a story concludes.

Characters

Stories require characters; otherwise, the telling is nothing more than a report. Characters move the plot along. They play out the themes in the story. Readers are interested in characters and sometimes wish them to be real rather than fictional. In film and television, such is true for *Star Trek's* Kirk and Spock; in literature, Sherlock Holmes lives and breathes in the hearts and minds of readers.

Characters are the most interesting element in stories. Some reflect us, the readers, and we in turn identify with them simply because they are so like us. Others intrigue us because they are different. Perhaps their cultural background, hard life, or joys engage the reader. Perhaps their universal appeal, which transcends place, space, and time, draws the reader in.

Protagonist is the literary term for the main character, commonly referred to as the hero or heroine. "Pro" means for, and "agonist" means one who struggles.

Thus, the protagonist is the person who faces the obstacles and overcomes them. The protagonist can be either good or wicked.

An **anti-hero** is a main character who defies the convention of his society, mocks it, and tries to live apart from it. This character may start out as a bad person but change by the end of the story. Readers are drawn to the anti-hero because of the heightened balance of good and evil within the character. An anti-hero is often used in satire or in comedy.

The **antagonist** is the dominant opposition to the protagonist. "Anti" means against, so an antagonist is someone who struggles against the hero but is not necessarily an evildoer.

Stories also need **supporting characters**. These "minor" characters are essential to the story. For example, Dr John Watson, Sherlock Holmes's companion, narrates most of the famous detective's adventures. Through Watson's eyes, the readers see the plot unfold and the hero make his astute deductions. Supporting characters often create the inciting incident that ultimately involves the protagonist. They also may be a moderating influence that makes the hero see the light. At other times, these characters help shape the story. Where would Frodo be without Sam, or Harry Potter without Hermione and Ron?

Supporting characters may be either stereotyped or rounded. In the case of stereotypes, the author does not flesh out traits and personalities. These characters do not "grow" or develop; their personalities remain static and unchanged. These characters function as short-form references, especially in short stories where there is no room to develop these characters.

Details in characterization

Characterization is the way the writer creates the person or persons in the story. Characterization is the details that make an invented person interesting, distinct, and plausible. Although often it is the skill and talent of the author that turn the character into a flesh and blood person, certain common techniques help in the process.

Recognizable character traits are archetypes. In literature, there are certain universal kinds of character, such as the leader, the warrior, the lover, the fool, the wise mentor, the apprentice, and the maiden.

The **names** of characters are important in literature. In "The Cask of Amontillado," the victim is ironically named Fortunato; he is anything but lucky. Not only does the protagonist in "The Moose and the Sparrow" have the nickname Sparrow, but his given name, Cecil, is one that you would expect for a weak, nerdy character. The meanings of names can easily be found in a baby name book or website. For example, Sarah means princess; Linda, pretty; Peter, rock; and Ali, greatest. Surnames, of course, often reveal ethnic origin.

The **physical features** of a character are also telling. Details such as physical size and hair colour help considerably. For example, a red-haired person is often portrayed as quick-tempered or quirky.

In addition to human characters, you must consider the non-human, such as talking pigs (as in George Orwell's *Animal Farm*) or the Jabberwock (as in Lewis Carroll's *Through the Looking Glass*). However fantastic or ordinary these other beings are, they share one common element: they have identifiable human traits or personalities. They can become angry, sad, happy, or thoughtful. They too fit into the roles of protagonist and antagonist, or rounded and stereotyped characters.

Setting

Setting is basically place, or "where." It is the location in which the story will be told. For example, in "The Moose and the Sparrow," Garner sets the story in a lumber camp in British Columbia. Poe's setting is atmospheric: he takes us from the "supreme madness" of the streets during Carnival to the deadly depths of the catacombs.

Setting includes time, or "when." An author may set his story in contemporary times—remember that this means the time in which the author lived. Historical fiction is set in the past, and science fiction is generally set in the future. The setting can be an unreal world, such as the fantasy of witches and muggles living side-by-side in contemporary England in the Harry Potter books.

Writers do not need to announce the setting. Hints may be given out in passing. For example, the technology used by characters often reveals the time setting. A person searching for a pay phone to make a call means the setting could be any time before the ubiquity of cell phones, but if he has to dial a rotary phone, then the story is set before the 1970s.

Themes

Theme is subject matter: what the story is about. The theme may be the message that the writer wishes to convey through plot and characters. Traditionally, moral standards prevail: good must win over evil, hope over despair. Contemporary writers may tweak the basic themes. Good may not always be good; evil is not necessarily that bad.

Many themes are universal and eternal because as human beings we all have similar emotional experiences and can identify with them in the stories: love, hate, anger, distrust, fear, pity, forgiveness, sacrifice, and so on. Certain topics are also universal: family, marriage, separation, work, friendship, growing up, revenge, winning and losing, age versus youth, appearance versus reality.

Often, the overriding theme of many stories is the struggle of the heart with the head, or **reason versus passion**. It is fundamentally an internal conflict. The protagonist must decide, make a choice, and do the right thing. The more interesting conflict is the dilemma: the lose-lose choice. For example, in Conrad's *Heart of Darkness*, the protagonist Charlie Marlow must choose between two evil forces, that of the Central Station manager and Kurtz.

How the writer develops a particular theme or themes is the important aspect in the study of literature. For example, with the universal and general theme of love, an author writing in the nineteenth century may only hint at homosexuality or not at all, whereas the twenty-first-century writer may investigate it in great detail. Moreover, a writer may combine two or three or more themes: love, friendship, and sacrifice go well together.

Narration and point of view

How a story is told is narration. A writer must make decisions about how to tell it. Narration requires a point of view: a perspective in the telling.

    First-person narration by main character: The story is told through the *I* narrator, who is the protagonist. Everything is seen from his or her perspective. The character makes observations and comments on the action and reports the actions of other characters. The protagonist cannot read the thoughts of others. This method engages the reader because often the reader identifies with the speaker.

    First-person narration by a secondary character: The *I* narrator tells the story, but he or she is not the main character. The benefits are that the reader follows the thoughts of the secondary character and is not privy to the thoughts of the protagonist. This method creates interest or curiosity in the reader because the reader does not know what the protagonist will do. Some things remain hidden, such as the actions of the Sparrow—we don't know whether he actually killed Moose Maddon because the narrator, Pop Anderson, only offers speculation.

    Third-person (omniscient): The most popular point of view is third person: *he* or *she*. The term *omniscient* means all-knowing. The writer can reveal the thoughts of all the characters but often does not. Stories work better when some aspects remain a mystery.

    Third-person (objective): Total objectivity in third-person narration is a challenge to many story tellers. It is the most limiting method because the writer can only recount what the characters say and do without going into their thoughts.

Style

Style is a distinctive way of saying something. It can depend on word choice or turn of phrase. For example, Oscar Wilde is known for his witty bon mots: "You don't seem to realize, that in married life, three is company and two is none." Ernest Hemingway is known for his minimalist writing and for not using *he said, she said* in lengthy dialogues between characters. In order to understand and appreciate style, the reader must be familiar with different works by the author and other authors to recognize variations in style.

Literary devices and techniques

Literature is not entirely literal. When we use language, we use both denotative and connotative meanings. For example, saying "the door is open" could simply be a comment on the fact that door is not closed, but it could mean any of the following:

- Close the door.
- Enter.
- Don't say anything. People may be eavesdropping.
- You can leave. No one is stopping you.
- You are welcome to come and talk to me.
- Opportunity awaits.

Writers use a host of literary devices to bring life to words, dialogue, and dramatic situations. Context has a lot to do with what is really meant and how it is meant.

A **symbol** is a concrete object that represents abstract qualities. For example, a ring is a piece of jewellery; however, when it is a wedding ring, it represents marriage, commitment, love, fidelity—all abstract qualities. In literature, symbols are plentiful and elusive. Some, of course, are standard and universal; others are time-specific and cultural. In "The Cask of Amontillado," Montresor's trowel represents vengeance.

It must always be remembered that the meaning of symbols is dependent on culture and situation. For example, in North America, the Statue of Liberty represents not only freedom but also the United States; the cross symbolizes Christianity. In literature, however, the meanings of symbols are often not so evident, especially to people unfamiliar with literature, with a particular time, and with that society. Moreover, a symbol whose meaning was common knowledge in the past may now be forgotten or viewed entirely differently. For example, in Biblical times, kissing someone's neck means that the person being kissed trusts the other enough as not to bite into the jugular vein and kill him, whereas, today, that act is symbolic of lovers' intimacy.

The meaning of **irony** is that what is said and done are diametrically opposite. To illustrate, on a cold and stormy day, someone comments, "Nice day out, isn't it?" What is said is not what is meant. This is verbal irony. In dramatic irony, the reader or spectator is aware of the disposition of a character and when the character acts or says something differently the spectator knows the difference. For example, when Montresor tells Fortunato how happy he is to have found the man, we are aware of the different meaning (whereas Fortunato is not).

Satire is ridicule with a moral purpose. Writers use satire to mock people, institutions, or ideas to illustrate how immoral, bad, or useless these things are. Political satire can be an agent of change. The tools of satire are exaggeration, sarcasm, and humour. The faults of the person or institution are made greater than they actually are in order to draw attention to them, as in editorial cartoons that attack politicians. One of the best-known satirical pieces is Jonathan Swift's "A Modest Proposal," in which he leads the reader into accepting the idea that the Irish should sell their babies to the English as food.

A **metaphor** is a comparison without the use of *like* or *as*. For example, the expression "he is a lion among men" makes the comparison of a lion to the person. *Lion* is used figuratively; the man is not a lion; rather some of the characteristics of the lion are conferred upon the man. The lion represents qualities of courage, strength, leadership, and power. Like symbolism, metaphors require of the reader the ability to think in the abstract and to understand literary tradition.

A **simile** is a comparison that uses "like" or "as" to preface the similarity. Like the metaphor, a simile draws out likenesses of one thing to another. For example, the expression "You are as lovely as a rose" compares the physical beauty in the flower to that of the person being complimented. Similes are easier to recognize because generally they are explicit comparisons rather than implicit.

An **allusion** is a reference. Often writers make references in passing to other works of literature, to history, to the arts, to anything that may have relevance to the material at hand. For example, a reference to a "Cheshire Cat smile" evokes a sense of mystery and fantasy; readers are expected to know that this cat can vanish, leaving only a smile visible, even if they have never read the literary work that introduced this character (Lewis Carroll's *Alice's Adventures in Wonderland*).

Allusions, however, are a quagmire for readers. The writer expects the readers to share the same background knowledge, but they may not. In the past, the writer could depend on those educated in their society to have common experiences and common frames of reference, such as the Bible or Greek mythology, or just everyday Western customs and traditions. Today, however, in a global village and multicultural society, the sheer diversity of authorship and readership can obscure what once was a universally recognizable allusion.

Writing about what you read

- Make sure you know whether the reading is fiction or non-fiction.
- If the reading has first-person narrative, refer to the "I" person by the author's surname if it is non-fiction and by the character's name or status if it is fiction.
- Make sure you understand what the assignment requires you to do.
- Understand the difference between summarizing and analyzing a reading.
- Quote from the reading sparingly—most of the time you will be paraphrasing.

- Paraphrasing and summarizing are valuable skills you need to practise.
- For most non-fiction readings, you should be able to distinguish the main ideas and supporting points.
- For fiction, you need to identify the theme, to follow the plot, and to understand the characters and setting. The author has used these elements deliberately; make sure you can see their purpose.
- To analyze poetry, you need to have a basic understanding of traditional forms and structures.

Research and Documentation

Many essays, such as the samples in Chapter 2, do not require any specific research. They are based on general knowledge and, perhaps, some background reading. However, if you do need to refer to a literary work or an article studied in class, you have to document it with a correctly formed citation. Generally, this means marking your quotation or reference in your essay so that the reader knows it was not your own words or your own ideas. A page of bibliographic references at the end of your essay gives the source information.

Research is something you have probably been doing since elementary school. You may have started with a project on snapping turtles, for instance, where you put together a booklet or a presentation that included pictures and facts you gleaned from an encyclopedia. You probably learned the rudiments of citation, such as listing the reference books you used for your project. As you progressed through school, your topics got more sophisticated and the demands of citation became more exacting.

For your college or university essays, your starting point is usually a reading (as discussed in Chapter 4). You may have studied a poem, literary essay, short story, or novel. These are considered **primary sources**. For essays on history or social studies, primary sources include witness accounts, memoirs, and autobiographies.

Sometimes you are asked to go beyond your course materials and do research to find other sources of information. These **secondary sources** are works written about the primary source, such as critiques and interpretations that appear in journals. Secondary sources include critical or explanatory notes about the primary source even if the notes are in the same book; for such notes it is especially important that you keep track of who said what so that you can document the source of the information accurately.

A distinction is sometimes made between secondary sources and **tertiary resources** ("third" sources), which include indexes and encyclopedias. They often distill information and can point the way to primary and secondary sources. However, for practical purposes, distinguishing between secondary and tertiary sources is unnecessary—it is just important to understand the difference between primary sources and all other sources of information.

Whatever sources you use, you have to refer to them in your essay, citing them correctly. The reader must be able to see clearly where the information came from and whose words or ideas are being used.

There are several **different citation styles**. In high school, you may have learned Chicago Style, which uses numbered footnotes instead of parenthetical references for in-text citations. The two most common styles used in college and university are MLA (Modern Language Association), which is used in the arts and humanities, and APA (American Psychological Association), which is used in the sciences and social sciences. This chapter includes explanations and examples of both these styles.

The rules of citation are very complicated—and can be maddening. This chapter cannot cover all the rules and examples. Professors generally give instructions with the assignment to get you started. You may have to consult your school's guides or official style handbooks. Do not hesitate to ask for help, especially if you are not comfortable doing research and citing sources. The school librarians can introduce you to the library resources and point you in the right direction. Often their resources include prepared handouts on citation styles, online tutorials, and links to helpful sites. You can also find electronic tools that will assemble citations for you, some in word-processing software and some as stand-alone programs. However, you must be wary of these and not just accept the output blindly. You cannot depend on the results being accurate. You can use the tools to give you a starting version, but you have to understand the rules so that you can check your citations. Ultimately, you learn the rules of citation with practice.

Research assignments can take several different forms. Your instructor may ask for an annotated bibliography (a list of references along with a one-sentence summary of each source) instead of a research essay. An instructor may guide you through a research essay by asking you to submit an outline or a list of references for feedback before you write your essay. Be sure to follow your instructor's directions carefully; don't just assume what is required.

This chapter goes over the basics of doing research and then deals with the specifics of MLA style and APA style.

Prepare for research work

Make sure you **understand everything about the assignment** before you begin. Obviously, a paper worth 20 per cent of your final grade in a course will require much less research than a master's thesis. The suggested length of the resulting research paper and the timelines you have been given also determine how much work you do. Sometimes professors give guidelines as to how many sources are required for a paper. If you are asked to cite at least three sources, for example, you should find at least two or three times that many, which you then narrow down to the most informative, reliable, relevant, and useful sources.

You may have chosen your research topic from a list your instructor has given you. Sometimes the topic is very broad, and you have to narrow it down to the question that interests you. Even a relatively narrow topic can be shaped and tweaked. Sometimes you have to come up with your own research topic. In this case, you will generally consult your instructor to make sure that your topic is acceptable and workable. In addition, as you research your topic, your focus might change. For instance, you may start out with a broad idea of writing about the generation gap between immigrants and their Canadian-born children. In your reading, you see that one bone of contention is the social life of teenagers and young adults. You might narrow it even further to talk about a specific ethnic group that you are familiar with, so that your essay focuses, for example, on dating in the South Asian community.

Before you begin your research, it is a good idea to **make some notes about what you already know and think about the topic**. This gives you a baseline. You will be better able to distinguish your own ideas and general knowledge from what you have absorbed in reading. You will also be able to see how your ideas have changed. Your notes will also help you distinguish your ideas and general information from what has to be cited.

If you are writing about a piece of literature, **read the primary source— the work itself—before consulting secondary sources**. Write down your thoughts about the work before you proceed with your research so that you have your own ideas to work with.

In the old days, researchers used index cards to record sources and the information gathered from the documents. They used card catalogues, microfiches, and periodical directories. Today, all of this sounds quaint and old-fashioned.

Students now work electronically. You should **open a document file for your research** and keep it separate from the file where you will be drafting your paper, so that you do not get your own writing mixed up with what you have copied from your sources (see "Avoid plagiarizing," p. 116). If it is a very large research project, you may need several document files for your sources, and you should put these files in a separate folder and name them appropriately for easy identification. In this folder, you can store electronic copies of any articles you need to consult frequently.

Be aware of the danger of cutting and pasting information—it is easy to get pieces out of order and mixed up. Be sure to keep quotations with the source information. You can use colours or different formatting to distinguish pieces of information. Instead of putting everything in a word-processing document, you may want to use specialized software to manage research notes. Make sure you can identify whatever you paraphrase or comment on to keep it separate from word-for-word sections copied from what you read. If you have this all in one file, use quotation marks or different fonts. Sloppy research can lead to accusations of plagiarism.

As you are setting up for your research, it is also a good idea to make a new bookmark folder in your browser. Bookmarking the Internet sources you use allows you to find them again easily.

Make sure you **back up all your files**. You can work with the files on your main computer and keep up-to-date copies on a flash drive, on an online file-hosting site, or in emails to yourself. Take into consideration that things can go wrong with electronic media—your Internet connection going down is not a valid excuse for lateness, and you do not want to lose your valuable work.

Remember that a research paper takes time—do not leave it until the last minute. You need time to find the sources, choose the best ones, absorb what is said, extract the information you need, document the sources, write the paper, revise your work, and format it correctly. Ideally, you need time to let your draft sit for a day or so before you revise it so that you can have a fresh view and spot errors and unclear writing more easily. **Make a work schedule** so that you space out the work and find the time to do it along with meeting all your other responsibilities.

Find suitable sources of information

Research involves looking for additional information. You are expected to know where and how to look, how to choose good sources of information, and how to document information and quotations correctly.

It is preferable to read thoroughly and completely the material you find. However, you do not have to do this for every source you find. Use the following **different reading techniques** to determine how relevant the source is and to find specific information you need:

- **Read a summary or abstract** of the article if it is available.
- **Read some parts of the article**, such as the introduction, the topic sentences, and the conclusion, to get an idea of the coverage.
- **Skim** the source material to get the main ideas.
- **Scan** for specific information, such as a name or a phrase.
- **Use the Find function** to search for specific words and phrases in electronic documents.

Avoid the temptation to just collect and hoard information. Successful research depends on quality of information—not quantity. Narrow your sources down to the ones that are relevant, sound, and useful. Don't just copy or bookmark every file you come across. Spend the time to read the material—even if it is a quick skim. Eliminate what is not useful right from the start. For example, if you are writing about Cirque de Soleil's success as a business, you do not need sites that tell people how to be an acrobat in the circus.

Avoid padding your research. Some students think that the more references they have, the better the paper is. Much of the time, they have not even read the information they cite. **A bibliography should list the sources actually used.**

Use a variety of sources

Because it is so easy to sit at the computer and type in search terms, most students rely on the Internet for all their research. Remember, however, that not everything has been digitized and made available on the Web. Look for physical books available in your library—both the school library and the local public library. Note that many periodical articles can be accessed through your school library. Although it takes more effort to search these databases, they will give you access to material, such as professional journal articles, that are not freely available on the Web.

As sources of information, both in print and electronic form, you can use

- dictionary entries and encyclopedia articles
- books
- articles in professional journals
- newspaper and magazine articles
- websites, blogs, online forums, wiki sites
- personal communication: lecture notes, interviews, letters, email, tweets
- videos, films, and documentaries

Thorough research requires the use of different kinds of sources. Moreover, the validity of the information can be verified if it appears in a variety of sources.

Search efficiently and thoroughly

Generally, you start your research with key words in an Internet search engine. Be sure to start with suitable search terms. You do not want to use a very general term, such as "social problems," which would net millions of hits. You can narrow your results by using more than one search term. For instance, "learning problems" with "hunger" would give you studies on how students' performance in school is affected by lack of food and poor nutrition. Depending on the results you get, you might have to change your search terms or add other words to your search. For example, you could add "Canada" as a search term to focus on the Canadian situation and eliminate the problems in developing countries from your research. As another example, a search for "lotteries" would bring up lottery results first; if you added the search term "gambling," results would include articles discussing the problems of gambling addiction and lotteries. In essence, when you do research, you move from general to specific, narrowing down your search terms and thus getting more relevant results.

Search engines have become very sophisticated and can predict what you want to find. You will probably not have to use quotation marks and Boolean operators to make your search more efficient. However, it is still useful to understand how different search engines work, especially when you are dealing with a more old-fashioned system. For instance, you may have to enter an author as "Last name, first name." Database directories can also be awkward to use. However, instructions and hints for using them are usually easy to find on the site.

Don't just take the first hit your search engine offers. Be aware that Google, for example, gives the most popular results first—but they may not be your best sources of information. For example, Wikipedia entries often come up first, but they are not considered to have the most reliable information. In addition, Google tailors results to the searcher's interests depending on a profile formed from search histories, so you should go beyond the first page of results.

Pay attention to what you are entering. Accuracy is important. If you misspell a name, you will not find what you are looking for.

Follow links to other websites. One source can lead you to many other good resources.

Choose the best sources

Essentially, in order to establish the credibility of a source, you have to determine who the authors are and which institution backs it. To see the relevance of this information, you have to understand the basics of publishing.

After someone writes a non-fiction book and submits it to a publishing company, it goes through many checks before it becomes a published book. Experts in the field review the manuscript, and editors check every word that is written. The reputation of the publishing company depends on the quality of the product that it puts out into the market.

However, keep in mind that this applies to books published by reputable companies. It is possible to self-publish and end up with a product that looks like a book but has not gone through the review and editing process. Look at the copyright page (after the title page) to find such information as the name and address of the publisher and the year of publication.

Newspaper and magazines also have reputations to protect. While fact-checking has become less thorough now, mainly because of time pressures exacerbated by the demands of cyberspace, reporters, columnists, editors, and publishers do what they can to ensure the accuracy of their reporting. Again, it is important to check the reliability of the publication. For instance, *The Globe and Mail* is a national newspaper with a long-established reputation; tabloid newspapers do not have the same credibility.

In contrast, websites have less authority because they do not go through the same kind of editing process. For instance, you could put up a website about how to play backgammon even if you knew nothing at all about the game. We have seen students cite online school projects written by ten-year-olds—obviously not authoritative sites. Although the Web has a way of regulating itself in that the better sites become more prominent, you still need to be careful. Information must always be taken with a grain of salt. Even the fact that the information exists on several different sites is not a guarantee that it is true. False information, like urban legends, spreads easily.

Some websites are written as a collaborative effort, perhaps by unpaid contributors whose qualifications and entries are not verified by fact checkers. For instance, you can look for the meaning of slang expressions in *Urban Dictionary*, where the terms are defined by readers. Many of these contributor-written sites are identified with the use of the word *wiki*, which comes from the Hawaiian word for "quick." Wikipedia is the best-known wiki site. Although Wikipedia is useful for a quick overview, it should not be depended on as an authoritative site. For instance, the site has often been hacked, and deliberately false information has been posted. Although the quality of its entries is improving with more stringent controls on editing, many instructors will not accept Wikipedia entries in bibliographies.

Look for credible sources: experts in the area, renowned scholars, established institutions such as universities, and reputable publishers. Some reliable sources of information are the *Encyclopedia Britannica* (with a well-established reputation for accuracy), the *Canadian Encyclopedia*, and the *Dictionary of Canadian Biography*. Starting with credible sources can also lead you to other reliable sources because many articles will have bibliographic references you can also use.

Check the URL to be sure that you are dealing with the actual site and not one that is pretending to be something it isn't. For instance, college and university websites are often identified by the *.edu* domain extension. Many websites include information about the authors in a section called something like "About us." Check this out to determine the reliability of the resource.

In general, trust your common sense. Be aware that the information may not be trustworthy, and watch out for red flags. For example, the Urban Dictionary entry for "meese" says that it is the "real plural of moose. Many people, including the dictionary and English teachers, will attempt to tell you that 'meese' is not correct" (www.urbandictionary.com). Dismissing the authority of dictionaries and teachers is an obvious red flag.

Use your school resources

One of the best places to start is your college or university library—both the actual building and the library's online resources. The reference librarians can help you start your search. Many libraries offer tutorials to teach you the basics. Most will have websites with reliable links to vetted sources.

College and university libraries subscribe to various **databases**, which give you access to professional journals as well as major newspapers and magazines. Through these databases, you can read a wide range of material, including dissertations and theses, statutes and regulations, and research studies. For example, ERIC is a source for education studies, the *Canadian Periodical Index* allows you to find articles in a wide range of Canadian newspapers and magazines, and the World Advertising Research Center focuses on marketing studies. These databases have different search engines, but each has instructions for use. In general, these databases have vetted sources, unlike the Internet as a whole.

Take notes as you research

Accumulating information does not directly translate into reading, digesting, and using it. Students sometimes fall into the trap of just finding and copying articles and websites, thinking they are doing research.

First, you need to manage the information you find. Decide which sources you are going to depend on the most. If there is only a small part of an article that is relevant, just copy that section, so you do not have to hunt through everything again. Highlight important ideas or possible quotations. Make sure you have marked copied sections so that you do not get them mixed up with your notes or your draft.

Write notes, summarizing what you read. Summaries are a useful study tool. They require you to comprehend what you are reading and to distinguish the main ideas from supporting ones. You have to paraphrase what you read, putting everything in your own words. That means you have to process and digest the information.

Follow the basic principles of documentation

As you do your research, you need to make sure you collect the information needed for the citation. Otherwise, you might have to go back and redo your work. You do not have to write everything in the proper citation style immediately, as long as you have all the information you need in your notes. You probably will not use all the sources in your notes, so you can focus on correct formatting just for the sources you have cited.

Proper documentation requires **attention to detail**. Make sure you have everything correctly recorded—title, author, publisher, date, page numbers, and other source information. Students often make copying errors when they have to write down such details. Even when they use cut-and-paste functions, they can end up with mistakes. Proofread everything carefully.

Essentially, a citation is the information that identifies the source you use. It should be correct and complete so that a reader can locate the same source. As you do your research, make sure you gather the **standard citation information**:

- the authors' full names (all the authors in the case of multiple authorship)
- title of the work itself, including any subtitle
- date of publication
- title of the source where an article was published
- publisher and place of publication
- any sponsoring website or database
- page numbers
- location information (URL or library call number)

Sometimes not all this information is available. A website may not have a recorded author or a date of publication, for example.

Distinguish the article information from the source-publication information. For instance, in this book are six readings. If you want to refer to the story "The Moose and the Sparrow" by Hugh Garner, you will also have to record that the source you used was in this book, *Essay Do's and Don'ts* by Lucia Engkent and Garry Engkent.

Note that works can exist in slightly different versions. You may find a newspaper article published with a slightly different title and even slightly different wording in two different newspapers. Be sure to cite the source you actually used.

Titles of articles, short stories, and poems are distinguished from titles of books, plays, films, newspapers, magazines, and journals. For example, the title of a newspaper article may be written in quotation marks, while the name of the newspaper is in italics. Italics and underlining are equivalent (so underlining can be used in notes or handwritten essays).

If you cite a newspaper or journal article, the same principle holds: the title of the article is in quotation marks, the name of the newspaper or journal is in italics.

Make sure you know where to **find this information**. A book's publishing information is on the copyright page, on the back of the title page. A website's publishing information may be on the bottom of the page, or you may have to go back to a home page to find the relevant identification.

Make it a habit to **date your research information**. For electronic sources, you need access dates (because websites can be changed and updated), but even for print sources, recording the dates can help you keep track of your work.

No matter what citation style you use, your research paper will have a **list of bibliographic references** on the final page. The style used determines the title of this page: it could be called "References," "Bibliography," or "Works Cited." Examples of bibliographic references in both MLA and APA citation styles are given in this chapter.

In the body of your essay, you will have references that mark quotations and passages where you took information from your sources. Instead of footnotes, MLA and APA use **parenthetical references** that give the author's name and page reference in parentheses (round brackets) after the work is cited. This is called **in-text citation**. It is a short-hand reference to the full citations found in your list of works. For example, if you see "(Keenan 105)" after a quotation or a reference, you need to look in the list of references at the end of the essay, and you will find a full entry for the author named Keenan. This entry will give you all the information you need—the title of the work, the date, and the source information. (The "105" is the page reference for a citation in MLA style.) Sometimes students have trouble with the words *quote* and *paraphrase*. For instance, if they are told to include a quotation in a research assignment, they choose one that already exists in the article—in other words, they end up quoting a quotation.

Quoting simply means taking the exact words of another author and putting them in your essay. Generally, this is shown by quotation marks for shorter quotations and indentation for longer quotations. You can read about choosing, using, and referencing quotations on page 118.

Sometimes, instead of quoting, you **paraphrase**—you report what the author said, but you do it in your own words. The paraphrase still needs to be documented with an in-text citation. A paraphrase can also be a **summary**, where the information you convey is only the main ideas of what the author said.

Cut-and-paste functions are useful, saving you the time it would take to retype something. However, remember to **correct the formatting** in your essay if you don't want your quotation to appear in a different typeface or size.

In addition, active links in online documents are generally underlined and appear in a different colour. This formatting is not correct for a printed essay, so you need to change the link to regular text. Make sure you know how to use the formatting functions of your word-processing program.

Determine what needs to be documented

All writing builds on previous knowledge and work by others. We assume a basic level of common knowledge that does not have to be documented. For example, you learned in elementary school that Canada has ten provinces and three territories—you do not have to cite a source for that information.

Facts that do not have to be documented include historical events, dates, and scientific facts. If the information appears undocumented in many reference books, it is accepted as general knowledge even if you did not know that fact before.

Reference any facts not generally known, quotations (words by another writer), expert information with specialized details, results of research studies, statistics, opinions of other writers, and ideas unique to someone else.

Jotting down some basic ideas before you begin your research can also help you decide what does need to be referenced. Whatever you come across that is new to you should be documented. It is better to be safe and over-reference than to be accused of plagiarism.

Avoid plagiarizing

Plagiarism is taking someone else's intellectual property without giving the original author credit for the work and misrepresenting that work as your own. It is an academic offence and is dealt with in your school's policy on academic dishonesty. There are severe penalties that come with the charge of cheating—ranging from a zero on a paper to expulsion from the institution.

Because of the sheer quantity of information for the taking through the World Wide Web, many people have come to believe that what is put out there is in the public domain and may be downloaded free and used without permission. They do not realize they are taking other people's intellectual property; that misconception creates problems for some students in college and university. A further cause of confusion is that in some cultures, copying another person's words is used as a learning technique, and quoting without acknowledging the author is standard procedure.

In North American education systems, students are expected to produce their own ideas in their own words in their essays. Even one copied sentence without a citation is enough for a student to be charged with plagiarism.

First, make sure you understand what kind of information has to be documented and what is considered common knowledge (as explained above).

Second, when you do your research, be careful to keep copied information separate from your own writing. When you cut and paste excerpts from electronic sources, put them in a separate file and make sure you can easily identify them as copied sections (either by the use of quotation marks or because they are in a different font or colour). Your own notes or paraphrasing should be clearly distinguished from the copied sections.

Third, paraphrase correctly. Don't just copy a sentence and replace some of the words with synonyms. A paraphrase should be in your own words, as you would naturally express those ideas. Understand what is standard English phrasing and what is the author's wording. The basics of paraphrasing are covered in Chapter 4. Remember that a paraphrase also has to be properly referenced.

It is sometimes difficult to determine what is copying and what is writing. Languages are full of set expressions, and it is easy to construct a unique English sentence by assembling such expressions. But is this actually writing? ESL learners sometimes work in this way, especially those who have memorized passages to repeat as needed. Constructed writing often lacks a natural flow and has jarring switches from the students' own writing to copied phrases. Native speakers of English often use set expressions in their sentences, but they do not go out and look for established ways to express specific ideas.

Finally, make sure you credit quotations, paraphrases, and information that you have taken from other works. This requires both an in-text citation and a full reference in the bibliography.

Academic dishonesty also includes submitting essays copied from the Internet or purchased from an essay service, recycling your own work from another course, and using another student's work. While tutors and classmates can help you, they should not be doing your work. It should be fundamentally your writing. Any collaborative writing should be clearly identified as a group effort.

Experienced writing instructors have read thousands of essays, they get to know their students' individual styles, and warning bells sound when instructors read something that sounds as if it is not the student's own work. The Internet has made it easier to copy, but it has also made it easier to find the copying.

Don't confuse authors' names

The author's name is one of the most basic pieces of information to record in a bibliographic citation, but it can be a minefield of problems, especially for English-language learners. For instance, students often mix up family names and given names. They may also use the wrong pronoun when they refer to authors in their essays (calling a female author "he," for example).

Note that names in English are usually written with the given names (first and middle names) followed by the family name (also called surname or last name). Some languages, such as Chinese, use the opposite order, but the surname first order is only used in alphabetical lists in Canada. In a bibliography, for example, the family name comes first, then a comma, and finally the given name or names. The comma indicates that the name has been reversed from the usual order.

Students learning English should learn common English names as part of their language study. This knowledge is useful for both social and academic reasons. Students should be able to distinguish family names from given names and recognize which names are generally used for males and which for females in order to use the correct pronoun when writing about the author. Although this is never 100 per cent reliable, it is helpful to know that someone named "Katrina," for instance, is probably female. When in doubt, students can check references to the author to see which pronoun is used in reading comprehension questions, for example. Other strategies include avoiding a pronoun or using *they* as a gender-neutral pronoun (see p. 180). If you are reading an article reprinted in a book, don't confuse the author of the article with the author of the book. Identify each separately and properly.

Quote effectively

Sometimes, instead of paraphrasing or summarizing the information you find, you may choose to use a quotation in your essay. A quotation can lend authority to what you are saying. You can quote to support your position. A quotation can also serve as a starting point for your argument, whether you choose to agree or disagree with the writer you are quoting.

Do not quote when the statement can be easily and effectively paraphrased. Quote when the author has said something succinctly, brilliantly, and power- fully. Quote when you want to analyze a statement, particularly in literature study. Do not quote plain, factual statements.

Record the quotation exactly. It must be verbatim—word for word. It must be exact even if there are mistakes in the quotation, such as spelling or typographical errors. (You note these mistakes by adding the Latin word *sic*, meaning "thus," after the mistake, in square brackets.)

Integrate the quotation smoothly into your own paragraph. Don't drop the quotation in or introduce it by an obvious phrase such as "Here is a quota- tion." It should fit in with what you are saying.

> In order to safeguard our privacy, it is important to realize that smartphones are essentially computers, not just communication devices. As Kowalski points out, "cellphones are the sites of our digital lives, and they contain an ever-increasing portion of our personal lives, making them much more than simply telephones in our pockets" (217).

You can see several examples of quote integration in the sample research essays in this chapter. Both the MLA and APA essays show the use of quotations even though the citation format is slightly different. You can also examine exam- ples of quotation use in the articles and essays you read.

Don't over-quote. Some students fill up their essays with quotations in order to meet the length requirement and minimize how much they actually have to write. An essay must be your ideas and your words—not a series of quotations.

Use ellipsis (marked with . . .) if you do not want to include the whole sentence or passage:

> Fortunato "prided himself on his connoisseurship in wine . . . in the matter of old wines he was sincere" (Poe 229).

Be careful not to change the meaning of the statement when reducing its length with ellipsis.

If you are **quoting a quotation**, be careful to show who originally said the words as well as the source where you found them, as in this example:

> Paul Godfrey insisted, "'OLG's Internet gaming program will stress responsible gaming while providing an enjoyable experience for Ontario players'" (qtd. in Sainsbury 221).

Note the tricky use of quotation marks. When you have a quotation inside a quotation that is set off with quotation marks, **use single quotation marks for the inside quotation**.

Quotations have to be properly cited, according to the style you are using. Both MLA and APA use **in-text citation**, which essentially means they give the information in the body of the essay and not as a footnote marked by a superscript number. Remember that the in-text citation points the reader to the full citation in your list of references, so it is only a short-form reference.

Use MLA citation style

MLA refers to the Modern Language Association, but people generally refer to the citation style by its initials alone. MLA style is used in arts and humanities courses and is therefore the one that you are likely to use in English courses. MLA covers more than referencing in essays; it also determines such features as date format, capitalization and punctuation, and writing style.

General guidelines for quoting and referencing are explained in the first half of this chapter. The rules for citation in MLA style (according to the 8th edition [2016] of the *MLA Handbook*) are explained below, with examples of common situations. The sample MLA essay (pp. 127–132) shows essay format and more examples. Your school library will also have citation guides to help you. If you have an unusual case that is not covered in the examples, you may have to do some research. Much of the information is online, including MLA's own site. Ultimately, follow the guidelines your instructor gives you for assignments. Instructors sometimes want slight alterations, such as including a cover page, which are not strictly MLA style.

Use in-text citation (MLA)

In an essay, you use in-text citation to show that the ideas or words you have used have come from another source. Basic guidelines for quoting and paraphrasing have been already discussed in this chapter. In MLA style, after the quotation or paraphrase, the author's name generally appears in parentheses followed by the number of the page where those words or ideas appeared. The in-text citation is a short form reference to the full citation which appears on the Works Cited page. Note that the period comes after the parentheses.

> People tend to dismiss privacy concerns by saying that innocent people do not have to worry. "It is not uncommon for people to be arrested or detained without ever being convicted of a crime" (Kowalski 218). The police can search phones on the flimsiest of excuses.

If the name of the author appears close to the reference, you do not have to repeat the name in parenthesis. You can simply give the page number.

> Keenan shows how easily memories can be manipulated when he refers to a study where mice where made "afraid of getting an electric shock. However, they had never actually experienced the shock. It was put there by interfering with cells in the hippocampus" (125).

If there is no page number (as on a Web page), just give the author's name. You may also be able to use other reference numbers to indicate the source of the quotation or information. For instance, some online articles have numbered paragraphs, and plays have numbered acts and scenes (as shown in the reference to *Hamlet* below).

If there is no author's name given, use the first few words of the title (ignoring *a, an,* or *the*) in quotation marks:

> Another argument for a national drug plan is that the current system needs repair. Canada "funds drugs through a hodgepodge of private plans and disjointed federal, provincial and territorial systems that still leave many people paying out-of-pocket" ("Canada needs").

If you are referencing more than one article by the same author in your essay, you add the first word of the title to the parenthetical reference to indicate which source you are quoting from.

Short quotations (four lines or fewer) are integrated into the text of the essay. Use quotation marks to show the exact words taken from the original, and give the reference information in parenthesis after the quotation, as in the examples above. Note that the period follows the parenthesis.

Quotations longer than four lines must be separated from the text of your essay and indented. Note that quotation marks are not used because you have already distinguished the passage by separating it from the paragraph. The reference information is given in parenthesis immediately after the completion of the long quotation. The long quotation should follow standard double spacing to conform to the format of an essay. You can see an example of long quotations in the sample research paper on page 128.

Show **line breaks** when quoting passages from poems or plays. Short quotations should have a forward slash at line breaks; longer quotations should follow the line structure of the original, as in this example from Polonius's famous speech in Shakespeare's *Hamlet*:

> Neither a borrower nor a lender be,
> For loan oft loses both itself and friend
> And borrowing dulls the edge of husbandry.
> This above all: To thine own self be true. (1.3. 75–78)

Prepare a Works Cited page (MLA)

As the finishing touch to the research essay, you need a bibliography listing the sources you used. The word *bibliography* means a list of books; it is a general term used for a list of references at the end of the essay. What the list is called and how it is formatted depend on the citation style you are using. In MLA, the heading "Works Cited" is used to show that these are the works you refer to in your essay; if you need or want to include other works that you used but did not refer to directly in the essay, you use the heading "Works Consulted." Remember that the in-text citations point to the full references in the bibliography. The entries on the Works Cited page must give enough information to allow someone to find the same source you used. In addition to the sample citations explained in this section, which are grouped in alphabetical order, you can see a full formatted Works Cited page at the end of the sample MLA essay (page 132).

Note these basic characteristics of MLA citation:

- The entries begin with the author's name followed by the title of the work. Next is the publication information which tells the reader where to find the work—whether it is in a collection of works, in an online source, or in a database.
- The first author's name is reversed with a comma showing this order; the other authors have their names in normal order (given names followed by surname).
- Citations begin with the author's name—or with the title of the work if there is no author's name given. Corporations and institutions can be listed as authors.
- In titles, all words are capitalized except articles, prepositions, and conjunctions (unless these are the first word in the title).
- Article and story titles appear in quotation marks; book titles and periodical names are in italics. Thus, a newspaper article would have quotation

marks around it while the name of the newspaper would be in italics, showing that the article is part of a bigger work. (Underlining in hand-written work is considered equivalent to italics.)

- URLs are included for online publications. You do not have to include the designations *http//* or *https//*. If there is a stable URL given in the form of a permalink or DOI (Digital Object Identifier), give that link.

Citing books

For books, you need the authors' names, full titles (subtitle appears after a colon), the publisher, and the year of publication. The publishing information can be found on the copyright page (the one after the title page). E-books found online are cited as electronic documents.

> *The Epic of Gilgamesh.* Translated by Maureen Gallery Kovacs, electronic edition by Wolf Carnahan, 1998, http://krishnamurti.abundanthope.org/index_htm_files/The-Epic-of-Gilgames.pdf
>
> Kamboureli, Smaro, editor. *Making a Difference: Canadian Multicultural Literatures in English.* 2nd ed., Oxford UP, 2007.
>
> Keenan, Thomas P. *Technocreep: The Surrender of Privacy and the Capital-ization of Intimacy.* Greystone Books, 2014.
>
> Tolkien, J.R.R. *The Hobbit.* HarperCollins, 2012.

Citing encyclopedia and dictionary entries

Note that some instructors do not accept Wikipedia as a reliable reference. How-ever, it is the most popular resource and can be useful if used with caution, so we have included a sample Wikipedia citation here.

> "J.R.R. Tolkien." *Wikipedia, the Free Encyclopedia,* 22 April 2016, en.wikipedia.org/wiki/J._R._R._Tolkien.
>
> Payne, Michael, Jack Brink, and Deborah Welch. "Head-Smashed-In Buffalo Jump." *Canadian Encyclopedia,* 16 June 2015, the www.canadianency-clopedia.ca/en/article/head-smashed-in-buffalo-jump/.
>
> "Underdog." *Oxford Dictionaries,* www.oxforddictionaries.com/us/definition/american_english/underdog.

Citing articles

Articles are printed in newspapers, magazines, and journals, both in print and electronic formats. It is important to reference the source you actually used. Note that the online article may have a different title than the print form. Short stories and poems are generally treated the same way as articles, as shown in the Arnason entry below.

Arnason, David. "The Sunfish." *Making a Difference: Canadian Multicultural Literatures in English*, edited by Smaro Kamboureli, 2nd ed., Oxford UP, 2007, pp. 98–106.

"Canada Needs a National Pharmacare Plan: Editorial." *thestar.com*, 19 July 2015, www.thestar.com/opinion/editorials/2015/07/19/canada-needs-a-national-pharmacare-plan-editorial.html.

Chemin, Anne. "Handwriting vs. Typing: Is the Pen Still Mightier than the Keyboard?" *The Guardian*, 16 Dec. 2014, www.theguardian.com/science/2014/dec/16/cognitive-benefits-handwriting-decline-typing.

Kim, Sandra, Matt Golding, and Richard H. Archer. "The Application of Computer Color Matching Techniques to the Matching of Target Colors in a Food Substrate: A First Step in the Development of Foods with Customized Appearance." *Journal of Food Science*, vol. 77, no. 6, 4 June 2012, pp. S216–S225, doi: 10.1111/j.1750-3841.2012.02744.x.

Picard, André. "Universal Pharmacare Touted as Way to Save Billions." *Globe and Mail*, 13 Sept. 2010, p. A1. *Canadian Newsstand*, libaccess.senecacollege.ca:2048/login?url=http://libaccess.senecacollege.ca:2073/docview/750302083?accountid=28610.

Citing other sources

Other commonly used resources are films, online videos, blogs, and government websites. Here are some example citations. Note the blog entry by Mair and the comment on that blog by Cragin.

Cragin, Dave. Comment on "Farcical Names." *Language Log*, 5 Apr. 2015, 5:41 p.m., languagelog.ldc.upenn.edu/nll/?p=18526.

Haggard Hawks. "10 Words Shakespeare Used that No One Can Work Out." *YouTube*, 21 Apr. 2016, www.youtube.com/watch?v=TldDmFQ1FaE.

The Hobbit: An Unexpected Journey. Directed by Peter Jackson, Performances by Martin Freeman, Ian McKellan, and Richard Armitage, New Line Cinema, 2012.

Mair, Victor. "Farcical names." *Language Log*, 3 Apr. 2015, languagelog.ldc.upenn.edu/nll/?p=18526.

Statistics Canada. *Aboriginal Languages in Canada.* 22 Dec. 2015, www12.statcan.gc.ca/census-recensement/2011/as-sa/98-314-x/98-314-x2011003_3-eng.cfm.

If you are using the articles and stories from Appendix A, you need to cite them as references from this textbook unless you find other sources, such as the original newspaper articles online or in databases. There are different ways to cite the readings in this textbook. One way is to cite the textbook itself with a separate entry; this works well if you are citing more than one reading.

Engkent, Lucia, and Garry Engkent. *Essay Do's and Don'ts: A Practical Guide to Essay Writing.* 2nd ed., Oxford UP, 2017.

Garner, Hugh. "The Moose and the Sparrow." Engkent and Engkent, pp. 222–28.

Sainsbury, John. "What If Dostoyevsky Had Been an Online Gambler?" Engkent and Engkent, pp. 219–21.

For a single citation, you could use:

Maharaj, Sachin. "Beware the Risks of Smartphones and Tablets in Schools." *Essay Do's and Don'ts: A Practical Guide to Essay Writing*, 2nd ed., by Lucia Engkent and Garry Engkent, Oxford UP, 2017, pp. 213–14.

Note that *Essay Do's and Don'ts* is an authored book, not an edited one. Most sample citations for articles in books are for anthologies, which are edited.

When you are dealing with reprinted articles and stories, the original date and location of the publication can be included if deemed necessary for the reader's understanding. This information is usually included in the anthology, whether after the reading selection itself or in a credits list.

Your Works Cited page should be formatted so that

- it is on a separate page, at the end of the essay
- it is paginated as part of your essay
- the heading is centred on the page
- citations are double-spaced with a hanging indent
- citations are in alphabetical order
- alphabetization is by the first word in the entry (unless it is *the*, *a*, or *an*)
- authors' names are alphabetized by the surname (for more than one author, it is the first author's name)

Sample research essay (MLA)

This sample research essay includes samples of what goes into the writing process: brainstorming notes, search terms, research notes, and outline.

The essay has been formatted to approximate what it would look like on a standard 8½ by 11 inch page, with the borders representing the edge of the sheet of paper. An actual essay would be double spaced. The Works Cited should be printed on a separate page.

Note the MLA-style headings and the format of the Works Cited page. Examine how quotations have been integrated into the essay and how the in-text citations are formatted.

MLA asks for the identifying information (such as the student's name and the course code) to be placed at the top left of the first page. However, some instructors prefer a cover page, similar to the one used for the APA research paper (page 138). These cover pages generally include this information: the title of the essay, the student's name and identification number, the course code, the instructor's name, and the date of submission. For MLA-style assignments, the cover page would not have a page number.

MLA Research Paper: Brainstorming

Topic: Examine how blood is used in Bram Stoker's *Dracula*.
- blood keeps the physical body alive; the lack of blood kills the body and takes away life in animals and in humans
- sustenance, to keep the vampire alive, return to youthful health
- sexual, metaphor for semen and sexual acts
- blood is red, and the colour has psychological effects: a violent colour, capriciousness
- blood language: cold-blooded, hot-blooded, blood brothers, bloody mess, blood sacrifice, blood lust (Berserker), blood is thicker than water
- the mentioning of blood produces queasiness, squeamishness in people
- paradox, blood is the fluid of life, and life giving, but people do not want to dwell on its practicality, use, and spillage. They would rather not think about blood.
- vampires take not only life but blood, the essence of the life force, and selfishly nourish their lives.
- colour of blood is red and red has symbolic meanings: danger, anger, passion, devil's eyes
- the taking of blood is the taking of life
- defiance of God's laws

MLA Research Paper: Sample search terms

- blood in Dracula
- vampire lore
- Stoker blood imagery

MLA Research Paper: Sample notes from source materials

Leviticus 17:10-12
  "Therefore I said unto the children of Israel, No soul of you shall eat blood, neither shall any stranger that sojourneth among you eat blood."

Skal, David J., editor. *Vampires: Encounters with the Undead.* Black Dog & Leventhal Publishers, 2001.

[from *The Book of Vampires* by Dudley Wright]
"According to primitive ideas, blood is life, and to receive blood is to receive life: the soul of the dead want [*sic*] to live, and, consequently, loves blood. The shades in Hades are eager to drink the blood of Odysseus's sacrifice, that their life may be renewed for a time. It is of greatest importance that the soul should get what it desires, as, if not satisfied, it might come and attack the living." p. 20

[marginalia from Skal]
"Blood, the ultimate human symbol, has the power to assume almost endless metaphorical forms—much like the vampire itself. As the primary vital fluid, blood has been held in awe since prehistoric times, and is prominent in the imagery of most religious and folk traditions. Blood represents the life force, the emotions and sexuality—but the sight of blood paradoxically signifies death. Blood is our connection to the atavistic past, as well as our immediate bond of kinship and fealty. The ancient belief that there is no essential difference between the physical reality of blood and the less tangible qualities of spirit, courage, and consciousness—that 'the blood is the life'—is notably at the root of cannibalism, blood sacrifice and vampire legends in a wide variety of cultures." p. 21

Stevenson, Jay. *The Complete Idiot's Guide to Vampires.* Penguin Group, 2009.

"In any case, the novel Dracula closely links sexuality and blood lust, as have many vampire stories ever since." p. 172

Porter, Ray. "The Historical Dracula." www.eskimo.com/~mwirkk/vladhist.html

The word for dragon in Romanian is "drac" and "ul" is the definitive article. Vlad III's father thus came to be known as "Vlad Dracul" or "Vlad the dragon." In Romanian the ending "ulea" means "the son of." Under this interpretation, Vlad III thus became Vlad Dracula, or "the son of the dragon." (The word "drac" also means "devil" in Romanian.)

"Vampires in history" dracula.cc/vampires/

"The history of the vampire begins in ancient Persia, where a vase was discovered depicting a man struggling with a huge creature which is trying to suck his blood. Then, there was discovered a deity known for drinking the blood of babies, lilitu or 'Lilith,' in Babylonian myth. During the 6th century BC, traces of the 'Living Dead' were also found in China."

MLA Research Paper: Outline

Working thesis statement: On the topic of blood, we will investigate how blood is used, how it violates the Christian ethos, and how it becomes a metaphor for sex.

Blood for the vampire
- Dracula and vampire Slavic meanings "blood drinker"
- what blood can do for the vampire: younger
- for female vampires, more beautiful

Judeo-Christian context
- interdiction about blood
- violation of commandments
- alliance to Satan, the devil and dark forces

Blood as metaphor for sex
- seduction
- references to sexuality

Conclusion

Miguel Santos

Professor J. Hammersmith
English 301 Section AB
25 November 2011

The Use of Blood in *Dracula*

In *Dracula*, published in 1897, Bram Stoker infused the horror genre with the vampire story and caught the imagination of the Victorian readers. This piece of popular literature then spawned a whole industry of blood-sucking tales with the vampire as anti-hero or hero in series such as *True Blood, Twilight*, and *Buffy the Vampire Slayer*. Moreover, as the lore and myth of the vampire expanded in series television, film, and books, some traditional elements that Stoker used in his classic work were incorporated, rejected, or modified. Blood, however, is the essential, universal ingredient in all vampire stories. In *Dracula*, Stoker used it to show the vampire's need for blood, the Judeo-Christian context, and the metaphor of blood for sex.

Blood sustains life. Without it, there can be no life. In vampire lore and in particular Dracula, vampires also need blood to continue their existence in the physical world. They can no longer consume food and enjoy beverages or even a good cigar (Stoker 24). Jonathan Harker in his first days at Dracula's castle makes this observation about the Count: "So I breakfasted alone. It is strange that as yet I have not seen the Count eat or drink" (Stoker 33). These creatures lust for the red liquid of life. The three brides of Dracula feast on the blood of a child. Dracula himself consumes a lot of blood. On the *Demeter*, he feasts on every sailor until the ship wrecks itself on the English shores.

Blood, however, does more than keep the vampire alive. It rejuvenates his physical appearance. When Jonathan Harker first meets the Count in Transylvania, he observes the man as "a tall old man, clean shaven save for a long white moustache" (Stoker 22), and "the general effect was one of extraordinary pallor" (Stoker 23). Yet, in his encounter with Dracula in London, according to Mina, her husband notices the total change:

[H]e gazed at a tall, thin man, with a beaky nose and black moustache and pointed beard . . . His face was not a good face; it was
hard, and cruel, and sensual, and his big white teeth, that looked
all the whiter because his lips were so red, were pointed like an
animal's. (Stoker 183)

Harker remarks that the Count has become younger in appearance
(Stoker 184). Similarly as a vampire now and living on the blood of children, Lucy Westenra also changes into an unearthly beauty: "She was, if
possible, more radiantly beautiful than ever; and I could not believe that
she was dead. The lips were red, nay redder than before; and on the cheeks
was a delicate bloom" (Stoker 213). Ingested blood then has the power
to transform the physical body of the vampire from old to young, and in
women, like Lucy and the three brides of Dracula in Transylvania, from
mere beauty to extreme sensual attractiveness.

Because the vampires depend so much on blood, they violate the laws
of God and willingly do so. Bram Stoker makes this point explicitly and implicitly throughout the story. The laws they break as they seek the sources
of sustenance are found in *Leviticus* and *Deuteronomy*. In the matter of
blood, *Leviticus* 17: 10-12 makes clear:

I will even set my face against that soul that eateth blood, and will
cut him off from among his people . . .

Therefore I said unto the children of Israel, No soul of you shall eat
blood, neither shall any stranger that sojourneth among you eat blood.

God forbids the improper use of blood, and good Christians obey this commandment. Holmwood, Sewell, Morris, and Van Helsing use their blood
in transfusions in order to preserve the life of Lucy Westenra. Dracula
defies God's law. He repeatedly depletes Lucy's body of blood for his own
selfish survival. Vampires are an anathema to secular and sacred society.
And as Dracula and his kind drain the blood in people, they commit further
violations of God's laws. Innocent children's blood is devoured by female

vampires and the children are left for dead; a shipload of sailors is drained of blood. In each case, they commit murder and thus break the fifth commandment: "Thou shalt not kill." In addition, Dracula himself violates the tenth commandment by seducing Lucy and committing adultery with Mina.

In addition, Dracula aligns himself with the dark forces. He subverts communion and the Eucharist. Through transubstantiation, Christ changes wine to his blood (and bread to his flesh) to save souls and remove sin. Dracula reverses the sacrament. He and other vampires consume the blood of the innocent and pervert their souls to the realm of the Undead. It is highly probable that the eating of blood gives Dracula the power to transform himself into lower order animals or to command them. Professor Van Helsing says:

> . . . he can, within limitations, appear at will when, and where, and in any of the forms that are to him; he can, within his range, direct the elements: the storm, the fog, the thunder; he can command all the meaner things: the rat, and the owl, and the bat—the moth, and the fox, and the wolf; he can grow and become small; and he can at times vanish and come unknown. (Stoker 252)

The name of Dracula reveals his demonic nature. "Drac" in Romanian means dragon (Porter). The dragon, in the West, has always been associated with the snake and with Satan. Moreover, "the word 'drac' also means 'devil' in Romanian" (Porter). In Judeo-Christian terms, Dracula the vampire is an anti-Christ figure.

Finally, blood becomes a metaphor for sex. Knowing the Victorian prudishness and repressed sexuality, Bram Stoker relied on blood to bypass the censors and to suggest the sexual aspect of the story. Because of their undead state, vampires no longer have the full function of their reproductive nature. In short, they cannot procreate; they cannot produce progeny in the normal sex act. Instead, they create other Undead as their children. Dracula has done this to the three female vampires and Lucy Westenra, and almost Mina Harker. The method is simple: he drains the natural blood from the body and induces the dying victim to suck in some of his vampire blood. Thus, they are reborn as the Undead and as vampires.

However, this is not to say that vampires have lost their sexual nature. Stoker makes it clear that vampires lust after human companionship. When Jonathan Harker first meets the three ladies in the castle, they stir his libido: "I felt in my heart a wicked, burning desire that they would kiss me with those red lips" (45). The repetition of the word *red* in relation to lips and tongue suggests sensuous sexuality. Blood is red, and the sanguine colour suggests sexual passion. These ladies use sex to obtain a blood feast in Harker (Stoker 45). Fortunately for the young solicitor, Dracula prevents his "wives" from indulging. From a slightly different perspective, Dracula exacts his revenge on Jonathan Harker by not only immobilizing him on the bed but also forcing him to witness the seduction of Mina, his wife. This scene of sexual seduction has the unwilling Mina sucking up Dracula's blood from the wound he opens in his chest.

> . . . his right hand gripped her by the back of the neck, forcing her face down on his bosom. Her white nightdress was smeared with blood, and a thin stream trickled down the man's bare breast which was shown by his torn-open dress. . . His eyes flamed red with devilish passion; the great nostrils of the white aquiline nose opened wide and quivered at the edge; and the white sharp teeth, behind the full lips of the blood-dripping mouth. . . . (301)

Stoker repeats the description of this scene (303) to reiterate blood as a metaphor for semen. The spurting of blood, whether it is from Lord Godalming pounding a stake into the vampirish Lucy (Stoker 230–31) or from Dracula releasing his essence to Mina, strongly suggests sexual activity. Moreover, Stoker combines sex and violence in the spray of blood.

In *Dracula*, Bram Stoker sets the standard in his portrayal of blood for all later vampire literature. Blood is the enduring ingredient. It paradoxically attracts and repulses the reader as it is siphoned away from the vampire's victims. The ingesting of blood from the vampire's perspective shows the lack of regard for the laws of God and society and the willingness to break them. Moreover, infused with other elements of perversity and passion, blood never fails to shock and surprise. With blood, Stoker taps into the prurient and forbidden interests of the Victorians that later writers of vampire literature adopt, adapt, and exploit.

Santos   5

Works Cited

The Bible. Authorized King James Version, Oxford UP, 1998.

Porter, Ray. "The Historical Dracula." 1992, ww.eskimo.com/~mwirkk/castle/vlad/vladhist.html.

Stoker, Bram. *Dracula.* Edited by Maurice Hindle, Penguin, 2003.

Use APA citation style

APA refers to the American Psychological Association, but people generally refer to the citation style by its initials alone. APA style is used in the sciences and social sciences. It sets a standard for citation, referencing, and bibliography, so scholars and scientists can use a common procedure to follow and to communicate with each other in various publications.

The *Publication Manual of the American Psychological Association* focuses on research papers for publication, not on student essays. These rules are subject to interpretation, so most schools and online resources offer modified rules to guide students. For example, author biographies and abstracts are unnecessary for student work, unless it is a major research paper or thesis. However, if your instructor requires you to include an abstract, perhaps along with key words, follow the format he or she gives you.

Use in-text citation (APA)

In an essay, when you use the words or ideas from another author, you have to reference the source with an in-text citation. You put the name of the author, the year, and the page reference in parentheses after a quote. Commas separate these three elements. If your work has two authors, use an ampersand instead of *and* between the authors' names in the parenthetical reference. If there is no page number, you can use paragraph or section numbers if they are given.

> The Internet has a long memory. "The computers at Amazon and Google usually have no reason to forget or purge any data, and every reason to hang onto it in perpetuity, a license you explicitly granted them when you agreed to the terms and conditions" (Keenan, 2014, p. 88).

If you have the author's name in your text, close to the quotation, you do not need to repeat it.

> The Internet has a long memory. As Keenan (2014) points out, "The computers at Amazon and Google usually have no reason to forget or purge any data, and every reason to hang onto it in perpetuity, a license you explicitly granted them when you agreed to the terms and conditions" (p. 88).

To cite a passage from a source with no authorship, use part of the title. If the citation comes from a book, italicize the title; if from an article, use quotation marks.

> Another argument for a national drug plan is that the current system needs repair. Canada "funds drugs through a hodgepodge of private plans and disjointed federal, provincial and territorial systems that still leave many people paying out-of-pocket" ("Canada needs," 2015).

Short quotations are integrated into the text of the essay and marked off with quotation marks. Longer quotations are indented and do not have quotation marks around them. If you are paraphrasing what an author said, you do not need a page reference. You can see quotations and paraphrases used in the sample APA essay which starts on page 138.

Prepare a References page (APA)

To format your page of citations, which is the last page of your essay, start a fresh page with the title "References" centred. Double-space each entry and use a hanging indent. Put your entries in alphabetical order by the first word in the entry (unless it is *the*, *a*, or *an*).

Note these characteristics of APA citation:

- Initials are used instead of authors' given names.
- Only proper nouns and the first word of the title or subtitle are capitalized.
- The year of publication is given in parentheses after the first element of the citation.
- Italics are used for titles of books and periodicals.
- Quotation marks are not used around article titles.
- For Internet sources, the URL is given, prefaced by "Retrieved from . . ."
- For articles from library databases, the DOI (Digital Object Identifier) is given if available.

More examples can be found on the formatted References page (p. 141) at the end of the sample APA essay.

Citing books

For books, you need the authors' names, full title (subtitle appears after a colon), the publisher, place of publication and the year of publication. The publishing information can be found on the copyright page (the one after the title page).

> Bryson, B. (2010). *At home: A short history of private life*. [Kobo]. Retrieved from https://store.kobobooks.com/
>
> Keenan, T. P. (2014). *Technocreep: The surrender of privacy and the capitalization of intimacy*. Vancouver: Greystone Books.
>
> Engkent, L., & Engkent, G. (2017). *Essay do's and don'ts: A practical guide to essay writing* (2nd ed.). Don Mills, ON: Oxford UP.

Citing encyclopedia and dictionary entries

These are citations from online reference sites:

> Demographics. (2016). In *Oxford dictionaries*. Retrieved from http://www.oxforddictionaries.com/us/definition/american_english/demographics
>
> Sir Tim Berners-Lee. (2016). In *Encyclopædia Britannica*. Retrieved from http://www.britannica.com/biography/Tim-Berners-Lee
>
> Smith, D. (2004). October crisis. *Canadian Encyclopedia*. Retrieved from http://www.thecanadianencyclopedia.com/index.cfm?PgNm=TCE&Params=a1ARTA00058

Note that encylopedia articles often do not have authors' names included, but the *Canadian Encyclopedia* is an exception.

Citing articles

Articles are printed in newspapers, magazines, and journals, and they can be found both in print and electronic formats. Sometimes you will be retrieving them from your school library database, in which case they may have a Digital Object Identifier (DOI) number.

> Canada needs a national pharmacare plan. [Editorial]. (2015, July 19). *Toronto Star*. Retrieved from http://www.thestar.com/opinion/editorials/2015/07/19/canada-needs-a-national-pharmacare-plan-editorial.html
>
> Chemin, A. (2014, December 16). Handwriting vs. typing: Is the pen still mightier than the keyboard? *The Guardian*. Retrieved from https://www.theguardian.com/science/2014/dec/16/cognitive-benefits-handwriting-decline-typing
>
> Geddes, J. (2004, August 16). A big step toward missile defence. *Maclean's*, 20–21.

> Kim, S., Golding, M., & Archer, R.H. (2012, June). The application of computer color matching techniques to the matching of target colors in a food substrate: A first step in the development of foods with customized appearance. *Journal of food science*, 77(6), S216–S225, doi: 10.1111/j.1750-3841.2012.02744.x

Citing other sources

Here are some other typical references. Note that the McWhorter entry is a TED Talk; it would have a different citation if retrieved from YouTube. The Mair entry is for a blog.

> Hunka, R. (Writer & Director). (2013, October 10). Ticked off: The mystery of Lyme disease [Television series episode]. In *The nature of things*. Canada: Merit Motion Pictures.
> Mair, V. (2015, April 3). Farcical names. *Language Log*. Retrieved from http://languagelog.ldc.upenn.edu/nll/?p=18526&utm_source=twitterfeed&utm_medium=twitter
> McWhorter, J. (2013, February). *John McWhorter: Txtng is killing language. JK!!!* [Video file]. Retrieved from https://www.ted.com/talks/john_mcwhorter_txtng_is_killing_language_jk?language=en
> Statistics Canada. (2015, December 22). *Aboriginal Languages in Canada*. Retrieved from http://www12.statcan.gc.ca/census-recensement/2011/as-sa/98-314-x/98-314-x2011003_3-eng.cfm

Sample research essay (APA)

Here is a sample essay in APA style, including a look at the process. The brainstorming shows the writer's preliminary thoughts on the topic—on both sides of the issue. The section on search strategies lists possible fruitful search terms. The sample notes include references to sources not ultimately used in the final essay because essay writers reference what they cited, not everything they read. Note that the outline consists of a draft of the thesis statement and the four topic sentences. While an outline can be in point form (as in the sample MLA essay on page 127), drafting the topic sentences can help you keep your body paragraphs on track.

The essay has been formatted to approximate what it would look like on a standard 8½ by 11 inch page, with the borders representing the edge of the sheet of paper. Note the use of a running head giving an abbreviated title of the essay in capital letters along with the page number. Pagination includes the title page. On the first page of the actual essay, the title appears centred on the page.

APA format includes the use of the actual words "Running head" in the header on the first page, preceding the title (i.e., "Running head: TITLE"); however, this is sometimes considered unnecessary for student papers. Likewise, an author bio and abstract are not included here because these elements are for published research work.

Examine how quotations have been integrated into the essay and how the in-text citations are formatted.

The topic is the same as that of Sachin Maharaj's essay "Beware the Risks of Smartphones and Tablets in Schools" (Appendix A, pp. 213–14). This allows you to compare a journalistic essay and an academic essay on the same topic.

APA Research Paper: Brainstorming

Topic question: Should students be allowed to use personal electronic devices in class?

Yes
- notes can be typed faster than handwritten
- e-books can be stored on laptops and tablets
- research info can be accessed on Internet
- devices can be used for classroom activities (e.g., quizzes on smartphones)
- some students prefer to participate in class with devices (like clickers) rather than speaking up
- students feel comfortable with and like using their devices

No
- writing notes by hand fires up different parts of the brain and helps people remember what they wrote
- reading from paper leads to slower, more thoughtful reading
- devices can be used for cheating on tests
- students don't pay attention to the instructor
- students spend a lot of time with irrelevant websites—checking Facebook, watching videos, etc.
- images, light, and sound from phones and laptops can distract other students
- instructors get distracted by students who are not paying attention
- students use technology too much already
- students need to develop skills that are not dependent on technology

APA Research Paper: Sample search terms

- laptop use in class
- cellphone use in school
- benefits of electronic reading devices (even though a positive word was used in the search term, the results showed both advantages and disadvantages)
- note-taking by hand vs. computer

APA Research Paper: Sample notes from source materials

"Beware the risks of smartphones and tablets in schools" by Sachin Maharaj
(in course textbook)
- move to use more electronic devices in classrooms
- teachers realize that personal devices often not used for educational purposes
- students already use technology too much
- technology is having effects on values—lack of empathy, desire for fame
- tech also affects intelligence, makes people impatient

"Why it's time to put your smartphone down. Seriously" by Zosia Bielski
Globe and Mail, Oct. 8, 2015
http://www.theglobeandmail.com/life/relationships/connected-to-our-phones-but-disconnected-from-each-other/article26715937/
- Bielski quotes Sherry Turkle's new book *Reclaiming Conversation: The Power of Talk in a Digital Age*: "As Turkle puts it in her book, 'We can become different kinds of consumers of technology, just as we have become different kinds of consumers of food. . . . What tempts does not necessarily nourish.'"
- "Teachers are setting aside class time for 'tools down' conversation, when students stop multitasking on laptops and actually listen and debate issues together." (mentioned by Turkle)

"Schools seek balance for cellphones in class: Are they a teaching tool or a distraction?" by Linda Matchan
Boston Globe, June 16, 2015
https://www.bostonglobe.com/lifestyle/style/2015/06/15/cellphones-school-teaching-tool-distraction/OzHjXyL7VVIXV1AEkeYTiJ/story.html

"It is the most vexing issue of the digital age for teachers and administrators: What to do about students' cellphones? Some maintain that smartphones and other devices in schools are crucial to being competitive in a global market, while others insist that phones and tablets distract students, compromising their learning and focus."

- study found that students' test scores were higher in classes that did not allow cellphone use

---

APA Research Paper: Outline

Thesis: Personal electronic devices should not be allowed in class.

1. Reading from the printed page is preferable.
2. Laptops are not necessarily better for note-taking.
3. Devices are distracting.
4. Students need a break from technology.

PERSONAL COMPUTING DEVICES   1

Personal Computing Devices in the Classroom
Lucy P. Eng
Classroom Management: EDU 251
Prof. M. Heinrich
October 20, 2015

Personal Computing Devices in the Classroom

Throughout the 20th century and into the new millennium, technology has been heralded as a means to revolutionize education. From television to language labs, learning with technology has been touted as the better way. The promised revolutions never happened, but now technophiles are making claims that computers are different. They are interactive devices and portals to the vast information stored on the Internet. Although computers have changed our world and have a very important place in education, a limit should be placed on the use of smartphones, tablets, and laptops. Students should not be allowed to use personal electronic devices during class lessons.

Although tablets and laptops allow students to use electronic textbooks in class, reading from screens is not the best way to learn. Print still has advantages. Even though eTextbooks are cheaper and more portable, many students prefer learning from printed textbooks (Baron, 2015). Some even print out pages from their eTextbooks. One reason is that the physicality of books is an important factor in learning. For example, people use the position of the information on the page as a guide to remembering it. In addition, reading on a screen is not as comfortable as reading from paper. Baron (2015) explains the different kind of reading people do from an electronic device where the "meaning of 'reading' increasingly becomes 'finding information'—and often settling for the first thing that comes to hand—rather than 'contemplating and understanding'" (p. 39).

The argument that laptops make for better note-taking is also weak. Research by Mueller and Oppenheimer (2014) showed that students taking notes on laptops did not remember the information as well as those taking notes by hand. This can be ascribed to both muscle memory and the need to process the information for hand-written notes. Many typists just mindlessly transcribe what they hear. Moreover, writing by hand gives students practice for the times they have to handwrite tests and exams in class.

Handwriting is a useful skill that should be practised no matter how many digital devices we have.

The use of personal computing devices distracts students from the lesson they are supposed to be paying attention to. Even when students are trying to do their work, they cannot resist the seductive pull of games, videos, and social media. A glance around any classroom where students are using phones and laptops shows this, as in this example:

> It was about five years ago that Paul Thagard, a professor of philosophy at the University of Waterloo, started noticing a "wall" of screens in his lectures. When he installed a graduate student at the back of the classroom to spy on his plugged-in students, he learned that 85 per cent of them were using their computers for something unrelated to class. (Andrew-Gee, 2015, p. A12)

Students may think they are multi-tasking when they have a small window open showing the hockey game while they are taking lecture notes, but the human brain is incapable of doing more than one thing at a time (Morrison, 2014). It can switch very quickly between two tasks, but each task is completed more quickly and thoroughly when one is the sole focus. Furthermore, students sitting near a laptop user can get distracted by whatever is on the screen—like second-hand smoke, the harm spreads.

Another reason to prohibit personal computing devices in class is that students need a break from the technology. People get addicted: They use their smartphones when they are dining with other people, walking down the street, and even using the bathroom. Students exhibit anxiety symptoms when they are away from their phones. However, the over-use of technology has many detrimental effects—impatience, lowered attention span, reduced critical thinking skills, loss of empathy for others, and

PERSONAL COMPUTING DEVICES   4

desire for gratification (Maharaj, 2017). Students want to use technology in class be-cause they want to be entertained, but study after study shows that digital technol-ogy has dumbed down higher education. They may make education more "fun" and "engaging." But that's only saying that they've turned education

> into a form of entertainment. Writing essays, reading difficult texts or figur-ing out complex mathematical problems have never been "fun"—and never will be. (Mann, 2012)

Students need to concentrate on the material and engage with classmates and the instructor to actually learn in class.

It is clear that the use of personal electronic devices in class is not as advanta-geous as it would seem, and so it should be limited. Obviously, this does not mean that classrooms must be technology-free zones. Instructors use smartboards and projectors linked to a computer to deliver information effectively. Students use their computers for specific tasks, such as research and essay writing. However, encour-aging more use of computers in the classroom is not a panacea for all educational problems, and instructors should not be forced to allow students to use personal electronic devices.

PERSONAL COMPUTING DEVICES   5

References

Andrew-Gee, E. (2015, August 22). Pulling the plug on classroom laptop usage. *The Globe and Mail*, p. A12.

Baron, N. S. (2015). *Words onscreen: The fate of reading in a digital world*. New York, NY: Oxford University Press.

Maharaj, S. (2017). Beware the risks of smartphones and tablets in schools. In L. Engkent and G. Engkent, *Essay do's and don'ts: A practical guide to essay writing* (2nd ed., pp. 213–14). Don Mills, ON: Oxford University Press.

Mann, D. (2012, October 6). Let's unplug the digital classroom. *Toronto Star*. Retrieved from http://www.thestar.com/opinion/editorialopinion/2012/10/06/lets_unplug_the_digital_classroom.html

Morrison, N. (2014, November 26). The myth of multitasking and what it means for learning. *Forbes*. Retrieved from http://www.forbes.com/sites/nickmorrison/2014/11/26/the-myth-of-multitasking-and-what-it-means-for-learning/

Mueller, P. A., & Oppenheimer, D. M. (2014). The pen is mightier than the keyboard: Advantages of longhand over laptop note taking. *Psychological Science*, 25(6), 1159–1168. doi: 10.1177/0956797614524581

Research guidelines

- Make sure you understand your topic and the assignment requirements.
- Follow whatever format your instructor asks for, and use whatever handouts and guidelines your instructor gives you.
- Organize your work, and schedule your time.
- Distinguish your words and ideas from the source material you used.
- Use authoritative sources and a variety of sources.
- Pay attention to detail when you quote from and refer to sources. Proofread carefully.

Vocabulary

Writing starts with words. Word choice is fundamental to the shape your writing takes. It determines sentence structure, style, and tone, as well as meaning.

English has a huge vocabulary at the disposal of the writer. It has three-quarters of a million words, more than any other language, even though we use only a small fraction of that number. Generally, we use ten times as many words in our writing than we use in our everyday conversation. Moreover, our **receptive vocabulary** (the words we understand, or our **passive** vocabulary) is about twice the size of our **productive vocabulary** (the words we use, or our **active** vocabulary).

Clear and concise writing depends on our ability to use the correct, precise word. Writing requires a larger vocabulary than speaking because we need to use the precise word to make our meaning clear. For example, we cannot get away with referring to a gadget as a "thingamajig" as we can in conversation when we can point to the actual thing we mean. Moreover, if we do not know what to call something, we often have to use an unwieldy phrase instead. For instance, someone might be forced to say "a place where rock is dug out of the ground" if he or she does not know the word *quarry*.

Initially, vocabulary is acquired in a person's first language through hearing and reading the language as he or she grows up. People who learn a language as adults do not have the luxury of years of vocabulary development through childhood, so they have to study vocabulary actively. In addition, native speakers who do not read much have not learned as many words as they need for academic studies because the spoken language uses far fewer words than the written language.

Why you need a good vocabulary:

- to understand, paraphrase, and summarize what you read
- to be able to write quickly and easily, with clarity and conciseness
- to vary your expression of ideas
- to reflect your education level

Another important point to consider is that **many writing errors are lexical rather than grammatical**. In other words, students misuse a word because they do not fully understand the meaning or the usage of the word. Both native speakers and English learners make such errors. Here are some example sentences from student work, with the incorrect words underlined:

✗ He <u>quit</u> the idea of buying a new laptop.
✗ Salespeople are sometimes rude or <u>effortless</u>.
✗ People are <u>reliable</u> on taking the easy way out.
✗ I look in the dictionary when I am <u>suspicious</u> about a word.

A vocabulary mistake is worse than a grammatical mistake. If you use a word incorrectly, your sentence may be unclear or misleading as the examples above show: in English, you cannot "quit" an idea—it does not mean the same thing as changing your mind. A person who does not make an effort is not "effortless." "Reliable" is not used to describe a general tendency and "suspicious" does not mean "curious." If you are not sure of the meaning or usage of a word, check it in the dictionary.

Knowing what a word means is not enough—you have to understand the way it is used. Words are like people: they belong to word families, they have different origins and ethnic backgrounds, and they can gradually change in meaning, use, and pronunciation. When you really know certain people, you know who they like to hang out with and how they behave in certain situations. When you really know a word, you know what words tend to appear with it (in collocations) and how it works in sentence structures.

Even though many students—both native speakers and English learners— struggle with word choice and usage in their essays, vocabulary is not often taught explicitly. This chapter goes over the properties of words so that you know the basics. These basics will help you decipher words you do not know and will help you build your vocabulary.

Recognize parts of speech

The part of speech determines the way the word works in a sentence. For instance, the word *success* is a noun, so you can say "the show was a huge success" but not "he did not success." It is essential to be able to recognize the different parts of speech in order to determine whether a sentence is correctly formed.

We can distinguish between function words (prepositions, conjunctions, pronouns) and content words (nouns, verbs, adjectives). Adverbs can be found in both categories, since words like *yesterday, however,* and *there* are function words, while adverbs formed from adjectives are content words (e.g., *softly, sweetly*). For vocabulary learning, we concentrate on content words.

Note the part of speech when you look up a word in the dictionary. The part of speech is abbreviated (*n., v., adj., adv.*) and usually comes at the beginning of the entry. Some words can be more than one part of speech; for example, *hand* can be both a noun (*a hand*) and a verb (*to hand*). Some dictionaries have one entry for the word and then subdivide it for the different parts of speech. Make sure you are looking at the correct part of the entry since the part of speech is crucial to understanding the meanings and sentence patterns.

Nouns

Nouns are words that refer to people (*doctor, Jane, girl*) and other beings (*dog, spider, elf*); places (*school, Montreal, house*); things (*chair, mountain*); activities (*golf, yoga*); and ideas and concepts (*beauty, truth, justice*). **Proper nouns** are names of individual people, places, and titles, and they are capitalized (*James, Canada, September*).

Most nouns have singular and plural forms. The most common plural ending is –s, but some nouns have irregular plural forms:

chair/chairs, box/boxes, mouse/mice, phenomenon/phenomena, passerby/passersby

Uncountable nouns are generally not used in the plural:

information, salt, luggage, advice, tea, sand, homework, water

Essentially, nouns act as subjects and objects in sentences:

The <u>students</u> passed the <u>books</u> around the <u>class</u>.

Nouns can also work as adjectives, defining a word and often forming a compound noun:

<u>computer</u> program, <u>student</u> teacher, <u>college</u> diploma, <u>mountain</u> bike

Some common noun endings:

-ance, -ence	acceptance, difference, fragrance, violence
-er, -or	adviser, baker, instructor, swimmer
-ism	criticism, optimism, racism, tourism
-ist	communist, scientist, terrorist
-ity	community, security, quality
-ment	agreement, environment, government
-ness	business, darkness, happiness
-ship	championship, citizenship, relationship
-sion, -tion	conclusion, decision, information, population

Verbs

Verbs describe actions, experiences, or states. Like nouns, they are essential to a sentence. Verbs can be more than one word. For example, they are often used with **auxiliary verbs**. Note the verbs (underlined) in the following sentences:

> The children play in the park every day.
> The race draws people from around the world.
> They both ran the half marathon on the weekend.
> The park was designed to handle big sporting events.
> The route seems difficult, but I have been training for weeks.
> He is the chair of the committee. He can make the changes.

Know the principal parts of verbs

In order to construct all the tenses and other forms of a verb, you need to know the three principal parts of the verb. The base form (the infinitive without the *to*) is used for the simple present tense (e.g., *I help, you help, he helps, we help, they help*). It is also the form that is used for the *–ing* form (*helping*). The past form is the simple past (*I helped*). The past participle is used in the perfect tenses (see p. 170) (e.g., *he has helped, they had wanted*), the passive voice (*it was discovered*), and adjectives (e.g., *the wanted man*).

Base Form	Past	Past Participle
help	helped	helped
want	wanted	wanted
sleep	slept	slept
fly	flew	flown
ring	rang	rung

The simple past and past participles of regular verbs are the same: both end in *–ed*. Irregular verb forms are listed in the dictionary in the entry for the base form.

It is important to know the correct forms of the verbs to avoid errors in using the verb tenses (see pp. 167–176).

Recognize transitive verbs

Dictionaries label verbs as either transitive or intransitive. Some verbs can be both, depending on the meaning and usage. Unlike intransitive verbs, transitive verbs require a direct object. Consider the following sentences—they would be incomplete without the object following the verb:

> Ellen sent the package.
> Jason forgot his homework.
> I bought the groceries.

Knowing whether a verb is transitive is also useful because a transitive verb can be put in the passive voice (p. 176). Look at your dictionary to see which abbreviations it uses to identify transitive and intransitive verbs.

Recognize verbals

Infinitives, gerunds, and participles are **verbals**. They are formed from verbs but do not function as main verbs.

- **Infinitives** are the base form of a verb, often preceded by *to*.
- **Gerunds** are the *–ing* form of a verb; they are used as nouns.
- **Participles** are the *–ing* and the *–ed* forms of a verb; they are used as adjectives (the *–ing* form is active participle; the *–ed* form is passive).

In the following sentences, the underlined forms are identified as either verbs or verbals:

> She is reading now. [verb—present continuous tense]
> Reading is the best way to increase vocabulary. [verbal—gerund (as subject of the sentence)]
> She likes to read every day. [verbal—infinitive]
> The sleeping boy looked so angelic. [verbal—participle (adjective describing *boy*)]
> They were planning a trip to Spain. [verb—past continuous tense]
> The trailer park was destroyed by the tornado. [verb—passive voice, simple past tense]

The main verb carries the action of the sentence. Any other verb form is probably a verbal.

Some verbals act as complements to the main verb; in other words, they complete the action of the verb. Whether the verb takes a gerund or an infinitive as a complement depends on the main verb itself. There is no grammar rule to explain it—it is a lexical property of the word itself. ESL learners, especially, often have difficulty with these complements.

- ✗ Ivanna enjoys to read on the beach. [*enjoy* is followed by a gerund, so it should be "enjoys reading"]
- ✗ Mahmoud promised visiting him again. [*promise* is followed by an infinitive, so it should be "promised to visit"]
- ✗ They suggested to try the other location. [*suggest* is followed by a gerund, so it should be "suggested trying."]

Learn the particles and prepositions that accompany verbs

Verbs are often accompanied by specific prepositions and particles. This can be confusing. Writers may have to pause and think whether they should say "specialize *in* something" or "specialize *at* something." (The former is correct.)

Phrasal verbs are multi-word verbs with particles (essentially prepositions and adverbs). A phrasal verb often has a different meaning from the verb by itself. Many of them are idiomatic or informal.

> She was <u>brought up</u> in Vancouver. [raised]
> The car <u>blew up</u> when it hit the guardrail. [exploded]
> I like to <u>sleep in</u> on the weekend. [sleep late]
> She <u>works out</u> at the gym near her job. [exercises]

In addition to learning the nuances of phrasal verbs, you have to know the **verb-and-preposition combinations** that require a noun or pronoun to complete the idea, such as these:

> He <u>depends on</u> his brother to drive him to his appointments.
> She was <u>staring at</u> him as if she did not <u>approve of</u> his behaviour.

If you are not sure which preposition is used with a certain verb, check the dictionary. It's easy to make mistakes. Here are some types of errors:

- ✗ He <u>referred on</u> Chapter 9 in the textbook. [using the wrong preposition—should be *referred to*]
- ✗ They finally <u>caught up him</u>. [leaving out a preposition—should be *caught up to him*]
- ✗ I always have to <u>wake up him</u> in the morning. [not recognizing a separable phrasal verb—should be *wake him up*]
- ✗ We need to <u>re-look at</u> our priorities. [putting a prefix on a phrasal verb—should be *re-examine*]

Prefixes and suffixes that make verbs:

be–	bejewel, belittle, bewitch
en–	enable, endanger, enjoy, enlarge, envision
–en	blacken, lighten, soften, toughen
–ate	activate, discriminate, motivate
–fy	identify, notify, signify, solidify, unify, verify
–ize*	idealize, maximize, realize, recognize, sympathize

Note that the *–ize* suffix is generally spelled *–ise* in British English. Verb tense, form, and use are explained in greater detail in Chapter 7.

Adjectives

Adjectives describe nouns. They can come before the noun or appear after a linking (or copula) verb.

> The <u>yellow</u> house is the house my grandfather built.
> The house is <u>yellow</u>.

That <u>big</u>, <u>black</u> dog terrifies me.
They had to deal with some <u>unfinished</u> business.

Some adjectives have **comparative** forms (for comparing two things) and **superlative** forms (for comparing more than two things):

long, longer, longest
small, smaller, smallest
bad, worse, worst
good, better, best

With longer adjectives, the comparative and superlative forms are made with *more* and *most* (or *less* and *least*):

She picked <u>the least expensive</u> notebook computer.
This option is <u>more practical</u>.

Don't use *more* and *most* with adjectives that are already in the comparative or superlative form:

✗ His results were <u>more better</u> this time.
✗ I need to find one that is <u>more cheaper</u>.
✗ Shakespeare was the <u>most greatest</u> dramatist of his time.

Some common adjective endings:

-able, -ible	believable, reachable (made from verbs)
-ful	beautiful, careful
-ic	heroic, Icelandic
-ive	attractive, descriptive
-less	careless, hopeless
-ous	wondrous, courteous
-ly*	friendly, lonely

*Note that most words that end in *–ly* are adverbs. Some common adjectives, however, are exceptions: *deadly, friendly, lively, lonely.*

Use adjectives wisely
A well-chosen adjective can make your writing clearer by adding information, but do not use too many adjectives, and do not use empty, filler adjectives that add little meaning. Overused, vague adjectives include *good, bad, great, amazing, awesome, nice,* and *interesting.*

It was an interesting movie. The plot was good. The special effects were awesome. The characters were nice. [weak]

It was a spectacular movie. The plot was intricate. The special effects were thrilling. The characters were intriguing. [better]

The movie had cutting-edge special effects that integrated well with the intricate plotting. Moreover, the characters' motives were hidden, keeping the audience guessing. [better]

Adverbs

Many adverbs are made by the addition of –*ly* to the adjective form (such as *quietly, hugely, wickedly*). These adverbs generally explain how something is done.

A few common adjectives end in –*ly* and do not have an adverb form: *friendly, lonely, lively*. Therefore, we cannot say, "the dog wagged its tail <u>friendlily</u>" but rather "the dog wagged its tail in a friendly way."

Note that *pretty* in front of an adjective is an adverb (as in "he's feeling pretty good"), but its use should be avoided in academic writing.

Adverbs can describe verbs, adjectives, other adverbs, or even a whole sentence:

He walks <u>slowly</u>.
She is <u>seriously</u> considering our proposal for a new workstation.
This game is <u>extremely</u> difficult to master.
<u>Essentially</u>, the story is about lost love.

Exercise 6.1 Review of parts of speech

Identify the parts of speech of the underlined words:

1. <u>Richard</u> went to <u>see</u> the <u>doctor</u>. He complained about a <u>sore</u> throat, insomnia, and <u>tiredness</u>. The doctor <u>told</u> him his <u>unhealthy</u> lifestyle was to blame. She <u>advised</u> him to <u>quit</u> smoking, get more <u>exercise</u>, and find a less <u>stressful</u> job.
2. The school <u>band</u> practised <u>diligently</u> every day last <u>week</u>. The band members <u>were</u> excited about performing in the opening <u>ceremonies</u> for the <u>new</u> community centre.
3. The <u>leader</u> of the Liberal Party <u>was chosen</u> because she is <u>charismatic</u> and dedicated. The party was pinning all its <u>hopes</u> of <u>re-election</u> on her star <u>power</u>. Most members <u>enthusiastically</u> <u>endorsed</u> her <u>selection</u>.
4. The Bank of <u>Canada</u> is issuing <u>new</u> bills made of a single <u>piece</u> of <u>poly-mer</u> with two <u>clear</u> panels. <u>Metallic</u> images and hidden numbers can be

seen through the windows when the bills are held up to the light. These features should make it more difficult for counterfeiters.

5. Graphic novels are not like children's comics. Generally, they have adult themes and tell complicated stories. Many people today prefer stories told through images rather than text.

Word families

Think of the noun *danger*, the verb *endanger*, the adjective *dangerous*, and the adverb *dangerously*. The verb, adjective, and adverb are all derived from the noun *danger* and together they can be considered a word family. Learning related words is an important aspect of vocabulary building.

Get to know the suffixes (and some prefixes) listed above for each part of speech to help you learn the members of a word family. For instance, the words derived from the noun *joy* include the verb *enjoy* (formed with the prefix *en-*), the adjective *enjoyable*, the adverb *enjoyably*, and another noun—*enjoyment*, which is derived from the verb. The suffixes *–able* and *–ment* are a common adjective and noun ending, respectively.

Using the different parts of speech can add variety to your writing. For example, in an essay on what students need to do to be successful, instead of repeating "to be successful" throughout, you could write "to achieve success" or "to succeed."

Note that the same word can be used as different parts of speech. For instance, *light* can be a noun, a verb, or an adjective, as in the following sentence:

She turned on the light, but she wanted to light the fire so she could take off her light jacket.

Here are some other examples:

They look at the new videos every day. [verb]
They take a look at the new videos every day. [noun]
The surface was smooth. [adjective]
She smoothed out the wrinkles. [verb]

Exercise 6.2 Complete the word family

Complete the table with the words related to each of the words given. Sometimes there will be more than one derivative of the same part of speech, and sometimes the same word can function as more than one part of speech. The first row has been completely filled in as an example.

Try to fill in the whole table without using a dictionary unless you cannot think of the right word on your own.

Table 6.1

	Noun	Verb	Adjective	Adverb
E.g.:	success	succeed	successful	successfully
1	beauty			
2		caution		
3	danger			
4				equally
5	falsehood			
6			high	
7		infect		
8			minimal	
9			personal	
10				safely
11	specialty			
12			stable	—

Recognize roots, prefixes, and suffixes

Understanding word formation can help you build your vocabulary. Many words have identifiable parts that can give you a clue to the meaning and properties of a word. In this chapter, we have already looked at the suffixes that are used to make derivatives for each part of speech. For example, if you see the word *generalize*, you can see the *–ize* ending which makes a verb from the common adjective *general*; therefore, *generalize* means "to form general principles."

While suffixes (word endings) generally show the part of speech, prefixes (word beginnings) alter the meaning of a word.

The most common negative prefixes are *in-* and *un-*, both of which are commonly used before adjectives, as in *inactive* and *unusual*. While the use of *un-* is fairly straightforward, the *in-* prefix is not. First of all, *in-* changes spelling depending on the letter that comes afterwards: *il-* before *l*; *im-* before *m*, *p* and *b*; and *ir-* before *r* (as in *illogical*, *immoderate*, *impossible*, *imbalanced*, and *irregular*, respectively). Another problem with the prefix *in-* is that sometimes it means *in* and is not negative, as in *inborn* and *indebted*.

Other prefixes that turn a word into its opposite include *a-/an-*, *de-*, *dis-*, *mis-*, and *non-* (as in *apolitical*, *debug*, *dislike*, *misunderstand*, and *non-toxic*, respectively).

Exercise 6.3 Using prefixes to show the opposite meaning

See how well you know negative prefixes. Add a prefix to each word in the list to make it opposite in meaning. For example, adding *dis* to *honest* makes *dishonest*—i.e., not honest.

1. legible
2. like
3. comfortable
4. typical
5. friendly
6. active
7. agree
8. grateful
9. passive
10. handle

In addition to negative prefixes, English has prefixes that specify such qualities as size, quantity, and direction. For example, *uni-*, *bi-*, and *tri-* when added to *cycle* show how many wheels the vehicle has. Dictionaries often have separate entries for such prefixes to explain their meaning, so keep an eye out for these handy prefixes.

Learning a few common Greek and Latin roots is also a good way to increase your vocabulary, especially for scientific and technical words. For example, *hemo/hema* (also spelled *haemo/haema*) are variants of the root word that refers to blood (as in *hemophiliac*). That is useful to know if you are in any health-related field.

Understand usage—the ways words are used

Words are much more than their meanings. To write clear, well-formed sentences, you have to understand how each word is used—both the grammatical structures that it works with and what other words are likely to appear with it. The technical terms for this are *colligation* (how words are tied to structures) and *collocation* (how words tend to occur along with other words, i.e., co-location).

Most of the time you form sentences without thinking much about what words go together. Certain word combinations just sound right. The problems arise for words that you do not know as well. When you learn a new word, pay attention to what is around it. Look at sample sentences in dictionaries.

Here are examples of such usage errors:

✗ The building dismantled. [should be "They dismantled the building" or "The building was dismantled"]
✗ Parents should stop hovering their children. [should be "hovering over"]
✗ We have to do the scientific method. [should be "follow the scientific method"]
✗ He went to the bank to borrow a loan. [should be "get a loan" or "borrow money"]

These types of errors tend to be more common in the writing of English-language learners, who have not had the benefit of hearing and reading the language for years, and therefore have less of a sense of what "sounds right." The errors can also be the result of translation from the student's native language. Another problem is that collocation is rarely taught in the classroom, so students are unaware that they have to be aware of this feature of language use. Native speakers also may have trouble with collocation for words they are less familiar with.

When you speak or write, each word choice you make determines the shape of the sentence. For example, if you want to say that people were talking about a problem, you can choose to use either the verb *discuss* or the noun *discussion*:

The group discussed the problem.
The group had a discussion about the problem.

The verb *discuss* is transitive—that means it takes a direct object without a preposition. However, the noun *discussion* requires a preposition, usually *about* or *of*. These characteristics of *discuss* and *discussion* limit our options for a grammatical sentence. For example, we cannot say:

✗ The group discussed about the problem. [common error]
✗ The group had a discussion to the problem.
✗ The group had a discussion the problem.
✗ The group discussed that the department had an organizational problem.

Likewise, we have only a few choices of verb to go before the noun. We can *have* or *hold* a discussion, but not *take* or *make* a discussion. The first two verbs collocate with *discussion*, while the second two do not. Adjectives that tend to modify *discussion* include *detailed, in-depth, long, lengthy, preliminary, informal, frank, open, lively, heated, serious, useful,* and *fruitful.*

If you want to continue the idea and say that the group discussion had a successful resolution, you would probably say: The group *solved* the problem.

Instead of the verb *solve,* you could use *fix* or *resolve,* but it would be unlikely that you would choose a verb like *repair* or *conclude,* even though these words are synonyms of *fix* and *resolve,* respectively. If, instead of the verb *solve,* you wanted to use the noun *solution,* you would need to use the verb *find* or *reach.*

The verbs *discuss* and *solve* are both transitive verbs; that means they require a direct object. You cannot say "the group discussed" or "the group solved" without using a noun structure after the verb.

Words tend to go together with other words in collocations, so your choice of any word limits the other words that can be used in the sentence.

Exercise 6.4 Complete the collocations

Fill in each blank with the correct word from the following list:

> break, casual, covert, detail, emotional, favour, hidden, itemized, meticulous, submit, substantial, throw, waste, well

1. It was a _____ operation, carried out with _____ attention to _____. No one saw it coming.
2. They must have a _____ agenda. They spent a _____ amount of money on a project most of the researchers saw as a complete _____ of time.
3. He made an _____ appeal as to why he deserved a _____, but I could tell Isabel was not convinced. She wanted to _____ the book at him.
4. I was asked to _____ a claim with an _____ list of expenses in order to get my refund.
5. I do not know him _____ enough to ask him to do me a _____. He is just a _____ acquaintance.

Use synonyms and antonyms

Because English has such a large vocabulary, there are many words that mean the same thing or almost the same thing. It is important to draw on this vocabulary to make your writing clearer and more interesting. You need to choose the right word to express your meaning clearly. You also need to vary your choice of words to avoid unnecessary repetition:

> Teachers teach a wider range of subjects at small schools.
> Instructors teach a wider range of subjects at small schools. [better because it avoids the repetitive phrase "teachers teach."]

Even simple choices such as using words like *item* and *product* instead of the broad term *thing* can make a difference, as in this example:

> All the damaged things were marked for the "as is" sale.
> All the damaged items were marked for the "as is" sale. [better]

Use a thesaurus effectively

Because your receptive vocabulary (the words you understand) is larger than your productive vocabulary, a thesaurus (a dictionary of synonyms and sometimes antonyms) is a useful tool to remind you of words you know that didn't occur to you and to introduce you to new words.

Don't try to pump up your writing by slotting in words from a thesaurus. Remember that you are writing to communicate, not to impress. **"Big words" don't make an essay better.** More important, you are likely to use unfamiliar words incorrectly. Words that are synonyms are not interchangeable. They may have different meanings when used in different contexts. For instance, *famine* is a synonym of *hunger*, but you cannot say, "He has a famine for fame."

Exercise 6.5 Find synonyms

With a partner or in a small group, consider synonyms for the underlined words or expressions. Use a thesaurus for help. Discuss any differences of meaning and choose what you think is the best word or expression. You may find the original word choice is best, and you may have to adjust the sentence structure to make the synonym fit. For example, you may have to add a preposition.

1. The new proposal puts the <u>manager</u> in a <u>predicament</u>. She has already <u>allocated</u> the <u>resources</u> and <u>hired</u> the <u>personnel</u>. However, the <u>new proposal</u> is such a good idea that she is <u>thinking</u> of adopting it even though it will <u>delay</u> the start of the <u>project</u>. Even with the <u>delay</u>, the company can save money in the long run.
2. City life often <u>requires</u> getting used to a variety of sounds. From the street come the <u>sounds</u> of construction, the <u>sounds</u> of transit, and the <u>sounds</u> of sirens. Those <u>unlucky</u> enough to have an apartment with thin walls may hear the <u>sounds</u> of their neighbours: the <u>sound</u> of footsteps, the <u>sound</u> of music, and the <u>sound</u> of voices.

Consider connotation

Words can have the same basic meaning but be quite different in connotation, the emotional implication of the word. For instance, if you describe someone as *thrifty*, it just means that the person likes to save money—it is usually thought of as a good thing. Calling the person *stingy*, however, has a negative connotation—it is an insult even though *stingy* has the same basic meaning as *thrifty*

Consider the connotations of the following groups of words. What are the differences in meaning? Which words are neutral, which are negative, and which are positive? How would you use the words?

- problem/ challenge/ issue
- stubborn/ strong-willed/ pig-headed
- slender/ thin/ scrawny/ slim/ skinny
- mentally ill/ crazy/ bonkers

Recognize jargon, register, dialect, slang, and idioms

Your essay writing should be in standard English. You can use elements from other types of language—but judiciously. Make sure you understand the use of these words and expressions.

Jargon is technical language. For instance, *myocardial infarction* is medical terminology, and *defamatory libel* is a legal term. The rule here is simple—you can use such technical language if you are writing for an audience that routinely uses the terminology and therefore would understand what you are saying. Note that the term *jargon* is often considered negative because many writers use too many technical terms and thus confuse their readers.

Register refers to such distinctions as formal and informal language. For example, the word *kids* for *children* is informal register. Essays should be in a more formal register than your conversational style.

Dialect differences can show up in vocabulary and grammar. For instance, British motorists might refer to their car's *boot*, *bonnet*, and *windscreen* whereas North Americans use *trunk*, *hood*, and *windshield*, respectively. Regional differences show up in conversational speech, but writing tends to be more standardized.

Slang is the language of the street, the language of specific groups. Here are some examples: *bucks, chillax, cop out, dude, jerk*. Do not use slang in your essays.

An idiom is an expression whose meaning is often quite different from the literal meaning of the words that make it up. For example, *spill the beans* means to reveal a secret—it has nothing to do with beans. Someone might lose her "train of thought" or finally "see the light." Some idioms are informal, even slangy, and thus should be avoided in essay writing. For instance, instead of saying "they were ripped off," you should say "they were taken advantage of."

Improve your spelling

Spelling is important. First, it leads to successful communication. Everyone has had the experience of struggling to read misspelled documents. Second, poor spelling creates a bad impression—that you cannot be bothered to attend to details. Imagine your chances of getting a job with a résumé full of misspellings. Spelling errors are usually the first mistakes noticed.

It is not surprising that most people struggle with English spelling because it often does not correspond to the pronunciation and there are many exceptions to the "rules." Because English vocabulary is a mix of other languages, spelling is also mixed up. For instance, words from Greek have letter combinations such as *ps* (as in *psychology*) and *ph* (as in *phonetics*). Moreover, English pronunciation changed after the spelling was standardized, so that letter combinations such as *gh* are no longer pronounced.

Another difficulty is that some words have more than one acceptable spelling. For instance, Canadians write *centre*, while Americans write *center*. British spelling of the *–ize* verb ending is *–ise* in such words as *organise* and *realise*. The most important thing is to be consistent. For example, if you write *color*, which is the American spelling, you should also write *neighbor* and *favor*. However, you should use Canadian spelling in your studies in Canadian colleges and universities.

All this means that spelling must be learned. Reading helps you improve your spelling because you get used to what the words look like in print. However, some avid readers are poor spellers, so direct study is also important.

You need to know your own weaknesses. Make a list of the words you have trouble with. Figure out ways to remember the spelling. Write the words out by hand dozens of times. (Muscle memory—whether from handwriting or typing the word—helps you spell correctly.) Give yourself spelling tests by having a friend read the words out for you as you write them down.

Use the spell checker in your word-processing program, but remember that this is not foolproof. Spell checkers flag words that are not in their database but do not tell you when you used the wrong word. For instance, a spell checker will not tell you that you should have used *principal* instead of *principle*. In addition, computer spell checkers tend to use American spelling by default. Sometimes a spell checker can even make things worse. One document we saw had the word *bicycle* appearing throughout even though it had nothing to do with bicycles—the writer wanted the word *basically*.

Check words in the dictionary—either electronic or paper-based. You may be wondering how you can look up a word you cannot spell, but the trick is to concentrate on the beginning of the word and you should be able to find it. You may have to guess at the first letters. Consider common letter combinations (given below). Don't give up too easily. The time you spend looking is time spent learning, which will make it easier next time.

Watch out for errors that are the result of carelessness. For instance, dropping the *y* at the end of *they* is a common mistake people make when they are writing quickly. Other mistakes are copying errors—the word or name may be right in front of you on the screen or in the article you are reading, so there is no excuse for spelling it incorrectly.

Exercise 6.6 Check your spelling

Correct the spelling mistakes in the following sentences:

1. Is the meeting time convenent for you? We could change it to acomodate your skedual if your going to have trouble makeing it. The commitee will develope the criteria for the evaluation. Once you recieve them, you can see weather they fullfill your expectashions. I expect we will be able to reach a concensus eventuelly. [13]
2. The proffessor told his students that they should of studied more for the exam. He offered extra tutorials for remedeal help for those who were struggling with the basic concepts. Some of the students were not greatful. They made the arguement that he should just bell curv the marks. Others acknowleged that they needed to improove, and they started studing write a way. [10]
3. The writting had alot of misteaks. It was embarasing to see that graduates wear going to go out in the work world doing work like that. Eventhough they had talent and skill, thier poor writing skills made a bad inpression. [7]

The number of mistakes for each group of sentences is given in brackets. Check your answers in the key (p. 248), and note the words you got wrong for further study.

Memorize the most common words

It is easy to find a list of the 2000 most common words in English (originally called the General Service List). Look online. Make sure you can spell all these words correctly. They account for about 80 per cent of the words in your writing. After you have mastered this list, you can work on the Academic Word List, which contains the words most often used in academic writing (not counting the 2000 most common words in English). Make sure you memorize words commonly used in your specific field.

Lists of commonly misspelled words and commonly confused words appear on the inside covers of this book. Highlight any that you tend to misspell.

Learn common letter combinations

Often you have to guess at a spelling and then check it in a dictionary or with a computer spell checker. Even though English spelling is not completely phonetic, it is helpful to know the possible spellings for certain sounds.

The *s* sound can be written with *s*, *c*, *sc*, and *ps* (as in *sign*, *cent*, *science*, and *psychology*, respectively).

Many scientific and technical words are from Greek. For these words, the *f* sound is spelled *ph* (from the Greek letter *phi*, ϕ) as in *philosophy*; the *k* sound is spelled *ch* (from the Greek letter *chi*, χ) as in *chaos*; and the *s* sound is occasionally spelled *ps* (from the Greek letter *psi*, ψ) as in *psyche* and *psychology*.

The *ch* combination is problematic in English because it is pronounced differently depending on the origin of the word. In simple, everyday words like *church*, *child*, and *choke*, the *ch* is pronounced like "tch." In words that come from Greek, the *ch* spelling represents the *chi*, χ, which is pronounced like a *k* sound. Examples include *chaos*, *character*, and *Christmas* (in the short-form *Xmas*, the *X* actually comes from *chi*, which looks like an *x*). The *ch* in French words is pronounced *sh* as in *chef*, *champagne*, and *château*.

The combination *ough* has many pronunciations (*rough*, *thought*, *through*), but it is a standard combination of letters to learn. For instance, it is never *uogh*. Sometimes it is followed by a *t*.

Watch out for silent letters. Words starting with an *n* sound may have a silent *k* before the *n* (as in *know* and *knife*). Those with an *r* sound may have a silent *w* (as in *wrestling* and *wrath*). Silent *w*'s also show up in *answer* and *sword*. Silent *b*'s are found in a variety of words (*debt*, *lamb*, and *subtle*). A few words start with a silent *p*: *pterodactyl*, *pneumonia*, and *psoriasis*. You do not have to remember all the cases of silent letters (of which this is just a basic list), but learn them in any words you have trouble spelling.

Learn some basic spelling rules

Most people remember the rule "i before e" rule from elementary school: "i before e, except after c, and when it says *ay*, as in *neighbour* and *weigh*." This rule is handy for remembering the spelling of some common words like *believe*, *receive*, and *beige*, but it has many exceptions (such as *caffeine* and *weird*).

The rule for doubling consonants before endings is difficult to remember. (In Canadian and British English, the final consonant is generally doubled if the word ends in a single vowel and single consonant and the last syllable is stressed, as in *stop/stopped* and *begin/beginning*.) Even if you find this rule confusing, it is important to recognize that a doubled consonant often signals a difference in pronunciation, as in these words:

    write, written
    filing, filling
    later, latter
    cuter, cutter

The silent *e* at the end of many one-syllable words signals that the vowel is what is often called a "long" vowel (it says its own name) whereas other vowels are short vowels, as shown in these pairs:

    fat/fate, bit/bite, cod/code, cut/cute

(For words with the *e* vowel, a double vowel is usually used instead of a silent *e* at the end, as in *bet/beat*. Sometimes this also holds true for the *o*, as in *cot/coat*.)

When endings are added, the silent *e* is generally dropped, so the double consonant signals the short vowel sound:

    hope → hoping; hop → hopping
    mope → moping; mop → mopping
    file → filing; fill → filling
    hate → hater; hat → hatter

Distinguish between commonly confused words

People often make spelling mistakes when they choose the wrong word of a pair that sound the same or almost the same but are spelled differently, such as *whether/weather* or *to/too*. Sometimes the pronunciation is not the same, but the words are close in spelling, such as *quite/quiet* and *desert/dessert*.

One of the most common spelling mistakes is the mix-up between *there*, *their*, and *they're*. Most of the time it is an easily correctable error—it is made when the writer does not stop to think which word is needed. If you have trouble distinguishing between these words, remember that *there* is an adverb (like its spelling mate *here*), *their* is the possessive pronoun (for something belonging to *them*), and *they're* is the contraction of *they are*. If you make this mistake often, pause for a second before you write one of these words to ascertain which one you need.

Another common mix-up is between *it's* and *its*. *It's* is a contraction of *it is* or *it has*; *its* is the possessive pronoun for something belonging to *it*. While an apostrophe generally signals a possessive (as in "Jane's book"), possessive pronouns (such as *its*, *his*, *hers*, *whose*) do not have an apostrophe. Think for a second when you write—if you can replace the *it's* with *it is* or *it has*, put an apostrophe in it. If you can't, don't.

A list of commonly confused words appears on the inside back cover.

Exercise 6.7 Choose the right word

Choose the right word from these commonly confused words:

1. I need to order some business _____ [stationary, stationery] for the office. I did not expect to _____ [lose, loose] a whole box. It should take a _____ [weak, week] or so.
2. He almost drove _____ [passed, past] his destination, but he hit the _____ [brakes, breaks] in time. I thought he would go _____ [threw, through] the red light _____ [to, too, two].
3. Camels are the best transportation in the _____ [desert, dessert], but _____ [there, they're, their] stubborn animals.
4. In a research essay, you have to be careful to _____ [cite, sight, site] your references _____ [to, too, two] show exactly _____ [wear, were, where] you got the information.
5. She always gives good _____ [advice, advise]. She does not receive _____ [complements, compliments] very graciously.
6. Those tours seem to be popular with _____[woman, women] travelling alone.

Use your dictionary for any words that you do not know, and check your answers in the key (p. 248).

Pay attention to word division

Other common spelling mistakes involve the incorrect separation of words. For example, many people write *a lot* as one word (which is sometimes corrected by spell checkers to *allot*, which is an entirely different word). Sometimes there are two correct forms, such as the adverb *maybe* and the verb *may be*, and the writer has chosen the wrong one. Sometimes, however, people write two words incorrectly as one, such as the common mistakes *infront* or *eachother*.

Exercise 6.8 One word or two?

Choose the correct word, words, or spelling to fit each blank:

1. He wants to be _____[a part, apart] of Howard's project. He does not like working _____ [a lone, alone]. He is _____ [all ready, already] to start.
2. It _____ [may be, maybe] time to redo the whole room _____[even though, eventhough] it will cost_____

[a lot, alot]. They should be able to do most of the work _____ [them selves, themselves].

3. I only wanted to buy a loaf of bread, but I could not resist the special on brownies at 50 cents _____ [a piece, apiece]. It's not an _____ [every day, everyday] indulgence.

4. The brothers do not look _____ [at all, atall] _____ [a like, alike].

5. They had to get the rooms _____ [all ready, already] for the guests. _____ [In spite, Inspite] of the short time they had, they tried to do _____ [what ever, whatever] their mother asked.

Build your vocabulary

Good writers have large vocabularies. They understand the nuances of meaning of different words and know the rules of usage. This doesn't mean that they fill their sentences with multi-syllable words, just that they know the precise word to express their meaning clearly.

People learn words by hearing them spoken and by reading them. Reading will expose you to more words.

Be curious about unfamiliar words—try to guess the meaning first and then look them up in the dictionary.

Use a dictionary

A dictionary helps you to study words actively. The best dictionaries, either electronic or paper-based, tell you not only the meaning, but also the properties and use of the word. For instance, a learner's dictionary, such as the *Oxford Advanced Learner's Dictionary*, often has examples of sentences that make the definition clearer. It also guides the writer in usage. For example, an entry for the adjective *reluctant* shows that it is often used with an infinitive—"reluctant to do something." Dictionaries also have entries for phrases, including idioms; look under the main word in the expression.

Some colleges and universities allow students to use book-form dictionaries for writing tests and exams. Make sure you take advantage of this opportunity if it is allowed. Note that electronic dictionaries are generally prohibited in test situations, so you may have to get used to a book dictionary before your test. Get to know your dictionary. Look over the introduction to see how the entries are organized. Practise using your dictionary so that you become proficient and do not waste time on a test.

Use precise vocabulary for clarity and conciseness

The purpose of building vocabulary is to communicate more effectively. Clarity in writing depends on correct word use. You need to know exactly what each word means and how it is used in a sentence. Check your dictionary if you are not sure.

Exercise 6.9 Correct word choice

Here are some sentences where the writer made a poor word choice. Correct the sentences:

1. She <u>debates</u> that plastic bags are not a huge environmental problem.
2. My car is in the shop because there is an <u>issue</u> with the brakes.
3. In Quebec, I could <u>exercise</u> my French.
4. In high school, students are <u>sponge-fed</u> by the teachers.
5. When his passport was <u>robbed</u>, he could not <u>show</u> his identity.
6. Being able to <u>articulate</u> with different <u>individuals</u> every day, one naturally begins to <u>inherit</u> interpersonal skills.

Vocabulary checklist

- Are you sure of the meaning and use of the words you used in your essay?
- Did you vary your word choice by using synonyms and derivatives?
- Did you use precise terminology instead of relying on vague words?
- Did you check your spelling?

If you cannot answer yes to each of these questions, reread your work, check the vocabulary you used, and edit your writing.

Grammar and Sentence Structure

The parts of speech and their characteristics were introduced in the previous chapter. Here, we see how these words work in sentences. We review the basics of sentence structure, focusing on areas students find problematic.

Being a good writer does not depend on a knowledge of grammatical terminology and the ability to explain rules of syntax. Many people can form correct sentences without being able to label a conjunctive adverb or a relative clause. However, grammatical terms are necessary when we try to explain how a sentence works or why a sentence is not well formed. Try to get a sense of what the term is describing by looking at the examples of sentences and the exercises. Note that the terminology can vary. For instance, continuous tenses are also referred to as progressive tenses.

Languages are not designed to follow rules—instead, the rules are written to describe what is considered correct usage by most educated speakers and writers. It is also worth noting that the rules are different for casual spoken language than for more formal uses, such as essay writing. What you say casually in speech may not be considered acceptable in written form. For instance, in conversation, we may say "There's the extra chairs" instead of the grammatically correct "There are the extra chairs."

What is important for you as an essay writer is to follow the standards of good, academic English. This includes following the standards your instructor adheres to. For instance, some instructors may object to the previous sentence because it ends with a preposition, while others will have more relaxed standards about some conventions. If this sounds confusing, be reassured that most of the rules will not be contentious. The majority of educated English speakers would generally agree on the correctness of most sentences.

Recognize subjects and predicates

A sentence needs a subject (what you are talking about) and a predicate (what you are saying about the subject). In the simplest sentences, the subject is a noun (or a pronoun) and the predicate is a verb. The verb may be completed by such elements as an object or an infinite. To this core of the sentence may be added many different elements—adjectives, adverbs, phrases, clauses—but you always need to have a subject and predicate. To help you check the grammaticality of a sentence it is useful to identify the simple subject (usually a noun or pronoun) and the simple predicate (the main verb along with any auxiliary verbs). In the following examples, the simple subject is underlined and the simple predicate is underlined twice.

> John sings.
> The school choir was singing at the performance.
> The outstanding children's choir from St Anthony's was invited to sing at the performance commemorating the town's anniversary.
> Stop! [In commands, the subject is understood to be you.]

If the verb is transitive (p. 146), like the verb *to buy*, an object is needed to complete the predicate:

> ✗ They bought. [incomplete and unclear]
> ✓ They bought a new trailer.

The subject can be compound, that is, consisting of more than one person or thing:

> Eli, Miriam, and Jeanette were on the winning team.

A sentence can also have more than one main verb:

> The children ran, skipped, and jumped in the schoolyard.

Usually, English sentences have the subject before the corresponding verb, but there are some exceptions:

> There are many opportunities to advance in the company. [*Opportunities* is the subject of the verb *are*; *there* is an adverb.]
> Deep in the heart of the woods howled a wolf. [*Wolf* is the subject; *howled* is the verb.]

It is easier to identify the main subject and verb if you discount the adjectives, adverbs, phrases, and clauses that work as modifiers. Identifying the core of the sentence lets you know if the sentence is grammatical and can help you understand a complicated sentence.

Exercise 7.1 Subjects and predicates

In the following sentences, underline the subject and double underline the main verb:

1. Jean changed the ring tone on her phone.
2. The signature on this page looks like a forgery.
3. Watching the game, he again felt the regret of his sports career ending so badly.
4. He has a good poker face.
5. On the back of the painting was a signature.
6. Signing the contract would have meant signing away all his rights to the material.
7. The option with the most leeway would be the best choice.
8. The person who collects the most points wins the game.
9. There are many new features on that phone.
10. Theresa and I went to the concert on Friday.

Use verb tenses correctly

In the previous chapter, we looked at the principal parts of the verb. These verb forms along with auxiliary verbs (*be, have, will*) and verb endings (*–ing, –ed*) are used to make the different verb tenses. Grammarians distinguish between *tense*, which refers to time (past, present, future), and *aspect*, which shows whether an action is completed (in the perfect tenses) or ongoing (in continuous or progressive tenses). However, these forms of verbs are generally grouped together as verb tenses:

Simple present:	They talk on the phone every day.
Simple past:	They talked on the phone yesterday.
Simple future:	They will talk on the phone tomorrow.
Present continuous:	They are talking on the phone right now.
Past continuous:	They were talking on the phone when the lightning hit.
Future continuous:	They will be talking on the phone forever!
Present perfect:	They have talked on the phone once already today.

Past perfect:	They <u>had talked</u> on the phone before they met in person.
Future perfect:	They <u>will have talked</u> on the phone for an hour by then.
Present perfect continuous:	They <u>have been talking</u> on the phone for an hour now.
Past perfect continuous:	They <u>had been talking</u> on the phone for an hour when I arrived.
Future perfect continuous:	They <u>will have been talking</u> on the phone for an hour by then.

This list may look intimidating, but you do not have to memorize the names of these verb tenses. Of these twelve tenses, you will mostly only use six. Moreover, you probably use verbs correctly in most of your sentences. English-language learners may have more difficulty, especially if the verb system in their own language is very different from English verbs. The basic uses are explained below.

Use the simple present tense to talk about general facts

The simple present tense is one that is often used in essays. It can convey general facts and habitual actions:

> Teenagers often <u>have</u> trouble understanding the consequences of their actions because their brain's reasoning power <u>is</u> not yet fully developed.
> Governments <u>rely</u> on lotteries and casinos to bring in much needed income.
> She <u>takes</u> the bus to school, but she often <u>gets</u> a ride home.

The simple present tense is also often used to tell or discuss a story:

> Shakespeare's *Macbeth* <u>tells</u> the story of an ambitious man who <u>kills</u> to gain the throne.

English-language learners, in particular, often have trouble with this "simple" tense. One reason is that there is an *s* ending on the third person singular (as in "he walks") that many non-native speakers leave off, both in speaking and in writing. In addition, some essay writers do not seem to trust in the tense alone to be general enough. They may add the unnecessary adverb *always* to the sentence or use the future form with *will*.

> Students who <u>always take</u> notes in class <u>will remember</u> the material better for tests.

Students who <u>take</u> notes in class <u>remember</u> the material better for tests. [better]

Whenever I see a mistake, I <u>will stop</u> reading.
Whenever I see a mistake, I <u>stop</u> reading. [better]

Use continuous tenses to show that an action continues

Continuous (also called progressive) verb tenses essentially show actions that continue over a period of time. They are formed with the auxiliary verb *be* and the present participle (the *–ing* form): as in *I am working, he is working, they are working, we will be working,* and *they were working.*

The present continuous shows a present action (as opposed to the simple present tense described above):

I <u>am studying</u> Russian at the university. [what I am currently doing]
The sun <u>is shining</u>, and the birds <u>are singing</u>. [Compare this to "the sun shines every day in California."]

The past continuous is often used with a simple past to show a past action that happened while something else was happening:

While they <u>were working</u> on the project, the fire alarm <u>went off</u>.
The student <u>answered</u> his cellphone while the teacher <u>was talking</u>.

Note that continuous tenses are also used to show future actions, sometimes with the verb *go*:

He <u>is</u> not <u>attending</u> that meeting tomorrow.
He <u>is</u> not <u>going to attend</u> that meeting tomorrow.

Continuous tenses are generally not used with verbs that describe states rather than actions. For example, we say "the wine <u>tastes</u> sour," not "the wine <u>is tasting</u> sour." However, we can use the verb <u>taste</u> if we are talking about the action of tasting, as in "he <u>is tasting</u> the wine." Here are some other examples of incorrect use of the continuous tense:

✗ I'm liking the orange one.
✓ I like the orange one.

✗ She is owning a car.
✓ She owns a car.

✗ We are wanting to clean the carpets.
✓ We want to clean the carpets.

Verbs that describe cognition, emotional states, and perception are usually not used in the continuous tenses. However, the movement towards more frequent use of the *-ing* forms in English has spread to these non-action verbs.

I'm thinking that orange would be the better choice. [conversational use]
I think that orange would be the better choice. [standard English]

This usage is more common in informal, spoken English and some regional dialects and should be avoided in essays.

Know when to use a perfect tense

The perfect tenses are formed with the auxiliary *have* and the past participle of the verb:

We <u>have finished</u> the assignment.
Dr Patel <u>has isolated</u> the gene responsible for that trait.

Use the present perfect tense for something that began in the past and is still true today:

I <u>have lived</u> in Vancouver for three years. [I am still living in Vancouver.]
She <u>has</u> never <u>tried</u> skydiving. [in all her experience, up until now]

In contrast, the simple past is used to describe completed actions that happened at a defined time in the past:

Yesterday I <u>washed</u> the windows.
He <u>studied</u> for the test all weekend.
I <u>lived</u> in Vancouver from 2005 to 2010.
She <u>went</u> skydiving last week.
I <u>planted</u> tomatoes in pots on my balcony in the spring.

Adverbs such as *already, just, ever, never,* and *yet,* as well as time phrases with *for* and *since,* often signal that a present perfect tense is required:

I have already washed the dishes.
Anita has just finished the report.
He has recently repainted the house but hasn't fixed the roof yet.
She has never been scuba diving.
Have you ever travelled in Europe?
I have been living in Halifax since 2006.

Use the past perfect tense to show that one action happened before another:

He <u>had studied</u> the map carefully before he left for the trip.
They <u>had</u> never <u>been</u> skiing until they moved to Whistler.

However, the use of the past perfect tense is declining, and often the simple past is used instead, especially in speech and less formal writing:

He <u>studied</u> the map carefully before he left for the trip.

Both native speakers and ESL students sometimes struggle with the present perfect and the simple past, making errors such as these:

- ✗ I have finished the assignment yesterday. [should be "I finished . . ."]
- ✗ He never been to Spain. [should be "He has never been . . ."]
- ✗ Liam has never flew in a jet. [should be "has never flown . . ."]

Because of the use of contractions in everyday speech (*I've, he'd*), the *have* form seems to disappear. This carries over to writing when people may leave it out, sometimes unaware that it is there at all:

- ✗ He seen the Eiffel Tower.
- ✓ He's seen the Eiffel Tower. [In speech, the two *s* sounds merge together.]

Sometimes, people use other tenses to try to convey the meaning of the present perfect:

- ✗ I am living here for six years.
- ✗ I live here for six years.
- ✓ I have lived here for six years.

Use the correct form of the past participle

The past participle seems to be a problem among students today, in both speech and writing. Even native speakers of English make mistakes. Here are some typical errors:

- ✗ I haven't <u>took</u> that course before. [taken]
- ✗ I <u>seen</u> this movie already. [have seen]
- ✗ They have <u>walk</u> to school before. [walked]
- ✗ They had <u>went</u> to the hospital. [gone]
- ✗ Was there homework <u>assign</u> for today's class? [assigned]

These types of errors do not happen as often with regular verbs because the simple past and the past participle are the same—both have *–ed* endings (*listened,* *occupied, carried*). However, the most commonly used verbs are irregular. Here are some common verbs where the simple past and the past participle are different:

Base Form	Past	Past Participle
be	was, were	been
become	became	become
begin	began	begun
break	broke	broken
choose	chose	chosen
come	came	come
do	did	done
drink	drank	drunk
drive	drove	driven
eat	ate	eaten
fall	fell	fallen
fly	flew	flown
forget	forgot	forgotten
get	got	got/gotten
go	went	gone
grow	grew	grown
know	knew	known
ring	rang	rung
rise	rose	risen
see	saw	seen
show	showed	shown
sing	sang	sung
speak	spoke	spoken
take	took	taken
throw	threw	thrown
wear	wore	worn
write	wrote	written

Remember that the past form is used for the simple past (as in "I wrote a letter") while the past participle is used for the perfect tenses with *have* and *had* (as in "I have written him a letter") and for the passive (as in "the pizza was eaten" and "the car was stolen").

Use the future tenses sparingly in essays

English has several ways of expressing future events:

> He <u>will take</u> the seven o'clock train. [usually shows a decision just made]
> He <u>will be taking</u> the seven o'clock train. [shows that something has been planned earlier]

He <u>is taking</u> the seven o'clock train. [already planned]
He <u>is going to take</u> the seven o'clock train. [already planned, informal usage]
The train <u>leaves</u> at seven o'clock. [shows a regular, scheduled event]

The distinction between these forms is slight. The ones that use continuous tenses are more common in speech. In your essays, you will probably use few future tenses, and when you do, you are more likely to use the basic future tense of *will* plus the base form of the verb.

Use the simple present tense, not the future, when you want to express general facts and common events (p. 168):

✗ Immigrants <u>will settle</u> in ethnic neighbourhoods at first when they <u>will need</u> the comfort of their own language and culture.
✓ Immigrants <u>settle</u> in ethnic neighbourhoods at first when they <u>need</u> the comfort of their own language and culture.

Use the conditional (the *would* form), and not the future, when you want to show what is likely to happen:

High-school students will benefit from college preparation workshops.
High-school students would benefit from college preparation workshops. [better]

Do not switch verb tenses unnecessarily

Changing from past to present tense or from present to past confuses the reader. Tense switching is especially common in narratives, because a story can be told in either the present or in the past tense, and student writers are sometimes inconsistent in the tenses they use.

✗ *The Hobbit* <u>tells</u> the story of Bilbo Baggins. The wizard Gandalf <u>gets</u> Bilbo to accompany thirteen dwarves on their quest to retrieve their treasure from the dragon Smaug. The group <u>encountered</u> goblins, elves, and spiders as they <u>travel</u> to the Lonely Mountain. Bilbo <u>found</u> the ring that <u>became</u> central to the sequel story, *The Lord of the Rings*. Because the ring <u>made</u> him invisible, he <u>helps</u> the dwarves escape from sticky situations. [with tense shifts]
✓ *The Hobbit* <u>tells</u> the story of Bilbo Baggins. The wizard Gandalf <u>gets</u> Bilbo to accompany thirteen dwarves on their quest to retrieve their treasure from the dragon Smaug. The group <u>encounters</u> goblins, elves, and spiders as they travel to the Lonely Mountain. Bilbo <u>finds</u> the ring that <u>becomes</u> central to the sequel story, *The Lord of the Rings*. Because the ring <u>makes</u> him invisible, he <u>helps</u> the dwarves escape from sticky situations.

Exercise 7.2 Verb tense

Insert the verb in brackets, using the correct tense:

1. First-year students _____[take] a broader range of courses, including English and math, before they _____ [specialize] in later years. This _____ [allow] them to have more time before they _____[decide] what they _____[want] to do and _____[give] them a broader base of knowledge.

2. Last week, we _____ [go] to see the school production of *Twelfth Night*. As we _____ [watch] the play, a drunken spectator _____[start] throwing things at the stage. Fortunately, the security guards _____ [lead] him away quickly, and the play _____ [continue].

3. In *King Lear*, the father _____[ask] his three daughters who _____[love] him the most. Two daughters _____ [respond] with flattery while the third _____ [be] reluctant to play the game. The father _____ [banish] her because she _____ [does] not _____ [offer] empty praise. Later he _____[realize] that she _____ [be] the most truthful and loving daughter.

Use the correct form of the main verb with auxiliary verbs

After the auxiliary verbs *do* and *will* and all the modal verbs (*can, could, may, might, should, would*), the main verb must be in the base form (the infinitive without *to*):

- ✓ He can speak French fluently.
- ✗ He can French.
- ✗ He can speaks French.

- ✓ I should stop by the store on the way home.
- ✗ I should stopped by the store on the way home.
- ✗ I should stopping by the store on the way home.

- ✓ I do not speak Russian.
- ✓ The students did complete all the homework.
- ✓ The bus will arrive at six.
- ✓ May I take another?
- ✓ We would never do that.

The auxiliary verb *have* is followed by the past participle:

✓ I have eaten chicken feet before.
✗ I have ate chicken feet before.

✓ They have walked a long way today.
✗ They have walk a long way today.

The verb *to be* is both an auxiliary verb and a linking verb. It is the most common verb in English. It gives some English-language learners difficulty because such a linking verb is not required in some languages. Moreover, it has the most irregular forms:

Infinitive and participles: be, being, been
Present tense: am, are, is
Past tense: was, were

The auxiliary verb *be* is followed by the *–ing* form of the verb for a continuous tense or by the past participle (the *–ed* form for regular verbs, the third principle part of the verb) for the passive voice:

She is studying calculus.
They were sleeping when the storm hit.
She was elected chair of the board.
The bear was shot with a tranquilizer dart.

Use modal verbs correctly

Modal verbs are used to show permission, advice, ability, possibility and probability, and conditions. The most common modal verbs are *can, could, may, might, should,* and *would*.

Modal verbs are also used to express politeness when asking permission or making requests:

May I borrow your pen?
Could you please send me an email to remind me?
Would you mind changing seats with me?

For expressions of ability, *could* is the past tense of *can*, and *be able to* is used for the future.

He can speak German very well.
I could speak French when I was younger, but I've forgotten most of it.
Once I finish this course, I will be able to speak Mandarin well enough to communicate on my trip to China.

Would is used in conditional sentences:

If it rains, we will cancel the picnic. [This is a real possibility, so the simple tense and the future tense is used.]
If the date could be changed, I would be able to come. [possible, but unlikely to happen]
If I had paid more attention in class, I would have passed the exam. [in the past—cannot be changed]

Exercise 7.3 Verb forms

Correct any errors in verb form:

1. The university run a special intensive language program in the summer. Students coming from all over the world to study English and to learns about Canadian culture.
2. They lives in the residence where they can meeting Canadian students. They are encourage to eat with the Canadians in the dining hall.
3. Social activities such as movie nights and a weekly soccer game let's students to mingle and speaking English. Students will also go on field trips to museums and the theatre.
4. Many students have already benefit from this program. They have found that learning a second language is not only an important part of education, but it can also been fun.

Use the passive voice effectively

A verb is said to be in the active voice when the grammatical subject does the action of the verb; a passive sentence has the subject acted upon. Only transitive verbs (verbs that take a direct object) can be made passive. The passive voice is formed with the auxiliary verb *be* and the past participle of the verb:

Jenny <u>blocked</u> the ball. [active]
The ball <u>was blocked</u> by Jenny. [passive]

We <u>corrected</u> the first draft of the report. [active]
The first draft of the report <u>was corrected</u>. [passive]

The passive can be formed in different tenses by changing the tense of *be*:

The report <u>is</u> written.
The report <u>was</u> written last week.

The report <u>will be</u> written next week.
The report <u>has been</u> written already.
The report <u>is being</u> written now.

The verb *get* is also used for passive constructions, but this form tends to be more informal:

They got arrested.
She got picked for the job.
How did the car get damaged?

Sometimes a form with *be* or *get* and the past participle has no real corresponding active form:

They got married in Jamaica. [Saying "Somebody married them in Jamaica" is unlikely.]
She was born in Saskatchewan.
I got lost. [Nobody did the losing.]

The past participle can also be used as an adjective:

We took the <u>broken</u> clock to the repair shop.
The <u>elected</u> officials were sworn in.

Do not try to put intransitive verbs in the passive

Transitive verbs have a direct object, but intransitive verbs do not. With a few exceptions, only transitive verbs can be found in the passive voice. The following errors are caused by the writers trying to make intransitive verbs passive:

- ✗ The accident was happened yesterday.
- ✗ She was succeeded in the competition.
- ✗ Bags are being littered on our city streets.

Do not overuse the passive voice

The passive is useful when you do not know who did the action or when you want to stress the action and not the actor. However, it can be more difficult for readers to understand, and so it can impede the flow of your writing. Here is a general rule to follow: if you have the actor in a *by* phrase, consider writing the sentence in the active voice instead. This does not always work; sometimes the *by* phrase is necessary or just sounds better.

The chair was kicked by the boy. [awkward]
The boy kicked the chair. [better]

The report was finished by John.
John finished the report. [better]

My sleep was disturbed by the fire alarm.
The fire alarm disturbed my sleep. [not really an improvement]

Exercise 7.4 Passive voice

Change the following sentences into the passive voice, where possible:

1. They tore down the community centre and are currently building a new one.
2. They designed it as a multi-purpose facility serving all members of the community.
3. The centre will be named after the long-time former mayor.
4. The local swim team will be using the pool for swim meets. The pool is one of the few in the city designed for competitive swimming.
5. The new facilities will also please the squash team.

Make sure pronouns have clear, correct antecedents

Pronouns take the place of nouns. The noun that a pronoun stands for is called the **antecedent**.

Peter was the first person across the finish line. He was surprised by the win. [*He* refers to *Peter*, and therefore *Peter* is the antecedent of *he*.]

Here is a list of pronouns, including subject, object, and possessive forms:

- first person singular: I, me, my, mine, myself
- second person: you, your, yours, yourself (singular), yourselves (plural)
- third person singular: he, she, it, him, her, his, hers, himself, herself, itself
- first person plural: we, us, our, ours, ourselves
- third person plural: they, them, their, theirs, themselves

Pronoun use in conversational speech is very loose and sometimes ungrammatical:

They say that dark chocolate is good for you. [Who are *they*?]
They told me to report here.

The company developed many successful products. Their bankruptcy came as a complete surprise. [*The company* is singular and should not be followed by a plural pronoun.]

In essays, it is important to avoid such usage and to make sure each pronoun has a clear antecedent.

Sometimes a pronoun can be confusing when its antecedent isn't clear. In the following example, *they* could refer to either *parents* or *children* because both are plural.

Helicopter parents protect their children so much that they may fail to become strong and independent adults. They need to recognize that this hovering is not doing them a favour.

Helicopter parents protect their children so much that the children may fail to become strong and independent adults. These parents need to recognize that this hovering is not doing their children a favour. [clearer]

Another reason to avoid using *you* in essays (see p. 8) is that it may not be clear who the *you* actually is:

✗ People believe you are entitled to have your cake and eat it too. You see it in those who insist on a full refund on merchandise that you have used for over six months.
✓ Many consumers believe they are entitled to a full refund on merchandise they have already used.

Avoid using *one* because it sounds stuffy and old-fashioned and because, again, the pronoun reference is tricky:

✓ One should be sure to keep one's equipment in good condition. [awkward]
✗ The only way young adults can deal with over-protective parents is by consistency in one's behaviour and actions. [should be *their*]

Pronoun shift is a common error in essays:

✗ As students, we need to organize our activities. When a student works at a grocery store, he or she knows that they have school and need to do their homework so the best days to work would be weekends because you still have two days to do the rest of your homework.
✓ Students need to organize their activities. Those who have part-time jobs know that they have school and need to do their homework on weekends when they have more time.

One of the trickier aspects of English is the use of *they* to refer to a singular antecedent:

Each student should get their own dictionary for class. [considered grammatically incorrect, but often heard]
Each student should get his own dictionary for class. [considered sexist]
Each student should get his or her own dictionary for class. [acceptable for limited use]

English lacks a gender-neutral singular pronoun, and saying "he or she" is awkward, especially if it has to be repeated many times. Some people resort to slashes (*he/she*, or even *s/he*), but again, this is not a satisfactory solution, especially in formal writing.

The *they* form is commonly used in conversational English. It is so pervasive that it shows up even when the sex is known:

The woman who wins the modelling competition receives a cash prize and a cruise, and they sign with a famous agency. [should be "she signs"]

Even though most English teachers will mark the use of singular *they* as an error, many linguists and editors are making the case for **the acceptance of singular, gender-neutral** *they* because it is practical and has historical and literary precedence. It is in common use because it is so convenient: it avoids the *he/she* awkwardness and the need to write in plurals to avoid marking for gender. It is also the pronoun of choice in the transgender community. Moreover, it has been used by renowned writers such as Charles Dickens and Jane Austen. Introducing a gender-neutral pronoun (such as *s/he*) has proven unsuccessful. Finally, English has already had a pronoun shift in meaning to encompass both singular and plural—*you* used to be only a plural pronoun (with *thee* and *thy* the singular). Although the use of *they* as a singular, gender-neutral pronoun is moving towards acceptability in English, avoid its use in formal essay writing.

Use singular and plural forms correctly

One of the most common grammatical mistakes is a mix-up with singular and plural forms of nouns and verbs. In most sentences, these errors are easily corrected by the writers themselves (if they are directed to the error) and therefore can be avoided.

While the basics of singular–plural agreement are fairly straightforward, there are some tricky bits. One problem is caused by the multi-functional *s* ending. Whereas an *s* at the end of the word usually denotes a plural, it is the third-person *singular* verb that carries the s ending in the present tense. This can be confusing for English-language learners. Note these examples:

> The <u>students</u> <u>walk</u> to the community pool every week for their swimming lesson.
> The new <u>student</u> usually <u>walks</u> alone.
> The <u>pool</u> <u>closes</u> at 10:00.
> The <u>pools</u> <u>close</u> in September for maintenance.

Note that the determiners *a, an, another, each, every,* and *one* always denote a singular:

> Each <u>student</u> <u>needs</u> a dictionary.
> I would like <u>another</u> <u>cup</u>.

This and *that* are singular; *these* and *those* are plural.

Remember that a subject can be compound (consisting of more than one person or thing):

> <u>Jake and Midori</u> <u>are</u> getting married next month.

Sometimes, however, a compound subject can be thought of as a single unit, in which case it takes a singular verb:

> <u>Peanut butter and jam</u> <u>is</u> my favourite sandwich.

It is important to identify the true subject of the verb and not to get distracted by prepositional phrases and other elements of the sentence:

> There <u>are</u> many <u>types</u> of fish in that lake. [*There* is an adverb; the noun *types* is the grammatical subject; since it is plural, the verb must be plural.]
> <u>One</u> of the soldiers <u>was</u> killed in the battle. [The subject is *one*.]

Irregular plurals of nouns can be confusing. For instance, one of the most common spelling mistakes is the confusion between *woman* (singular) and *women* (plural). (Part of the problem is that *women* is not pronounced as it is spelled.) Here are some examples:

> analysis/analyses
> child/children
> criterion/criteria
> deer/deer

knife/knives
mouse/mice
tooth/teeth
wife/wives

You can check for irregular plurals in the dictionary if you are unsure of the correct word to use.

Watch out for uncountable nouns

Some nouns in English cannot be made singular or plural. They are referred to as uncountable nouns. These include liquids (*water, milk*), gases (*air, oxygen*), and items found in tiny grains (*salt, sand*). Abstract qualities (*beauty, sportsmanship*) are also generally uncountable.

> Humans need air, water, and food to survive. [not "airs, waters, and foods"]
> The beaches on the island are famous for their white sand. [*beach* is countable, but not *sand*]
> Honesty is important in a relationship. [*relationship* is countable, but not *honesty*]

Some uncountable nouns are used in a countable sense for a different meaning or in an ellipsis (where words are left out):

> Would you like to meet for a coffee? [*coffee* is short for "a cup of coffee"]
> That horse is a real beauty. [*beauty* is not used in an abstract, uncountable sense]
> He has a lot of homework. He has to read the complete works of Shakespeare. [*work* is usually uncountable unless it refers to works of art or literature]

Uncountable nouns that give English-language learners difficulty include *advice, information, work,* and *research.*

> ✗ He gave me a good advice, based on many informations.
> ✓ He gave me some good advice, based on much information.

Some dictionaries mark nouns as countable [C] or uncountable [U], even distinguishing between countable and uncountable uses of the same noun, so check your dictionary if you are unsure whether a noun can be made singular and plural.

Form possessives correctly

The possessive is formed with an apostrophe and an *s*:

> Sean's car is in the shop.
> The dog ate the cat's food.
> The president's speech was very moving.

If the noun is a regular plural, the apostrophe appears after the *s*:

The students' laptops were damaged by the sprinkler system.
The Whites' cottage is spectacular.
The children's toys were spread all over the house. [note that *children* is an irregular plural form]

Sometimes, especially for inanimate objects, an *of* phrase is used:

✓ The top of the fridge is dusty.
✗ The fridge's top is dusty.

Possessive pronouns have two forms—one that appears before the noun, another that is used to replace the noun: *my/mine, your/yours, his/his, her/hers, its/its, our/ours, their/theirs*.

We have three bank accounts: this one is <u>my</u> money, that one is <u>hers</u>, and the third is <u>ours</u>.

Don't confuse *s* endings

English uses the *s* ending for different purposes, and so it is easy for writers to get confused.

The main *s* ending is a plural form, as in *horses, knives, boxes*, and CDs. Occasionally, an apostrophe is used with plural forms—if the word would be confusing otherwise:

The instructor only gave A's and B's.

Normally, an apostrophe with *s* shows possession:

John's brother borrowed Nina's car.

An *s* ending also appears on verbs in the third-person singular form of the present tense: *he swims, she whistles, he tries, it goes*.

An apostrophe with *s* can also be part of a contraction of *is*, as in *it's, who's, he's, what's, there's*, and *she's*. This is not actually an *s* ending, but it comes into the mix of *s* confusion. This construction also adds to the confusion between *it's* and *its*, and *who's* and *whose*. Remember that possessive pronouns (*his, hers, its, whose*), unlike possessive nouns (*Paul's, the students'*), do not have an apostrophe.

Double-check *s* endings and apostrophes:
• Are you talking about more than one thing, and does the noun have a regular plural form (ending in *s* or *es*)?
• Do you need the third-person singular form of the verb?

- Are you talking about something belonging to someone?
- Are you using a contraction of a verb and pronoun?

Exercise 7.5 Word endings

Correct any errors in word endings (paying particular attention to *s*'s and apostrophes):

1. The student's reading assignment's were poorly done. The whole class needed an extra classes. The instructors had a meeting to scheduled the tutorial.
2. The trades offers good jobs. Plumbers can easily make more money than teacher's do.
3. The Miller's house is up for sale. It should selling quickly because its' in a good neighbourhood with fine schools and a wide range of recreational facilitie's.
4. She try's to help the abandoned pets she find in the field's behind her house.
5. The childrens' choir is the highlight of this years Christmas pageant.

Understand the use of prepositions

Common prepositions include

> about, above, across, after, against, along, among, around, at, before, behind, below, beneath, beside, between, beyond, by, despite, down, during, except, for, from, in, inside, into, like, near, of, off, on, onto, out, outside, over, past, since, through, throughout, to, toward, under, underneath, until, up, upon, with, within, without

The basic meanings of prepositions are fairly straightforward. For example, a key can be <u>on</u> the desk or <u>in</u> the desk drawer, or have fallen <u>under</u> the desk.

Use prepositional phrases to add information to the sentence

A prepositional phrase is formed with a noun, along with its modifiers. It can state where, when, or how something is done. Here are some sentences with the prepositional phrases underlined:

> I walk <u>in the park</u> <u>in the morning</u> and work out <u>in the gym</u> <u>after work</u>.
> <u>During an election</u>, all political parties make extravagant promises <u>to the electorate</u>.
> <u>Before class</u>, we meet <u>in the library</u> and go <u>over our reading notes</u>.

Prepositional phrases are add-ons to the core sentence. When you are trying to find the subject and predicate to ensure agreement (see p. 180), look at the sentence without the prepositional phrases.

✓ The boys [in the band] are very young.
✓ One [of the students] was late.
✗ Each [of the books] are expensive. [*Each* is singular and requires the singular verb *is*.]

Make sure you use the correct preposition after nouns, verbs, and adjectives

Although the basic meanings of prepositions to describe position are relatively clear, it can be difficult to learn which prepositions are used in combination with a particular verb, noun, or adjective. There are no rules to govern these combinations, so they must be memorized or found in the dictionary.

Here are some examples.

With verbs:

I don't like to <u>rely on</u> the bank machines when I travel.
If we need it, can we <u>call upon</u> you for help? ["Call on" could also be used here.]
She is <u>liable to</u> make another mistake.
He <u>suffers from</u> malaria.

With nouns:

What is the <u>reason for</u> his absence?
He tried to pay <u>attention to</u> the lesson, but he kept daydreaming.
I received a <u>notification of</u> the change of date by mail.
It was good to see his <u>influence on</u> his nephew.

With adjectives:

They were found <u>innocent of</u> the crime.
I'm <u>encouraged by</u> your progress.
She is <u>famous for</u> her rousing speeches.
This option is <u>superior to</u> that one.

It is also important to note that the right prepositions to use with a particular word may depend on the part of speech of the word in question. For instance, whereas the verb *lack* does not generally take a preposition, the noun *lack* is often followed by *of*.

✓ She was surprised by the <u>lack of</u> agreement on the issue.
✓ The company <u>lacked</u> a contingency plan.
✗ He <u>lacked of</u> the information required to finish the report.

Here are some other examples where preposition use depends on the part of speech of a word:

- ✓ They discussed the problem all night.
- ✓ They had a long discussion <u>about</u> the problem but could not find a solution.
- ✗ They discussed <u>about</u> the problem.

- ✓ You need to put more emphasis <u>on</u> the history of the project.
- ✓ You need to emphasize the history of the project.
- ✗ You need to emphasize <u>on</u> the history of the project.

The use of a preposition after a transitive verb such as *discuss, emphasize,* and *explain* is a common error among both native speakers and English-language learners.

Exercise 7.6 Prepositions

Correct the use of prepositions in the following sentences. You may change the underlined preposition, eliminate it entirely, or leave it as is.

e.g.: He accused her <u>for</u> taking his idea and presenting it <u>to</u> the supervisor.

      ✗   of   ✓

1. While he was unemployed, he depended <u>for</u> handouts <u>by</u> his parents. They were happy <u>to</u> help him out because he had helped <u>to</u> his nephews <u>for</u> their schooling.
2. <u>At</u> his new book, he describes <u>about</u> the customs <u>of</u> the nomads who live <u>on</u> the desert.
3. The students did not participate <u>at</u> the social activities because they were busy playing <u>at</u> video games.
4. She expects <u>of</u> Jack to finish the project, but she could assign it <u>for</u> someone else.
5. Because he didn't understand <u>of</u> financial matters, he depended <u>with</u> John <u>for</u> help.
6. <u>With</u> all the noise, he cannot concentrate <u>at</u> his reading. He went <u>in</u> the library.
7. I applied <u>to</u> the desk job, but James said I wasn't qualified <u>in</u> it and advised <u>to</u> me to take some classes <u>at</u> the university.
8. The new bridge will affect <u>on</u> the traffic patterns, but we will gain <u>of</u> a bike lane.

9. The loss <u>of</u> his bike did not bother <u>to</u> him. He always used an old one because the possibility <u>of</u> theft was so high.
10. She never complained <u>at</u> the extra work. She was glad <u>of</u> the opportunity to learn <u>to</u> new skills.

Recognize phrasal verbs

Sometimes a preposition becomes part of the verb, forming a phrasal verb combination as in these sentences:

I have to <u>get up</u> at five tomorrow.
I will <u>call back</u> when you are not so <u>tied up</u>.
If you <u>fall down</u>, you just have to <u>get up</u> and <u>start over</u>.

Note that, technically, prepositions that form part of the verb are called *particles*, but since they are essentially the same words, it is simpler to use the word *preposition* to cover these words in both functions.

Phrasal verbs tend to be more idiomatic and more common in conversational speech and informal writing. In other words, do not use them often in your essays.

Join words, phrases, and clauses with coordinating conjunctions

Conjunctions are used to join parts of sentences or complete sentences. The **coordinating conjunctions** are *and, or, but, yet, so, for,* and *nor.*

The school offers both arts <u>and</u> science programs.
Hiro could take algebra <u>or</u> calculus to fulfill the requirement.
The new phone has a lot of features, <u>but</u> it is very expensive.
They spent hours on the problem, <u>yet</u> they could not solve it.

Do not use a comma instead of an *and*:

✗ They like swimming, biking.
✓ They like swimming and biking.
✗ Yesterday, Sandra walked on the beach, went snorkelling.
✓ Yesterday, Sandra walked on the beach and went snorkelling.

Generally, if the conjunction joins two words or phrases, there is no comma:

> They were tired but happy.
> The keys could be in the desk or on the dresser.
> We spent the day playing cards and watching TV.

If the coordinating conjunction joins two clauses that could each be a complete sentence, a comma is used after the first clause:

> Roberto has to get the materials, and Elise has to clear the work space.
> It was raining, so they cancelled the picnic.

In a series, the items are separated by a comma and the *and* or *or* comes before the last one. Commas separate items. The last comma, before the *and or or*, is called a serial comma and is optional:

> She added cucumbers, radishes, and celery to the salad.
> She added cucumbers, radishes and celery to the salad.

The serial comma can make a complicated sentence more readable:

> The winter camp included snowshoeing, cross-country skiing, skating on the pond, and an overnight camping excursion.
> I could serve canapés, vegetables and dip, or cheese and crackers as an appetizer.

Refer to Chapter 8, "Punctuation and Format," for more examples of commas used with coordinating conjunctions.

Don't start sentences with coordinating conjunctions

In speech and informal writing, people use simple sentences and string them together with coordinating conjunctions:

> In Ottawa, we took a bus tour. And then we went to the Parliament Buildings. And we wanted to see the Changing of the Guard. But we missed it. So we went inside to take a tour.

In your essays, avoid starting sentences with coordinating conjunctions. It is conversational style. Instead, write complex sentences with **subordinating conjunctions** or use conjunctive adverbs:

> Students take on internships to get valuable work experience. But often they end up doing menial jobs for no pay. [conversational style]

Students take on internships to get valuable work experience, but often they end up doing menial jobs for no pay.
Although students take on internships to get valuable work experience, they often end up doing menial jobs for no pay.
Students take on internships to get valuable work experience; however, they often end up doing menial jobs for no pay.

Use parallel structure

When you use a coordinating conjunction, you have to make sure that you are joining words or phrases with the same grammatical structure:

✗ In his leisure time, he likes playing video games and to watch movies.
✓ In his leisure time, he likes playing video games and watching movies.
✓ In his leisure time, he likes to play video games and watch movies.

✗ Success requires hard work and being determined.
✓ Success requires hard work and determination.

✗ We changed the program not because we wanted to but having to.
✓ We changed the program not because we wanted to but because we had to.

✗ She added celery, carrots, potatoes, beets, and then seasoned the soup.
✓ She added celery, carrots, potatoes, and beets, and then she seasoned the soup.
✓ She added celery, carrots, potatoes, beets, and seasonings.

Note that in the last example (middle statement) the first *and* is needed to complete the list of vegetables and the second *and* is needed to join the verbs *added* and *seasoned*.

Student writers often make mistakes in parallelism when they form thesis statements that list the three arguments in the essay (see p. 24):

✗ Marriage is a valuable institution because it fosters social stability, creates wealth, and so the population is maintained.
✓ Marriage is a valuable institution because it fosters social stability, creates wealth, and maintains the population.

✗ Social networking sites make people isolated, egocentric, and they actually become less involved in social activities.
✓ Social networking sites make people isolated, egocentric, and anti-social.

Exercise 7.7 Parallel structure

Correct any errors in parallel structure:

1. To stay healthy, people should eat well, get plenty of exercise, and they should get enough sleep.
2. In his spare time, he enjoys hiking, to watch movies, and woodwork.
3. The ingredients of the pasta sauce include Italian sausage, eggplant, red peppers, and they put some canned tomato sauce in it.
4. The problems of underground economies include the loss of tax revenue, labour lacks protection, and the consequent downgrading of the economy.
5. The yoga exercise requires participants to sit with legs crossed, breathing deeply, and to think only of their mantra.

Make adverb clauses with subordinating conjunctions

These are some common subordinating conjunctions:

> after, although, as, because, before, even though, if, since, so (that), unless, until, when, where, whereas, whether, while

The dependent (or subordinate) clause (the one that starts with the subordinating conjunction) is less important than the main clause:

> Even though the computer system was down, Henri gave the customers the correct change.

Putting the less important idea in the subordinate clause is a useful writing technique. It allows the writer to emphasize the main idea:

> Although famous people get a lot of perks, they have to give up their privacy. [for an essay on the disadvantages of being famous]
> Although famous people have to give up their privacy, they get a lot of perks. [for an essay on the advantages of being famous]

When the subordinate clause comes first, use a comma to tell the reader that the subordinate clause is finished and the main clause is beginning. If the subordinate clause comes after the main clause, you do not need a comma because the subordinating conjunction is the signal that a new clause is beginning.

Without the comma after the subordinate clause, a sentence can be confusing:

✗ When the car approached the girl ran around the corner.
✓ When the car approached, the girl ran around the corner.

Use *although* correctly

The subordinating conjunction *although* has a "but" meaning. It is a common conjunction, but it is sometimes used incorrectly.

Do not use *although* and *but* together (you only need one of them):

✗ Although he is the oldest brother, but he is less successful than his siblings.
✓ Although he is the oldest brother, he is less successful than his siblings.
✓ He is the oldest brother, but he is less successful than his siblings.

Do not put a comma after *although*:

✗ Although, Olivia has been with the company longer, Michael got the promotion.
✗ Although, I would really like to go. [also incorrect because it is an incomplete sentence]

Recognize the differences between *although, though,* and *even though.* Unlike *although, though* can appear at the end of a sentence as an adverb. It is also used with phrases to mean *but.*

I really needed more time, though.
She was a friend, though not a close one.

Even though (note that it is spelled as two words) is stronger than *although*—use it for emphasis:

Although I worked hard, I did not finish the assignment.
Even though I worked all night, I did not finish the assignment.

Don't confuse conjunctions and conjunctive adverbs

A conjunction can join two sentences to make one grammatical sentence. A **conjunctive adverb** (also called an adverbial connective) is an introductory phrase that is usually followed by a comma. The most common mistake is thinking that *however* and *therefore* work the same as *although* and *so.*

✗ One of the engines failed however the pilot was able to land safely. [run-on sentence]
✓ Although one of the engines failed, the pilot was able to land safely.

✓ One of the engines failed, but the pilot was able to land safely.
✓ One of the engines failed; however, the pilot was able to land safely. [Note the use of the semicolon which properly joins these two sentences—the *however* alone cannot do so.]

✓ He knew the scandal would ruin his chances for re-election, so he resigned.
✓ Because he knew the scandal would ruin his chances for re-election, he resigned.
✗ He knew the scandal would ruin his chances for re-election, therefore he resigned.
✓ He knew the scandal would ruin his chances for re-election; therefore, he resigned.
✓ He knew the scandal would ruin his chances for re-election. Therefore, he resigned.

One way to distinguish conjunctions from conjunctive adverbs is that conjunctions can only be placed at the beginning of one of the clauses whereas conjunctive adverbs (like other adverbs) can be placed in different positions in the sentence. Note that in the following sentences, *although* and *but* cannot be placed in any other position, whereas *however* can be moved:

Although they went through the whole factory, they could not find the source of the contamination.
They went through the whole factory, but they could not find the source of the contamination.
They went through the whole factory; however, they could not find the source of the contamination.
They went through the whole factory; they could not find the source of the contamination, however.
They went through the whole factory; they could not, however, find the source of the contamination.

Use adjective clauses to add information

Adjective clauses, which are also called relative clauses, are used like adjectives to modify nouns. Adjective clauses start with *who, what, which, where, when,* and *that.* (Note that the first sentence in this paragraph contains an adjective clause.) They allow the writer to add information, such as definitions, to a sentence without distracting from the main idea:

Jason, who is a long-time member of the Liberal Party, was hired to work in the deputy minister's office.
The recession has caused more cases of boomerang kids, young adults who are forced to move back to their parents' home.

An adjective clause is separated from the main part of the sentence when it is used to give extra information that is not absolutely essential. However, when the information is essential to the meaning of the sentence, no commas are used.

> Children whose parents did not attend college or university are less likely to pursue post-secondary education. [The clause is necessary to identify which children.]
> John's children, who are in French immersion, helped their parents communicate on their Quebec vacation. [We already know who John's children are.]

Use noun clauses as subjects or objects

In addition to adjective and adverb clauses, English has noun clauses. Instead of consisting of a single noun, the subject or object of a sentence can be a noun clause:

> That the attempt at cloning was a failure was evident to all.
> The main idea of the reading is that education for women leads to improved living conditions for the whole society.

English prefers short subjects and long predicates, and a long or complex noun clause or phrase can be awkward in a sentence. Therefore, an empty *it* (also called a dummy *it* or a non-referential *it*) is used instead:

> Why the glass panels on the condo balconies started cracking and plummeting to the ground puzzled the engineers.
> It puzzled the engineers why the glass panels on the condo balconies started cracking and plummeting to the ground.

> How he passed that course without attending most of the classes is impossible to understand.
> It is impossible to understand how he passed that course without attending most of the classes.

Avoid putting a long noun clause at the beginning of your sentence.

Reduce clauses to phrases for conciseness

A clause has a subject and verb. If the subject of both the main clause and the subordinate clause are the same, the subordinate clause can often be reduced to a phrase using a participle (an *–ing* or *–ed* form of the verb):

> As Elena was going through the reports, she spotted a discrepancy.
> While going through the reports, Elena spotted a discrepancy.
> Going through the reports, Elena spotted a discrepancy.

Another reduction is to take out the pronoun and the verb *to be*:

> Ivan, who was the chair of the committee, requested the investigation.
> Ivan, the chair of the committee, requested the investigation.

It is important that the subject of the main clause be the same as the subject of the reduced clause:

- ✓ While Nick was cleaning out the eavestrough, it started raining.
- ✗ While cleaning out the eavestrough, it started raining. [This cannot be reduced because the subjects of the two clauses, *Nick* and *it*, are not the same.]

Avoid misplaced modifiers

Modifier is a general term that includes anything you can add to a sentence to describe something. Modifiers can be adjectives, adverbs, and phrases. They should be next to the noun or phrase they modify so that there is no ambiguity in the sentence.

- ✗ Boomerang children live at home with their parents sitting idle. [The children are idle, not the parents.]
- ✓ Sitting idle, boomerang children live at home with their parents.
- ✗ Mohammad often received information on his cellphone that was useless.
- ✓ Mohammad often received useless information on his cellphone.

Correcting a misplaced modifier requires rewriting the sentence:

- ✗ Running towards the moving curtain, Hamlet's rapier struck Polonius.
- ✓ Running towards the moving curtain, Hamlet struck Polonius with his rapier.

- ✗ She wondered whether she could get a raise often.
- ✓ She often wondered whether she could get a raise.

Use clauses and phrases effectively

Conversational speech uses short, simple sentences, making it easier for listeners to follow what is being said. Written English, especially academic style, uses more complex sentences, with more clauses and phrases. It is easier to follow complicated sentences in writing than in speech.

An advantage of complex sentences is that the writer can express more subtle meanings. An adverb clause, for instance, relates an idea that is less important than the idea expressed in the main clause. Adjective clauses are useful for adding clarifying information. Remember that clauses can sometimes be reduced to phrases, retaining the information but making the sentence concise.

In conversational English, we tend to join ideas with *and* instead of using subordinate clauses. Note how these sentences move to more formal styles:

> My sister is a court clerk, and she says they rarely pick teachers for jury duty.
> [conversational]
> My sister, who is a court clerk, says they rarely pick teachers for jury duty.
> [informal written style]
> My sister, a court clerk, says that teachers are rarely chosen for jury duty.
> [more formal]

Avoid anecdotal examples in simple sentences

When you give an example to support your point in an essay, do it concisely. Do not drag it out into a narrative of short, simple sentences—use complex sentences instead:

✗ Sometimes failure leads to knowledge. For example, a student does his homework. He makes some mistake. His teacher points out the mistake and gives him some advice. The student then will understand the lesson better.

✓ Sometimes failure leads to knowledge. For example, when a student receives corrections and advice on his homework, he understands the lesson better.

Exercise 7.8 Sentence structure

Correct any errors:

1. By reading the chapter before class, it helps students understand the lecture better.
2. Although the divorce rate for arranged marriages is low, but many couples are unhappy in their relationship.
3. The instructor presented a concept which the students did not understand it.
4. Even the study group worked hard together, only one member passed the bar exams.
5. If it will rain tomorrow, the wedding can be moved indoors.

Ensure sentences are complete

A sentence needs a subject and a predicate in order to be a complete sentence. In other words, we need to have something we are talking about (the subject) and something that we say about the subject (the predicate). (See p. 165.)

Probably the most common errors in sentence structure are sentence fragments (incomplete sentences) and run-on sentences. Although fragments and run-ons are common in informal writing, you should avoid them in your essay writing.

Don't write sentence fragments

A sentence fragment is an incomplete sentence. A sentence needs both a subject and a predicate, and these have to be in the main clause. Here are some examples of fragments, along with the corrections:

    ✗ Swimming across the lake.
    ✓ Swimming across the lake would be a good challenge.

    ✗ The students who finished the assignment first.
    ✓ The students who finished the assignment first received bonus marks.

    ✗ Because she could not find the screwdriver.
    ✓ Because she could not find the screwdriver, she tried using a coin.

    ✗ Which is a problem because he does not know the correct procedure.
    ✓ It is a problem because he does not know the correct procedure.

You should recognize most fragments because they sound incomplete. Often the predicate is missing. For instance, a fragment might be a noun phrase without a verb (as in the first example above) or a relative or subordinate clause lacking a main clause (as in the next two examples). The fourth example starts with the relative pronoun *which*, which should be used to join clauses, not to start a sentence.

Note that some teachers tell their students not to start a sentence with *because*. This advice is based on the propensity of students not to finish the sentence. However, a sentence can start with *because* as long as it has a main clause.

Don't write run-on sentences

We use the general term **run-on sentence** even though grammarians distinguish between different types. One kind of run-on is two independent clauses with nothing to join them:

    ✗ Jack fell off the ladder he sustained a concussion.

A **comma splice** has a comma between the two independent clauses—but it is still incorrect:

    ✗ Jack fell off the ladder, he sustained a concussion.

Sometimes a run-on sentence can be grammatically correct, but stylistically weak and difficult to read:

> When Jack fell off the ladder, he landed hard and hit his head with a loud crack, so we were worried and we took him to the hospital even though he objected, saying that he wasn't really hurt badly, but we were glad the doctor saw him because the doctor confirmed that Jack had sustained a concussion and needed to be careful not to aggravate the injury. [grammatical, but awkward]

There are three ways to fix a run-on sentence. You can make it into two complete sentences, use a semicolon, or add a conjunction:

> ✗ Jack fell off the ladder, he sustained a concussion.
> ✓ Jack fell off the ladder. He sustained a concussion.
> ✓ Jack fell off the ladder; he sustained a concussion.
> ✓ When Jack fell off the ladder, he sustained a concussion.

Make sure you add a conjunction, not a conjunctive adverb (see p. 191) to fix the run-on problem.

> ✗ The series host was running late, the shoot had to be rescheduled.
> ✗ The series host was running late, therefore the shoot had to be rescheduled.
> ✓ The series host was running late, so the shoot had to be rescheduled.
> ✓ Because the series host was running late, the shoot had to be rescheduled.
> ✓ The series host was running late; therefore, the shoot had to be rescheduled.

Exercise 7.9 Run-ons and fragments

Correct any sentence errors:

1. The attack ads that offend the viewers and insult their intelligence.
2. Because he drank too much at the wedding. He insulted the hosts.
3. Poseidon wants to avenge the hurt Odysseus caused to his son he creates a storm to destroy the hero's raft.
4. He writes, she edits. The book that they just finished which was nominated for an award.
5. Fewer movies are adult-oriented today. For example, horror films and gross-out comedies currently running in the theatres.

6. They did not want to get married. Even though they had lived together for so many years.
7. Wanting to be the first to get the new smartphone, he waited in line all night.
8. Count Dracula first sucks his victims dry of blood, then he turns them into vampires.

Correct your mistakes

Before you hand in your essay, look it over for grammar, spelling, and punctuation mistakes. Use a dictionary to check words you are not sure of. Look for errors that you tend to make. The checklist below focuses on some common grammatical errors to look for.

Grammar checklist

- Does your sentence contain a subject and a verb?
- Are the verbs in the correct tense and formed correctly?
- Are singular and plural forms correct and in agreement?
- Do pronouns have clear, correct antecedents?
- Are complete sentences joined by conjunctions, not commas?
- Did you use the correct prepositions?

Punctuation and Format

Written language depends on punctuation marks to help the reader follow what is being said. They are used to distinguish between words, phrases, sentences, and paragraphs. Punctuation takes the place of the pauses, tone of voice, and gestures of the spoken language.

Punctuation can be complicated and even controversial. Grammarians can get into heated discussions about serial commas and the use of semicolons. However, we are not going to jump into the fray. Instead, we focus on the basic rules that you need to apply in your essay writing—rules that we often see students struggle with. Some of these rules were mentioned in the explanation of sentence structure in the previous chapter, but they are here again as a reference for punctuation rules.

Mark the end of each sentence

Sentences end with a period, a question mark, or an exclamation mark. What is expressed with tone of voice in speech is expressed with punctuation in writing:

> It's over. [neutral tone, giving a factual statement]
> It's over! [emphatic tone, showing surprise or insistence]
> It's over? [questioning tone; has a rising inflection in speech]

Most sentences end with a period. Note that the period should come right after the last word and that there should be a single space after the period. (In the days of typewriters, two spaces after periods was standard practice, but that has changed because computers have proportional spacing.)

Note that periods are also used with many abbreviations, such as e.g. and M.A., and with personal initials, such as J.K. Rowling. Abbreviations consisting of the initials of words are generally written without periods, such as NATO, AIDS, ESL, CBC, and RCMP. If you are not sure whether an abbreviation is usually written with periods, consult a dictionary. Note that there are different styles for using periods with abbreviations and so you may see the same abbreviation written different ways. It is important that you be consistent and follow whatever style guide (such as MLA) is required.

Use a **question mark** at the end of questions:

What is the best way to improve the transit system?

Make sure you are using question marks with actual questions, not indirect questions:

- ✓ Where was the meeting? [direct question]
- ✓ She asked, "Where was the meeting?" [direct question, which uses the speaker's exact words]
- ✗ She wondered where was the meeting? [indirect question—should not have a question mark and word order is incorrect]
- ✗ She wondered where was the meeting. [incorrect word order]
- ✓ She wondered where the meeting was.

Rhetorical questions are sometimes used in essays to pique the curiosity of the reader and to make the person think for a moment. The reader is not expected to answer; the writer supplies the response:

What are the benefits of dual citizenship? First, immigrants can keep connections with their native country while still making a commitment to their new home.

In essays, use questions sparingly, or not at all. Questions can make the tone of your essay too conversational.

Do not use **exclamation marks** in essay writing. They are used in dialogue and less formal writing to show surprise, anger, or excitement.

Text messaging may be changing the use of punctuation marks. Because of its conversational style, senders use more exclamation marks than in other kinds of writing. Moreover, ending messages with periods can be interpreted as showing a lack of sincerity. This usage may eventually influence standard English, but use periods and avoid exclamation marks in academic English.

Capitalize proper nouns and the first word of a sentence

Capital letters should be clearly distinguishable in your writing. If you write your in-class essays in block printing, for example, write the capital letters larger. Your instructor wants to see that you know how to capitalize.

The first word of every sentence is capitalized, as you can see in all the sentences here.

The first-person singular pronoun (I) is always capitalized:

Elizabeth and I volunteered for the project.

Proper nouns are capitalized:

- names of people (Margaret Atwood, Wayne Gretzky)
- place names (Canada, St. John's, Algonquin Park)
- languages and nationalities (English, French)
- titles (Prime Minister Trudeau, Major General Johnson)
- titles of publications and movies (*A Tale of Two Cities*, *Canadian Living*, *The Shining*) (see Chapter 5, "Research and Documentation," for more on titles)
- holidays and special occasions (e.g., Christmas, Mardi Gras, Mother's Day)
- days of the week (e.g., Monday, Tuesday, Wednesday)
- months of the year (e.g., January, February, March)

Adjectives derived from proper nouns are also usually capitalized:

English class, Spanish onions, Japanese art, French horn

While course titles (and course codes) are capitalized, the subject is not:

I need another biology class for my schedule. I'm thinking of taking Introductory Cell Biology, BIO 200.

Capitalization in titles of books, articles, and stories varies according to the style used. For example, MLA capitalizes all major words in titles, while APA does not. See the sample bibliographies in Chapter 5 for examples of these two styles.

Separate sections of a sentence with commas

Commas are used to separate certain parts of the sentence. When used correctly, commas improve the readability of sentences because a reader can more easily see which words go together. The way commas are used can vary according to regional style and even the age of the writer. Many modern writers, for instance, omit the comma after an adverb or adverbial phrase at the beginning of a sentence. Some writers do not use commas after subordinate clauses. However, the conventions described in this chapter are ones that almost everyone agrees on and that you should follow in your essays.

A comma separates **items in a list**, whether they are individual words or phrases:

Sayid brought apples, cherries, peaches, and bananas.
The children ran into the park, headed for the playground, and jostled for the swings.

A comma before *and* in a series of items is used in some writing styles, such as MLA. It is called a **serial comma** (for a series). If you choose to use it, be consistent.

Note that a comma is not needed if there are only two items and that a comma cannot replace *and*:

    ✗ She is studying biology, chemistry.
    ✓ She is studying biology and chemistry.

A comma can also come **after an introductory word or phrase** that precedes the main clause:

> In addition, students need to develop time management techniques.
> Therefore, they should use a calendar.
> Having never travelled before, they were looking for opportunities to study abroad.
> As a celebrity chef, he travels all over the world.
> Although the trip would be very costly, it would be a valuable addition to their education.

Many of these adverbial elements can also be placed in the middle or at the end of a sentence, in which case they may be set off by commas:

> A subway extension would be beneficial, of course.
> They go mall walking, for instance.
> The students, however, thought the plan hurt their chances.

Note that these are basic rules for separating adverbial elements with commas. Whether to use commas or not can also depend on the actual element, the length, and individual style. Look at some examples if you are unsure. Do not break up your writing with too many commas, but use them when they make the sentence more readable. Watch out for cases where commas can change the meaning of the sentence, as in this example:

> Students come to school to learn, not to socialize.
> Students come to school to learn not to socialize.

For **subordinate clauses** (see p. 190), the comma marks the end of the clause. However, if the main clause comes first in the sentence, the comma is unnecessary because the conjunction shows where the sentence is divided:

> When the clause comes first, the comma is used.
> The comma is not used when the clause comes second.

> Because it was late, we decided to finish the next day.
> We decided to finish the next day because it was late.

Make sure the sentence has a conjunction; joining two independent clauses with a comma is incorrect, resulting in an error called a **comma splice** (see p. 196):

   ✗ The manager wanted the procedures changed, we had to review everything.

One of the trickiest uses of commas is to separate **adjective clauses** (also called relative clauses—see p. 192) from the rest of the sentence. With these clauses, the commas can change the meaning of a sentence:

   The junior students who had trouble with the exercise asked for extra help.
   The junior students, who had trouble with the exercise, asked for extra help.

In the first example, the relative clause is restrictive—in other words, it restricts or defines who is being referred to: only those junior students who had trouble asked for help. In the second sentence, the relative clause is non-restrictive; that means the information between the commas is not essential to the meaning of the sentence and can be removed—in other words, all the junior students asked for help.

Don't place commas after *although*, *such as*, and *that*:

   ✗ Although, he was trained as an engineer, he worked as a designer.
   ✓ Although he was trained as an engineer, he worked as a designer.
   ✗ She wrote a letter informing them that, the property had changed hands. [no comma required in the sentence]
   ✗ They planned many improvements to the property such as, installing a second bathroom, remodelling the kitchen, and removing the carpet. [comma should go before *such as*, not after]

Commas are also often used incorrectly as breath stops, especially when the grammatical subject is long and complex. No commas should be used in these examples:

   ✗ Coming in second in the race after training so hard, was a crushing disappointment to him.
   ✗ The movie starring Matt Damon that I wanted to see, is no longer playing.
   ✗ The point is, he's much too old for the job.

Note that commas are also used in English names when the order of names is inverted for an alphabetical list, such as a bibliography or class list. The comma shows that the family name is given first, so it should not be used when the name is in the normal order of given names followed by family name. This use of the comma is sometimes confusing for students from countries where different naming conventions are followed.

The members include GangYue Eng, Abdul Sayid, and Mary Smith.

<u>Membership List</u>:
  Eng, GangYue
  Sayid, Abdul
  Smith, Mary

Exercise 8.1 Punctuate and capitalize

Place commas, periods, and capital letters where required:

1. parents do not have to feel obliged to pay for their children's university education if they have the money they can help their children pay for tuition but university students are adults and should be responsible for their own schooling moreover they will value their education more if they have paid for it themselves especially if that payment has required sacrifice on their part
2. i have to change my course schedule the psychology course i want to take is not offered this semester but i can finish off my english credits this course introduction to the canadian novel sounds interesting
3. the students had much more work to do on their oral presentation so they set up more meeting times it was difficult to work around everyone's timetables but they managed to find some time when everyone was free

---

Distinguish between semicolons and colons

A semicolon is used to join two related sentences:

Harry never drives after drinking; he takes a taxi.

A semicolon is used in a sentence with a conjunctive adverb—most commonly with *however* and *therefore*:

The characters are unbelievable; however, they are lovable as caricatures.

Sometimes a semicolon can be used instead of a comma between items in a list when the individual items are very long or contain commas:

For the potluck supper, the participants delegated the menu: Rudi and Mia brought salads and appetizers; Kyle and Ryan, bread and dessert; Miguel and Leah, lasagna and pizza; Lorne and Annie, beef stew.

Don't use a semicolon where a comma is needed:

✗ For example; the car should get a regular tune-up.

If you are not sure whether you have used a semicolon correctly, try replacing it with the word *and*. ("For example and the car should get a regular tune-up.") If the sentence no longer sounds right, the semicolon is probably incorrect.

Use a **colon** to introduce an explanation:

Losing weight hinges on one fundamental principle: burning more calories than we take in.
Writing an essay requires three basic stages: planning, drafting, and revising.

Colons are often used in this book to introduce examples.

Use a colon to signal the beginning of a list if the part of the sentence preceding the colon is a complete independent clause:

We visited many tourist sites in Nova Scotia: the Halifax Citadel, Pier 21, the Cabot Trail, the Fortress of Louisbourg, and Peggy's Cove.

Don't use a colon if the list is a grammatical part of the sentence:

✗ The dessert selection includes: ice cream, apple pie, crème caramel, and fruit cake.
✗ The eligible candidates are: Diego, Sergei, Leslie, and Mona.
✗ She participated in a number of different extra-curricular activities, such as: the chess club, volleyball, and the yearbook committee.

If you are not sure how to use colons and semicolons, avoid using them. You can write perfectly good sentences without them.

Use apostrophes for possession and contractions

Apostrophes show possession, contractions, and, occasionally, plurals. They are probably the most misused punctuation mark today, not just in student writing, but also in official signs and published documents. We have seen incorrect words such as *wan't's*, *concert's*, and *pie's*.

Apostrophes are used to show **possession**—before the *s* in a singular form and after the *s* in a plural:

Jorge's car
the dog's tail
the boys' rooms [more than one boy]

Irregular plurals are made possessive with *'s*:

> the men's room
> the children's toys

Apostrophes also take the place of a missing letter or letters in **contractions**:

> can't = cannot
> should've = should have
> they're = they are
> let's = let us

On rare occasions, the apostrophe is necessary to show a plural where the word would be hard to read without it:

> I got mostly A's and B's in high school.

The title of this book has two apostrophes. In *Essay Do's and Don'ts*, the first apostrophe is used for a plural form that could otherwise be misleading and the second apostrophe is in the contraction.

Apostrophes are often mistakenly used for plural forms and sometimes in the third-person singular verb form, as in these examples where there should be no apostrophes:

> ✗ The Viking's raided England.
> ✗ In the story, the old woman give's the panhandler five dollars.
> ✗ The Sheridan's [on a sign in front of a house]

Exercise 8.2 Using apostrophes

Put apostrophes where required and delete unnecessary ones:

1. The childrens toys were scattered all over the room.
2. The instructor leaves the last minute's of class for questions.
3. When the going get's tough, the tough get's going.
4. The super let's the tenant's leave their bikes in the back room.
5. The mens room and the ladies room needed cleaning.

Use space correctly

A space is an element of punctuation because it shows the reader where words, sentences, and paragraphs begin and end. Spaces are also important to the legibility of a document.

Speech does not have spaces between words; the last sound of a word blends into the first sound of the next word. As a result, students sometimes do not know where words are divided, as in the underlined words in these examples:

✗ Failure, dis grace, dis appointment—all words people don't want to hear.
✗ There were alot of people infront of the building.

Space can distinguish between similar words:

It may be the best time to go. Maybe we won't have another chance.
A lone man was walking down the street.
I dislike going to restaurants alone.

Note, however, that compound nouns often start out as two separate words that may be then joined by a hyphen or just joined into one word. For example, "web site" is now generally written as "website."

Spaces between words can become large, unsightly gaps if you use full justification in your document. (Full justification means that the words make a straight margin on both the right and the left sides of the page.) Most books and many other publications use full justification, but they also allow words to be broken at the end of the line so that there are no big gaps in the line. However, words cannot be split just anywhere; there are rules for hyphenation. For unpublished documents, such as your essays, it is better to use **left justification** with a ragged right margin.

It is also important to use spaces correctly **around punctuation marks**. For example, there is no space before commas, periods, semicolons, and colons, but there is one space after these marks. (Note that it was customary to use two spaces after a period because of fixed-width fonts on typewriters, and many people who were trained to type this way cling to this practice. Because computers use proportional spacing, a single space after a period is proper.) Apostrophes and hyphens have no spaces around them.

Space is important to show the beginning and end of a paragraph. **Indent** five spaces at the beginning of a paragraph. (You can also use the Tab key; the default spacing is five spaces, or half an inch.) In handwritten in-class essays, you might have to leave a larger space to make the paragraph boundaries clear. Business writing often uses single-spaced block paragraphs with a blank line between paragraphs and no indentation. Published documents often do not use paragraph indentation after a title or subtitle because it is unnecessary to show that this is the start of a new paragraph.

Line spacing is also important in formatting essays. Most instructors prefer double spacing so they have space for corrections. To double-space, leave a blank line between each line of writing. This is done automatically with word-processing programs; use the double-space setting under paragraph formatting. If you are writing an essay by hand for an in-class test or exam, double spacing gives you room to write in corrections and changes and makes your work easier to read.

Margins are another requirement of spacing. Do not cram your writing to the edges of the page. A one-inch margin on all sides is standard.

Show quotations

When you are quoting the words someone else said or wrote, you have to show it clearly in your essay. You can learn more about quotation in Chapter 5, "Research and Documentation."

Use quotation marks in pairs (". . .") at the top of the line. In North American styles, they are double marks, rather than single.

Quotation marks go around the part that is quoted, with a comma separating the quotation from the rest of the sentence after a speech tag:

> We are now living in what Marshall McLuhan dubbed "the global village."
> McLuhan also said, "The medium is the message."

Note that the period is placed before the closing quotation mark in this example. In North American style, a period or comma is always put before the closing quotation mark.

The words between quotation marks must be *exactly* what was said or written by the person being quoted. If you add **explanatory words** to the quotation, you put them in square brackets:

> "Like all compulsive gamblers, [Dostoyevsky] was captive to his addiction, with nearly devastating consequences" (Sainsbury, see Appendix A, p. 220–21).

If you want to omit some words, you must insert three periods (called ellipsis points) to show the **ellipsis** (i.e., the omission):

> "It came close to ruining his marriage to the long-suffering Anna . . . and it kept him a virtual exile for many years in the decadent fleshpots of Western Europe, all the while pining for Mother Russia" (Sainsbury, see Appendix A, p. 220).

A quotation within a quotation is shown with single quotation marks:

> Sainsbury remarks on the effect of the change in terminology: "The 'bling' has been taken out of 'gambling,' so it becomes merely 'gaming,' a much more innocent-sounding activity" (see Appendix A, p. 220).

Recognize other uses of quotation marks

Note that another use of quotation marks is for titles of articles and short stories (the titles of books and periodicals are italicized or underlined):

"The Cask of Amontillado" by Edgar Allan Poe is reprinted in *Essay Do's and Don'ts.*

Distinguish hyphens from dashes

Hyphens are used inside words, while dashes are used between words in a sentence.

The hyphen is on a regular keyboard, while dashes are not. Dashes can be inserted as special symbols. The em dash (the width of the letter *m*) is used as a parenthetical dash—as in this sentence. The en dash (the width of the letter *n*) is used in number ranges (as in 1939–1945). Some word-processing programs replace two hyphens typed in a row with an em dash.

A **hyphen** unites two or more words together to create a unit of meaning:

French-Canadian, Johnny-come-lately

When a phrase is used as an adjective, it is hyphenated:

a three-metre pole, the newly-elected president

Note that singular forms are used in these adjective compounds:

The boy is six years old.
The six-year-old boy was lost.

Hyphens are used with some prefixes and in some compound words. Usage can vary and evolve. Hyphenated prefixes often lose their hyphen, and compound words often start out as two separately written words, then become hyphenated, and finally become one word, as in these examples:

co-ordinate/coordinate, e-mail/email, proof reading/proof-reading/proofreading

Hyphens are also used when a word has to be divided and written on two lines. The split has to be placed at a syllable break. While words hyphenated this way are common in publications such as books and newspapers, avoid dividing words in your own writing. Just go to the next line.

Parenthetical dashes signal shifts in thought that interrupt the sentence:

When I first met your sister, it was May—no, it was Valentine's Day—she was wearing a blouse with hearts.

Parenthetical dashes can also separate extra information from the main part of the sentence. In this way, they function like parentheses (round brackets)

and commas, but they add more emphasis. Don't overuse dashes; sometimes a comma or semicolon will do the job adequately.

Use italics for words used in special ways

Italic print is used for words from another language:

> A Latin phrase expressing personal fault or failure is *mea culpa*.

Titles of books and periodicals are generally italicized (see Chapter 5 for examples.):

> That article came from *Maclean's* magazine.
> *Essay Do's and Don'ts* is a guide to essay writing.

Words that are discussed as words (as is often the case in this book) are italicized:

> The idiom dictionary had 14 pages on phrasal verbs with *get*.
> I always have trouble spelling *relevant*.

Like boldface, underlining, and all caps, italics are sometimes used for emphasis. Avoid using any of these techniques in academic essays.

Underlining is the equivalent of italics. Underlining is used in handwritten work and was used in typewritten documents because most typewriters could not produce italics.

Exercise 8.3 Correct punctuation

Correct the faulty punctuation:

1. The traditional horror tales of vampire's werewolves and witches are finding new life in popular literature today
2. Although, rain was forecast the wedding was held outdoors without a problem.
3. Before she could paint the room she had a lot of prep work to do; emptying the closets, moving the furniture; and cleaning the walls.
4. Elizabeth and Hiro hold the same value's even though, they were raised in different cultures.
5. I was surprised to hear that she didn't know what the problem was? Its usually a simple case of following the instructions—in the manual.

Format your essay

Most instructors tell their students how they want essays formatted. For instance, some may prefer electronic submissions, while some will only accept a hard copy. Some want a cover page even though MLA style does not require one. Generally, handwritten essays are not accepted except for in-class assignments. Two features that are important to all instructors are that the work be easy to read and that there be room for corrections and comments (this usually requires double spacing).

Here are some **general guidelines** for formatting essays:

- Use white, letter-size (8½ by 11 inch) paper.
- Print in black (not faded) ink.
- Print on one side of the page.
- Use a standard typeface such as Times New Roman or Arial—not fancy fonts like those that imitate handwriting.
- Use a standard type size—usually 12 pt—and make sure there are no shifts in font or point size.
- Leave 1-inch margins on all four sides.
- Double space (leave a blank line between each line).
- Indent paragraphs with five spaces (the default tab setting).
- Use left justification and a ragged right margin (to avoid uneven gaps between words).
- Use standard punctuation and capitalization.
- If you are following MLA style for the first page (with no cover page), put your name, your instructor's name, the course title or code, and the date in the left-hand corner, double-spaced; put your essay title at the beginning of the essay, centred (see sample on p. 128).
- If you are including a cover page, put the title of your essay, your name and student number, the course code and section, the instructor's name, and the date all on the cover page, not on the essay itself.
- For an APA style essay, remember to include a running head of the title.
- Number your pages (MLA style is with your family name and the page number in the upper right-hand corner).
- Do not paginate the cover page, if you are including one.
- Staple the pages together in the top left-hand cover; do not use a cover or folder unless your instructor has asked for one.
- Avoid unnecessary graphics and pictures.
- Make sure your work has a neat, professional appearance.

Punctuation and format checklist

- Are paragraph beginnings and endings clearly shown with correct spacing such as indentation?
- Are sentence boundaries clearly shown with a capital letter at the beginning and final punctuation at the end?
- Are commas used correctly to separate the parts of sentences?
- Is spacing around punctuation marks correct (for instance, so that there is no space before a comma or period)?
- For pairs of punctuation marks (commas, brackets, quotation marks), did you remember to put the second one in?
- Are capital letters used for proper nouns?
- Did you double-space your essay?

Selected Readings

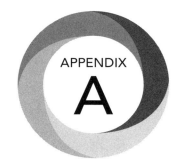

Beware the Risks of Smartphones and Tablets in Schools

by Sachin Maharaj

1   After initial reluctance, school systems appear to be rapidly embracing the use of electronic devices in classrooms. In 2010, former premier Dalton McGuinty reversed an earlier position and publicly supported the use of smartphones in schools, touting their ability to be used as learning tools. In 2011, the Toronto District School Board followed suit and overturned its previous ban of devices in classrooms.

2   Tablets like the iPad, once considered an expensive luxury, are increasingly becoming a must-have learning item. The Los Angeles Unified School District recently decided to spend more than $1 billion to give every one of its students an iPad. Many schools across Canada are now either buying iPads for their students or actively encouraging them to bring their own smartphones and tablets to class.

3   The momentum appears to be unstoppable. But while electronic devices certainly offer many learning benefits, we should be cognizant of the potential downsides.

4   First, as many teachers will know from first-hand experience, while these devices can be valuable learning tools, they are often not used that way. Instead of focusing on the lesson or task at hand, many students find the compulsion to use their phones to play Candy Crush or browse Facebook, Twitter, Vine, Instagram et al. much too tempting. This should be no surprise given what we know about impulse control and the developing adolescent brain.

5   And even when safeguards are put in place to ensure the devices are used for learning, they are often no match for students' ingenuity. Almost immediately after students in Los Angeles were given their iPads, the tablets were hacked, loaded up with social media apps, and students started accessing unauthorized websites.

6   Apart from these issues, given how pervasive electronic use is in all of our lives already, should we really be encouraging even more of this in our schools? Canadians with smartphones already spend an average of eight hours per day staring at electronic screens, not including time spent on computers or mobile devices for work. One Stanford University study found that 75 per cent of iPhone users regularly fall asleep with their phones in their bed. Another study found that almost a third of 16- to 25-year-olds check and update their social media accounts while in the middle of using the bathroom.

7   Perhaps most worrying are the effects that all of this constant technology use can have on students' cognitive and emotional development. As noted in a recent feature on CBC's The National, such high amounts of screen time reduce opportunities for quiet reflection, a key to developing empathy for others. This may go some way to explaining the prevalence of cyberbullying among teens.

8   It is also having an impact on the values our children hold. Whereas teens used to be mostly concerned with fitting in with their social groups, their primary concerns now seem to be acquiring attention and fame. As one Grade 6 Nova Scotia student put it: "I like it when people like my pictures, it makes me feel really good . . . who doesn't want to be famous?"

9   Constant electronic use can also carry a significant cognitive cost. Indeed, researchers in Britain found that excessive use of technology reduces people's intelligence more than twice as much as heavy marijuana use. The incessant barrage of electronic information also makes us less patient. A study by Microsoft and Google found that just a mere 250-millisecond delay in the time it takes to load a web page is enough for most people to abandon it entirely.

10   Other studies have shown that as our devices and networks get even faster, our impatience only grows. It also seems to be reducing our attention span. Consider the finding that people who read newspapers read for an average of 25 minutes, whereas people who read news online read for an average of 70 seconds.

11   The implications for our students are profound: it can make them less likely to want to experience things that take long periods of time or that do not provide instant gratification. But learning about and truly appreciating the natural world, as well as the great works of humanity, often require both significant time and patience. It is also what is necessary for students to engage in deep and creative thinking of their own. So while electronic devices may have benefits, perhaps we should rethink embracing them with such open arms in our schools.

[*The Toronto Star*, 3 April 2014, A17. https://www.thestar.com/opinion/commentary/2014/04/02/beware_the_risks_of_smartphones_and_tablets_in_schools.html]

Discussion and Writing Topics

1. What are the educational benefits of using electronic devices such as smartphones, tablets, and laptops in the classroom?
2. Why do people want to be famous?
3. Research one of the problems Maharaj mentions (such as less time for reflection or a reduction of attention span). Write an essay explaining causes and effects.
4. Explain the learning benefits of doing things without technology, such as taking notes by hand and using paper textbooks and dictionaries.
5. What do you see as the future in education when digital devices become smaller, wearable, and even implanted in the brain? For instance, will exam-taking have to be changed completely when students can easily get information from the Internet?

Why Are We So Scared of Eye Contact?

by Katrina Onstad

[1] Surely there's a word for this: You are mid-sentence and suddenly the listener's eyes slide southward to her own hand or the table or her lap. Whether she glances back immediately or—and this hurts—begins pecking away at whatever device proved more important than the final part of your sentence, the moment of connection that came before has been snapped like a twig. Let's call the ensuing sensation of vague humiliation and invisibility "techerruption."

[2] Eye contact is vanishing and even I miss it—and I'm constitutionally shy, prone to ducking people by hiding behind pillars and shrubs in a cowardly Scooby Doo fashion. It's harder to catch a gaze these days; the mass focus is inward, toward the electronically curated self. Try it: Walk with the head up, scanning faces and buildings and trees. Now look at people bustling by—how many are looking down at their phones or are caught in their cones of silence beneath headphones and sunglasses?

[3] In conversation, non-verbal cues matter as much as words, and the most potent tool of body language is eye contact, at least in most Western cultures. Human mothers and infants require eye contact to bond; one study showed that human babies fixate on the face and eyes of their caregivers twice as long as apes do. Evolutionary scientists propose that eye contact came to be the cornerstone of communication because of the "cooperative eye hypothesis," which suggests that collaboration and cooperation are optimized when our

eyes are locked. Today, life coaches and public-speaking gurus push eye contact as a business strategy, a gesture of sincerity to close the deal.

4   If eye contact is done properly—neither staring like a stalker, nor flitting like a butterfly—it's almost invisible. But its absence is immediately noted: the scurrying waiter in the busy restaurant; the fake-out at a crowded party: "Oh, you're here! I didn't see you!" Forbes reported a study in which a hospital analyzed its complaint letters to find that 90 per cent concerned lack of eye contact from doctors. Clearly, to feel unseen is to feel a lack of care.

5   And that, perhaps, is why I hate Skype. It gives the illusion of eye contact without actual eye contact. Unlike a phone call, where communication is a simple oral-aural proposition, Skype confuses all signals. It's a herky-jerky, distorted version of a real moment with someone. Software and robotic engineers know that when human replicas seem almost like actual human beings but not quite, real humans respond with revulsion. This is called "the uncanny valley" and it's where Skype lives.

6   In robotics, they're working on filling the valley. In her book *Alone Together: Why We Expect More from Technology and Less From Each Other*, MIT professor Sherry Turkle writes about the evolution of social robots ready to step in for humans, some of whom are caretakers, pets, even sex partners. Turkle describes eye contact in artificial intelligence as a key to human acceptance of robots; a patient in a nursing home might bond with a robot if she can feel connected to it at the eyes.

7   Last month, a small town in New Jersey became an international media sensation when it was widely reported that police were issuing $85 tickets for walking while texting. Naturally, this notion created an online maelstrom as appalled commenters decried the bylaw on freedom-to-be-an-idiot grounds. Safety was the motivator, but the potential for accidents when walking while texting seems almost less urgent than the lack of eye contact. When the gaze is broken, so is something larger—some corner of the social contract gets torn. The imperative notion that we are looking out for one another is harder to believe when we don't see each other's eyes. The socially networked self arrives tidily edited; Facebook is an exercise in selective broadcasting. I don't advocate returning to tablet and hammer but I'm not happy about how I've been changed by my own reliance on technology. Certainly I'm more distracted and only partially present when my attention is required. I suspect I'm more cautious in my real interactions too, accustomed instead to polishing a thought, transmitting and retreating. The time I spend with people has dwindled, though large parts of my day are doing something that passes for interacting. So it feels urgent to pocket the devices from time to time and raise the head.

8   The messiest—and, I suspect, richest and most complex—parts of the self tumble forward when eye to eye with another person. A conversation of ungroomed opinion could go anywhere; imagine the possibilities in a mutual gaze. Imagine not just seeing, but being seen.

[*The Globe and Mail*, 30 June 2012 , A14. http://www.theglobeandmail.com/life/relationships/why-are-we-so-scared-of-eye-contact/article4375470/]

Discussion and Writing Topics

1. What is Onstad's thesis?
2. Eye contact rules can vary from culture to culture. Discuss the differences you know about.
3. Compare Skype to other methods of communication. What are the advantages of using Skype?
4. Why do so many people continue to text while walking—or, even worse, while driving—even though it is such a dangerous activity?
5. Studies show that adolescents are still learning to read facial expressions. Will extensive use of smartphones and other digital devices impair their ability to learn to read faces? Why or why not?
6. Discuss the advantages and disadvantages of using robots to take care of human beings.
7. Onstad admits, "I'm not happy about how I've been changed by my own reliance on technology. Certainly I'm more distracted and only partially present when my attention is required." How has reliance on technology changed you?

We All Should Worry about Cellphone Searches

by William Kowalski

1   Imagine police being able to access your communications, private photographs, call logs, records of places you've been and other minute and private details of your life. On Dec. 11, 2014, the Supreme Court of Canada effectively made this information available when they ruled that police can, without a warrant, search the cellphones of people under arrest in certain conditions. This decision is another backward step in the ongoing struggle to protect digital privacy.

2   First, cellphones are the sites of our digital lives, and they contain an ever-increasing portion of our personal lives, making them much more than simply telephones in our pockets. Cellphones are portals into every aspect of our existence: What we've written to whom, what pictures we have taken, who's in our contact list, which websites we have viewed. If your phone is linked to your home computer, social networks or cloud storage accounts, it's possible to find out nearly everything about you through a search of your phone.

3   In the wrong hands, that kind of power is something to fear. The court decision states that searches must be directly related to an arrest and that the officer must keep detailed notes. But who is to say, in the heat of the

moment, what "directly related" means? And what if an officer sees an intimate photo, a draft of a sensitive business document, an e-mail outlining sensitive political views, and doesn't make a note of it? Can the officer forget she saw it? Can the arrestee forget the feeling of violation? What protection do "detailed notes" offer against invasion of privacy, and how does the absence of such notes prove that privacy wasn't violated?

4   We should not be made complacent by the fact that only "criminals" will have their digital lives laid bare. It is not uncommon for people to be arrested or detained without ever being convicted of a crime. This means that anyone whom the police suspect of committing an offence is at risk. You might be marching in a protest in downtown Toronto and arrested for failure to disperse—or, as happened to many during the G20 protests, for no reason at all—and the police would then be able to go through your phone.

5   In a time when government cybersurveillance has become a cause for major concern, this decision seems to be yet another blow against the laws that used to protect us. Should the current trend continue, Canadians will soon have no right to digital privacy at all. Already we know that the government has the ability, if not the legal right, to find out anything it wants about us, simply by making use of information-sharing agreements with other Five Eyes nations as well as CSEC surveillance capabilities. The Supreme Court's ruling makes such invasions of privacy possible through our physical devices as well—police officers can now remove our phones from our pockets and peruse them at their leisure. All they need to do is find a reason to arrest us first.

6   Officers being human, susceptible to both error and bad judgment, there is no reason to assume that every instance of this kind will go strictly by the book. What will be done with the information they gather? Who will they be reporting it to? How do we trust that it won't be misused and added to the millions of megabytes of data and metadata that are already collected about Canadians every day through projects like Levitation? How do we know photographic or audio evidence of police misconduct won't be deleted?

7   There are a few things you can do to protect yourself against this kind of intrusion, but your privacy is not guaranteed. A simple step is to password-protect your phone. For now, the police cannot compel you to give up your password, although they may use other means to access your data. It would also be wise to create a video or audio record of your encounters with police, and to connect your smart phone to a cloud storage service, so that pictures and audio are immediately uploaded. However, this does not necessarily protect your files from "accidental" deletion during a search, and it may allow police to access your other documents online.

8   But the best protection against intrusive laws is not to have them in the first place. Unfortunately, in this case, this is no longer an option.

[*The Globe and Mail*, 16 March 2015. By permission of Bill Kowalski.]

Discussion and Writing Topics

1. Do you agree with Kowalski's argument? Is he being too alarmist? Do you worry about your privacy? What do you do to protect it? For example, how careful are you about what you share on social media?
2. Research one of the references in this article: the Five Eyes intelligence agreement; the Canadian Communication Security Establishment (CSEC) and its project Levitation; or police actions at the 2010 G20 protests in Toronto. Write a research essay with a clear thesis giving your opinion of such actions. You could also write about WikiLeaks or Edward Snowden.
3. The police and government agencies do not need physical access to your phone to get your private information. Social media sites and telecommunications companies routinely give the government information on their users. How should privacy laws protect users?
4. Some people argue that only criminals and terrorists need to worry about the police actions, yet there are many examples of innocent people being accosted and detained. For instance, most of the people detained in the G20 police action were innocent. In addition, young black men are routinely stopped on city streets in police actions such as carding and "stop and frisk." Choose one issue and write your opinion about whether such actions are justified.
5. How worried are you about losing your smartphone or about someone accessing the information on it? What do you do to protect your information? What is more important to you—convenience or privacy?
6. The camera function on cellphones has been instrumental in exposing injustice and criminal activity. Does that give a person the right to violate the privacy of others on the streets and in public?
7. In the investigation of the mass shooting on 2 December 2015 in San Bernardino, California, the FBI asked Apple to create a way to break iPhone encryption so the authorities could unlock the work phone of one of the perpetrators of the crime. Apple refused, arguing that it had to protect its customers' security and that it wasn't a case of just one phone being unlocked. In the end, the FBI managed to unlock the phone without Apple's help. Research the arguments in this case, and write an essay siding with either Apple or the FBI.

What if Dostoyevsky Had Been an Online Gambler?

by John Sainsbury

1   Feodor Dostoyevsky, the great 19th-century Russian novelist, was a gambler who squandered vast sums at the roulette tables of Paris and Baden-Baden. Like all compulsive gamblers, he was captive to his addiction, with

nearly devastating consequences. It came close to ruining his marriage to the long-suffering Anna, whose jewellery he once sold to pay his gambling debts, and it kept him a virtual exile for many years in the decadent flesh-pots of Western Europe, all the while pining for Mother Russia.

2   Yet, Dostoyevsky had a quality of genius that distinguished him from the run-of-the-mill gambling addict. Even as he was psychologically chained to the gaming tables, his imagination roamed free in a way that enabled him to hover above himself and dissect his own condition. In his novella *The Gambler*, Dostoyevsky lays bare his own gambling compulsion (embodied in the fictional Alexei Ivanovich) so convincingly that even prosaic behavioural psychologists remain in awe. While Dostoyevsky's greatest novels don't have casino gambling as a significant theme, their antiheroes (Raskolnikov in *Crime and Punishment*, for example) are gambling addicts in the larger sense of being souls trapped by irrational cravings, while in a desperate quest for redemption.

3   Would Dostoyevsky's novels have been so compelling (and timeless) had he not been a casino gambler? The answer is probably no. Does this in itself make casinos a good thing? Definitely no. After all, the most evil institutions can inspire great literature. To take an extreme case, no one in their right mind would argue that Auschwitz was a good thing because it meant that Elie Wiesel wrote *Night*.

4   Yet, casinos, for all the misery they cause, are at least human institutions in the sense that they provide space for the all-too-human rituals of greed, shame, degradation and (occasionally) triumph. They can facilitate what anthropologists, with things such as Balinese cockfighting in mind, call deep play, activity that enacts communally humanity's most profound conflicts and concerns. I concede this is more evident in literature (to come back to Dostoyevsky) and movies (think of Stanley Kubrick's *Barry Lyndon*, where, in candlelit casinos, European aristocrats seek to preserve their sang-froid after losing the family estate on the turn of a card) than in your average Canadian casino. There, a typical scene would be a busload of people from a seniors' home, some with oxygen tanks in tow, being deposited in front of slot machines until they're driven back to their residence (where they're doubtless told by their caregivers that they all had a very nice time).

5   So, if there's a case for bricks-and-mortar casinos, it's a weak one, in which theory is confounded by practice. But at least casinos inspired Dostoyevsky's great literature. But what if Dostoyevsky had been chained to a computer screen in his basement? What if he'd been addicted to online gambling?

6   The questions are prompted by Ontario's decision to follow British Columbia's lead and launch a provincial online "gaming" site, projected to begin operations in 2012. (Notice a subtle linguistic amendment: The "bling" has been taken out of "gambling," so it becomes merely "gaming," a much more innocent-sounding activity.) The curious rationale for the venture is that it will redirect to government coffers the $400-million that Ontarians currently spend on out-of-province gambling sites.

7   Ontario Lottery and Gaming chair Paul Godfrey offers this reassuring message: "OLG's Internet gaming program will stress responsible gaming while providing an enjoyable experience for Ontario players." He makes it sound like a moral crusade, as if having the province take over a questionable racket somehow makes everything all right. Yet, as with any gambling operation, it will be the irresponsible gambler (the heirs of Dostoyevsky) who will drive the revenues. It's bad enough living in a nanny state, but it verges on the intolerable when nanny herself slips a narcotic into the baby formula for her own money-grubbing purposes.

8   All the evidence suggests that online gaming will prove an irresistible temptation to those who already have the gambling bug (while probably making some new recruits). Put a time-travelling Dostoyevsky in front of a computer screen and chances are he'll soon be maxing out his credit card on a cyberspace roulette wheel, rather than completing the rewrite of *The Brothers Karamazov*.

9   And at what a dreadful cost. The most terrifying outcome of Internet gambling is isolation, estrangement from friends and family, estrangement even from the company of strangers in traditional casinos. Dostoyevsky would be bereft of the rich cast of characters who populate the pages of *The Gambler*. And his evocation of gambling as a metaphor for the human condition would fade to nothing in the face of the bland tyranny of the computer screen. Perhaps Anna, confused by her husband's odd behaviour, would finally leave, driving Feodor to find solace in Internet pornography, online gambling's evil twin.

10   Is this the way the world will end, to the whimpering sound of Internet gamblers and pornography addicts? Feodor, you've got to switch off the computer and come out of the basement. Right now.

[*The Globe and Mail*, 21 August 2010, A17.]

Discussion and Writing Topics

1. How is Internet gambling different from casino gambling? Write a comparison essay.
2. Explain the difference between gambling and gaming. Why is the terminology so important?
3. Should the government be making money from lotteries and casinos? Is it not immoral to prey upon vulnerable people when a government is supposed to protect its citizens? Write an essay arguing for or against government participation in the gambling business.
4. Why does Sainsbury call Internet pornography "online gambling's evil twin" [paragraph 9]? Explain the connection.

5. Explain the point Sainsbury is making by using Dostoyevsky as representative of an obsessive gambler.
6. Fantasy sports leagues used to be social activities in workplaces or among friends. Now they have moved to the realm of online gambling. Research the topic, choose a point of view, and write an argumentative or comparative essay.
7. "Nanny state" [paragraph 7] is a term that refers to a government that tries to control and protect its citizens too much, like a parent. For example, the introduction of seat belts was criticized as an example of the nanny state at work. What is the role of government in keeping citizens safe? If a person wants to gamble, smoke, drink too much, or drive recklessly, when is government intervention in the form of laws and regulations necessary?

The Moose and the Sparrow

by Hugh Garner

1   From the very beginning Moose Maddon picked on him. The kid was bait for all of Maddon's cruel practical jokes around the camp. He was sent back to the tool-house for left-handed saws, and down to the office to ask the pay cheater if the day's mail was in, though the rest of us knew it was only flown out every week.

2   The kid's name was Cecil, and Maddon used to mouth it with a simpering mockery, as if it pointed to the kid being something less than a man. I must admit though that the name fitted him, for Cecil was the least likely lumberjack I've seen in over twenty-five years in lumber camps. Though we knew he was intelligent enough, and a man too, if smaller than most of us, we all kidded him, in the good-natured way a bunkhouse gang will. Maddon however always lisped the kid's name as if it belonged to a woman.

3   Moose Maddon was as different from Cecil as it is possible for two human beings to be and still stay within the species. He was a big moose of a man, even for a lumber stiff, with a round flat unshaven face that looked down angrily and dourly at the world. Cecil on the other hand was hardly taller than an axe-handle, and almost as thin. He was about nineteen years old, with the looks of an inquisitive sparrow behind his thick horn-rimmed glasses. He had been sent out to the camp for the summer months by an distant relative who had a connection with the head office down in Vancouver.

4   That summer we were cutting big stuff in an almost inaccessible stand of Douglas fir about fifty miles out of Nanaimo. The logs were catted five miles down to the river where they were bunked waiting for the drive. Cecil had signed on as a whistle punk, but after a few days of snarling the operation

with wrong signals at the wrong time and threatening to hang the rigging slingers in their own chokers, he was transferred to Maddon's gang as a general handyman. Besides going on all the ridiculous and fruitless errands for Moose, he carried the noon grub to the gangs from the panel truck that brought it out from the camp, made the tea and took the saws and axes in to old Bobbins, the squint eye, to be sharpened.

5   For the first two weeks after he arrived, the jokes were the usual ones practised on a greenhorn, but when they seemed to be having little or no effect on his bumbling habits and even temper Moose devised more cruel and intricate ones. One night Moose and a cohort of his called Lefevre carried the sleeping Cecil, mattress and all, down to the river and threw him in. The kid almost drowned, but when he had crawled up on shore and regained his breath he merely smiled at his tormentors and ran back to the bunkhouse, where he sat shivering in a blanket on the springs of his bunk till the sun came up.

6   Another time Moose painted a wide mustache with tar on Cecil's face while he slept. It took him nearly a week to get it all off, and his upper lip was red and sore looking for longer than that.

7   Nearly all of us joined in the jokes on Cecil at first, putting a young raccoon in his bunk, kicking over his tea water, hiding his clothes or tying them in knots, all the usual things. It wasn't long though until the other men noticed that Moose Maddon's jokes seemed to have a grim purpose. You could almost say he was carrying out a personal vendetta against the kid for refusing to knuckle under or cry "Uncle." From then on everybody but Moose let the kid alone.

8   One evening as a few of us sat outside the bunkhouse shooting the guff, Moose said, "Hey, Cecil dear, what do you do over on the mainland?"

9   "Go to school," Cecil answered.

10   Moose guffawed. "Go to school? At your age!"

11   Cecil just grinned.

12   "What school d'ya go to, Cecil? Kindergarten?" Moose asked him, guffawing some more.

13   "No."

14   "You afraid to tell us?"

15   "No."

16   "Well, what school d'ya go to?"

17   "U.B.C."

18   "What's that, a hairdressin' school?"

19   "No, the university."

20   "University! You!"

21   Moose, who was probably a Grade Four dropout himself, was flabbergasted. I'm sure that up until that minute he'd been living in awe of anybody with a college education.

22   "What you takin' up?" he asked, his face angry and serious now.

23   "Just an arts course," Cecil said.

24   "You mean paintin' pictures an' things?"

25   "No, not quite," the kid answered.

26   For once Moose had nothing further to say.

27   From then on things became pretty serious as far as Moose and Cecil were concerned. On at least two occasions the other men on the gang had to prevent Moose from beating the boy up, and old Bobbins even went so far as to ask Mr Semple, the walking boss, to transfer the youngster to another gang. Since learning that Cecil was a college boy, Moose gave him no peace at all, making him do jobs that would have taxed the strength of any man in the camp, and cursing him out when he was unable to do them, or do them fast enough.

28   The kid may not have been an artist, as Moose had thought, but he could make beautiful things out of wire. Late in the evenings he would sit on his bunk and fashion belt buckles, rings and tie clips from a spool of fine copper wire he'd found in the tool shed. He made things for several of the men, always refusing payment for them. He used to say it gave him something to do, since he couldn't afford to join in the poker games.

29   One evening late in the summer as I was walking along the river having an after-supper pipe, I stumbled upon Cecil curled up on a narrow sandy beach. His head was buried in his arms and his shoulders were heaving with sobs. I wanted to turn around without letting him know he'd been seen, but he looked so lonely crying there by himself that I walked over and tapped him on the shoulder.

30   He jumped as if I'd prodded him with a peavey, and swung around, his eyes nearly popping from his head with fright. The six weeks he'd spent working under Moose Maddon hadn't done his nerves any good.

31   "It's all right kid," I said.

32   "Oh! Oh, it's you, Mr Anderson!"

33   He was the only person in camp who ever called me anything but "Pop."

34   "I don't mean to butt in," I said. "I was just walking along here, and couldn't help seeing you. Are you in trouble?"

35   He wiped his eyes on his sleeve before answering me. Then he turned and stared out across the river.

36   "This is the first time I broke down," he said, wiping his glasses.

37   "Is it Moose?"

38   "Yes."

39   "What's he done to you now?"

40   "Nothing more than he's been doing to me all along. At first I took it—you know that, Mr Anderson, don't you?"

41   I nodded.

42   "I thought that after I was out here a couple of weeks it would stop," he said. "I expected the jokes that were played on me at first. After all I was pretty green when I arrived here. When they got to know me the other men stopped, but not that—that Moose."

43   He seemed to have a hard time mouthing the other's name.

44   "When are you going back to school?" I asked him.

45   "In another couple of weeks."

46   "Do you think you can stand it until then?"

47   "I need all the money I can make, but it's going to be tough."

48   I sat down on the sand beside him and asked him to tell me about himself. For the next ten or fifteen minutes he poured out the story of his life; he was one of those kids who are kicked around from birth. His mother and father had split up while he was still a baby, and he'd been brought up in a series of foster homes. He'd been smart enough, though, to graduate from high school at seventeen. By a miracle of hard work and self-denial he'd managed to put himself through the first year of university, and his ambition was to continue on to law school. The money he earned from his summer work here at the camp was to go towards his next year's tuition.

49   When he finished we sat in silence for a while. Then he asked, "Tell me, Mr Anderson, why does Maddon pick on me like he does?"

50   I thought about his question for a long time before answering it. Finally I said, "I guess that deep down Moose knows you are smarter than he is in a lot of ways. I guess he's—well, I guess you might say he's jealous of you."

51   "No matter what I do, or how hard I try to please him, it's no good."

52   "It never is," I said.

53   "How do you mean?"

54   I had to think even longer this time. "There are some men, like Moose Maddon, who are so twisted inside that they want to take it out on the world. They feel that most other men have had better breaks than they've had, and it rankles inside them. They try to get rid of this feeling by working it out on somebody who's even weaker than they are. Once they pick on you there's no way of stopping them short of getting out of their way or beating it out of their hide."

55   Cecil gave me a wry grin. "I'd never be able to beat it out of the—the Moose's hide."

56   "Then try to keep out of his way."

57   "I can't for another two weeks," he said. "I'm afraid that before then he'll have really hurt me."

58   I laughed to reassure him, but I was afraid of the same thing myself. I knew that Moose was capable of going to almost any lengths to prevent Cecil leaving the camp without knuckling under at least once; his urge seemed to me to be almost insane. I decided to talk to George Semple myself in the morning, and have the boy flown out on the next plane.

59   "I don't think Moose would go as far as to really hurt you," I told him.

60   "Yes he would! He would, Mr Anderson, I know it! I've seen the way he's changed. All he thinks about any more are ways to make me crawl. It's no longer a case of practical jokes; he wants to kill me!"

61   My reassuring laugh stuck in my throat this time. "In another two weeks, son, you'll be back in Vancouver, and all this will seem like a bad dream."

62   "He'll make sure I leave here crippled," Cecil said.

63   We walked back to the camp together, and I managed to calm him down some.

64   The next day I spoke to Semple, the walking boss, and convinced him we should get the boy out of there. There was never any thought of getting rid of Moose, of course. Saw bosses were worth their weight in gold, and the top brass were calling for more and more production all the time. Whatever else Moose was, he was the best production foreman in the camp. When Semple spoke to Cecil, however, the kid refused to leave. He said he'd made up his mind to stick it out until his time was up.

65   Though my gang was working on a different side than Maddon's, I tried to keep my eye on the boy from then on. For a week things went on pretty much as usual, then one suppertime Cecil came into the dining hall without his glasses. Somebody asked him what had happened, and he said there'd been an accident, and that Moose had stepped on them. We all knew how much of an accident it had been; luckily the kid had an old spare pair in his kit. Few of his gang had a good word for Moose any more, which only seemed to make him more determined to take his spite out on the kid.

66   That evening I watched Cecil fashioning a signet ring for one of the men out of wire and a piece of quartz the man had found. The way he braided the thin wire and shaped it around a length of thin sapling was an interesting thing to see. Moose was watching him too, but pretending not to. You could see he hated the idea of Cecil getting along so well with the other men.

67   "I was going to ask you to make me a new watch strap before you left," I said to Cecil. "But it looks like you're running out of wire."

68   The kid looked up. "I still have about twenty-five feet of it left," he said. "That'll be enough for what I have in mind. Don't worry, Mr Anderson, I'll make you the watch strap before I leave."

69   The next afternoon there was quite a commotion over where Maddon's gang were cutting, but I had to wait until the whistle blew to find out what had happened. Cecil sat down to supper with his right hand heavily bandaged.

70   "What happened?" I asked one of Maddon's men.

71   "Moose burned the kid's hand," he told me. "He heated the end of a saw blade in the tea fire, and then called the kid to take it to the squint eye to be sharpened. He handed the hot end to Cecil, and it burned his hand pretty bad."

72   "But—didn't any of you—"

73   "None of us was around at the time. When we found out, big Chief went after Moose with a cant hook, but the rest of us held him back. He would have killed Moose. If Maddon doesn't leave the kid alone, one of us is going to have to cripple him for sure."

74   Moose had been lucky that The Chief, a giant Indian called Danny Corbett, hadn't caught him. I made up my mind to have Cecil flown out in the morning without fail, no matter how much he protested.

75   That evening the kid turned in early, and we made sure there was always one of us in the bunkhouse to keep him from being bothered by anybody. He refused to talk about the hand-burning incident at all, but turned his head to the wall when anybody tried to question him about it. Moose left shortly after supper to drink and play poker in Camp Three, about a mile away through the woods.

76   I woke up during the night to hear a man laughing near the edge of the camp, and Maddon's name being called. I figured it was Moose and Lefevre coming home drunk from Camp Three, where the bull cook boot-legged home brew.

77   When I got up in the morning, Cecil was already awake and dressed, sitting on the edge of his bunk plaiting a long length of his copper wire, using his good hand and the ends of the fingers of the one that was burned.

78   "What are you doing up so early?" I asked him.

79   "I went to bed right after chow last night, so I couldn't sleep once it got light." He pointed to the plaited wire. "This is going to be your watch strap."

80   "But you didn't need to make it now, Cecil," I said. "Not with your hand bandaged and everything."

81   "It's all right, Mr Anderson," he assured me. "I can manage it okay, and I want to get it done as soon as I can."

82   Just as the whistle blew after breakfast one of the jacks from Camp Three came running into the clearing shouting that Moose Maddon's body was lying at the bottom of a deep narrow ravine outside the camp. This ravine was crossed by means of a fallen log, and Moose must have lost his footing on it coming home drunk during the night. There was a free fall of more than forty feet down to a rocky stream bed.

83   None of us were exactly broken-hearted about Moose kicking off that way, but the unexpectedness of it shocked us. We all ran out to the spot, and the boys rigged a sling from draglines and hauled the body to the top of the ravine. I asked Lefevre if he'd been with Moose the night before, but he told me he hadn't gone over to Camp Three. Later in the day the district coroner flew out from Campbell River or somewhere, and after inspecting the log bridge made us rig a hand-line along it. He made out a certificate of accidental death.

84   When they flew the body out, Cecil stood with the rest of us on the river bank, watching the plane take off. If I'd been in his place I'd probably have been cheering, but he showed no emotion at all, not relief, happiness, or anything else.

85   He worked on my watch strap that evening, and finished it the next day, fastening it to my watch and attaching my old buckle to it. It looked like a real professional job, but when I tried to pay him for it he waved the money aside.

86   It was another week before Cecil packed his things to leave. His hand had begun to heal up nicely, and he was already beginning to lose the nervous

twitches he'd had while Moose was living. When he was rowed out to the company plane, all the boys from his bunkhouse were on the river bank to see him go. The last we saw of Cecil was his little sparrow smile, and his hand waving to us from the window.

87   One day in the fall I went out to the ravine to see how the handline was making it. It still shocked me to think that Maddon, who had been as sure-footed as a chipmunk, and our best man in a log-rolling contest, had fallen to his death the way he had. Only then did I notice something nobody had looked for before. In the bark of the trunks of two small trees that faced each other diagonally across the fallen log were burn marks that could have been made by wire loops. A length of thin wire rigged from one to the other would have crossed the makeshift footbridge just high enough to catch a running man on the shin, and throw him into the ravine. Maddon could have been running across the log that night, if he'd been goaded by the laughter and taunts of somebody waiting at the other end. I remembered the sound of laughter and the shouting of Maddon's name.

88   I'm not saying that's what happened, you understand, and for all I know nobody was wandering around outside the bunkhouses on the night of Maddon's death, not Cecil or anybody else. Still, it gives me a queer feeling sometimes, even yet, to look down at my wrist. For all I know I may be the only man in the world wearing the evidence of a murder as a wristwatch strap.

[The Moose and the Sparrow, from: Hugh Garner, *Men and Women*, Ryerson Press, 1966. Reproduced with permission of McGraw-Hill Ryerson Ltd.]

Discussion and Writing Topics

1. Did Cecil kill Maddon? Write an essay arguing that Cecil is innocent of the crime.
2. Write an essay comparing the workplace bullying in this story with cyberbullying or another modern form of harassment.
3. The narrator is a secondary character in the story. Explain why this is an effective method of telling this tale.
4. Show the steps in which Maddon's "practical jokes" become increasingly more injurious.
5. Explain the motives in bullying, including why Maddon picked on Cecil.
6. Explain the effects of bullying.
7. How would Maddon's bullying be treated in today's society?
8. Is cyberbullying worse than traditional schoolyard bullying?
9. Compare bullying in school to bullying in the workplace.

The Cask of Amontillado

by Edgar Allan Poe

1   The thousand injuries of Fortunato I had borne as I best could, but when he ventured upon insult, I vowed revenge. You, who so well know the nature of my soul, will not suppose, however, that I gave utterance to a threat. *At length* I would be avenged; this was a point definitively settled—but the very definitiveness with which it was resolved precluded the idea of risk. I must not only punish, but punish with impunity. A wrong is unredressed when retribution overtakes its redresser. It is equally unredressed when the avenger fails to make himself felt as such to him who has done the wrong.

2   It must be understood that neither by word nor deed had I given Fortunato cause to doubt my good will. I continued as was my wont, to smile in his face, and he did not perceive that my smile *now* was at the thought of his immolation.

3   He had a weak point—this Fortunato—although in other regards he was a man to be respected and even feared. He prided himself on his connoisseurship in wine. Few Italians have the true virtuoso spirit. For the most part their enthusiasm is adopted to suit the time and opportunity to practise imposture upon the British and Austrian *millionaires*. In painting and gemmary, Fortunato, like his countrymen, was a quack, but in the matter of old wines he was sincere. In this respect I did not differ from him materially; I was skillful in the Italian vintages myself, and bought largely whenever I could.

4   It was about dusk, one evening during the supreme madness of the carnival season, that I encountered my friend. He accosted me with excessive warmth, for he had been drinking much. The man wore motley. He had on a tight-fitting parti-striped dress and his head was surmounted by the conical cap and bells. I was so pleased to see him, that I thought I should never have done wringing his hand.

5   I said to him—"My dear Fortunato, you are luckily met. How remarkably well you are looking to-day! But I have received a pipe of what passes for Amontillado, and I have my doubts."

6   "How?" said he, "Amontillado? A pipe? Impossible! And in the middle of the carnival!"

7   "I have my doubts," I replied; "and I was silly enough to pay the full Amontillado price without consulting you in the matter. You were not to be found, and I was fearful of losing a bargain."

8   "Amontillado!"

9   "I have my doubts."

10   "Amontillado!"

11   "And I must satisfy them."

12   "Amontillado!"

13   "As you are engaged, I am on my way to Luchresi. If any one has a critical turn, it is he. He will tell me—"

14   "Luchresi cannot tell Amontillado from Sherry."

15   "And yet some fools will have it that his taste is a match for your own."

16   "Come let us go."

17   "Whither?"

18   "To your vaults."

19   "My friend, no; I will not impose upon your good nature. I perceive you have an engagement, Luchresi—"

20   "I have no engagement; come."

21   "My friend, no. It is not the engagement, but the severe cold with which I perceive you are afflicted. The vaults are insufferably damp. They are encrusted with nitre."

22   "Let us go, nevertheless. The cold is merely nothing. Amontillado! You have been imposed upon. And as for Luchresi, he cannot distinguish Sherry from Amontillado."

23   Thus speaking, Fortunato possessed himself of my arm. Putting on a mask of black silk and drawing a *roquelaure* closely about my person, I suffered him to hurry me to my palazzo.

24   There were no attendants at home; they had absconded to make merry in honour of the time. I had told them that I should not return until the morning and had given them explicit orders not to stir from the house. These orders were sufficient, I well knew, to insure their immediate disappearance, one and all, as soon as my back was turned.

25   I took from their sconces two flambeaux, and giving one to Fortunato, bowed him through several suites of rooms to the archway that led into the vaults. I passed down a long and winding staircase, requesting him to be cautious as he followed. We came at length to the foot of the descent, and stood together on the damp ground of the catacombs of the Montresors.

26   The gait of my friend was unsteady, and the bells upon his cap jingled as he strode.

27   "The pipe," said he.

28   "It is farther on," said I; "but observe the white webwork which gleams from these cavern walls."

29   He turned towards me and looked into my eyes with two filmy orbs that distilled the rheum of intoxication.

30   "Nitre?" he asked, at length.

31   "Nitre," I replied. "How long have you had that cough!"

32   "Ugh! ugh! ugh!—ugh! ugh! ugh!—ugh! ugh! ugh!—ugh! ugh! ugh!—ugh! ugh! ugh!"

33   My poor friend found it impossible to reply for many minutes.

34   "It is nothing," he said, at last.

35   "Come," I said, with decision, "we will go back; your health is precious. You are rich, respected, admired, beloved; you are happy as once I was. You

are a man to be missed. For me it is no matter. We will go back; you will be ill and I cannot be responsible. Besides, there is Luchresi—"

36 "Enough," he said; "the cough is a mere nothing; it will not kill me. I shall not die of a cough."

37 "True—true," I replied; "and, indeed, I had no intention of alarming you unnecessarily—but you should use all proper caution. A draught of this Medoc will defend us from the damps."

38 Here I knocked off the neck of a bottle which I drew from a long row of its fellows that lay upon the mould.

39 "Drink," I said, presenting him the wine.

40 He raised it to his lips with a leer. He paused and nodded to me familiarly, while his bells jingled.

41 "I drink," he said, "to the buried that repose around us."

42 "And I to your long life."

43 He again took my arm and we proceeded.

44 "These vaults," he said, "are extensive."

45 "The Montresors," I replied, "were a great numerous family."

46 "I forget your arms."

47 "A huge human foot d'or, in a field azure; the foot crushes a serpent rampant whose fangs are imbedded in the heel."

48 "And the motto?"

49 *"Nemo me impune lacessit."*

50 "Good!" he said.

51 The wine sparkled in his eyes and the bells jingled. My own fancy grew warm with the Medoc. We had passed through walls of piled bones, with casks and puncheons intermingling, into the inmost recesses of the catacombs. I paused again, and this time I made bold to seize Fortunato by an arm above the elbow.

52 "The nitre!" I said; "see it increases. It hangs like moss upon the vaults. We are below the river's bed. The drops of moisture trickle among the bones. Come, we will go back ere it is too late. Your cough—"

53 "It is nothing" he said; "let us go on. But first, another draught of the Medoc."

54 I broke and reached him a flagon of De Grave. He emptied it at a breath. His eyes flashed with a fierce light. He laughed and threw the bottle upwards with a gesticulation I did not understand.

55 I looked at him in surprise. He repeated the movement—a grotesque one.

56 "You do not comprehend?" he said.

57 "Not I," I replied.

58 "Then you are not of the brotherhood."

59 "How?"

60 "You are not of the masons."

61 "Yes, yes," I said "yes! yes."

62 "You? Impossible! A mason?"

63 "A mason," I replied.

64   "A sign," he said.

65   "It is this," I answered, producing a trowel from beneath the folds of my *roquelaure*.

66   "You jest," he exclaimed, recoiling a few paces. "But let us proceed to the Amontillado."

67   "Be it so," I said, replacing the tool beneath the cloak, and again offering him my arm. He leaned upon it heavily. We continued our route in search of the Amontillado. We passed through a range of low arches, descended, passed on, and descending again, arrived at a deep crypt, in which the foulness of the air caused our flambeaux rather to glow than flame.

68   At the most remote end of the crypt there appeared another less spacious. Its walls had been lined with human remains piled to the vault overhead, in the fashion of the great catacombs of Paris. Three sides of this interior crypt were still ornamented in this manner. From the fourth the bones had been thrown down, and lay promiscuously upon the earth, forming at one point a mound of some size. Within the wall thus exposed by the displacing of the bones, we perceived a still interior recess, in depth about four feet, in width three, in height six or seven. It seemed to have been constructed for no especial use in itself, but formed merely the interval between two of the colossal supports of the roof of the catacombs, and was backed by one of their circumscribing walls of solid granite.

69   It was in vain that Fortunato, uplifting his dull torch, endeavoured to pry into the depths of the recess. Its termination the feeble light did not enable us to see.

70   "Proceed," I said; "herein is the Amontillado. As for Luchresi—"

71   "He is an ignoramus," interrupted my friend, as he stepped unsteadily forward, while I followed immediately at his heels. In an instant he had reached the extremity of the niche, and finding his progress arrested by the rock, stood stupidly bewildered. A moment more and I had fettered him to the granite. In its surface were two iron staples, distant from each other about two feet, horizontally. From one of these depended a short chain. From the other a padlock. Throwing the links about his waist, it was but the work of a few seconds to secure it. He was too much astounded to resist. Withdrawing the key I stepped back from the recess.

72   "Pass your hand," I said, "over the wall; you cannot help feeling the nitre. Indeed it is *very* damp. Once more let me *implore* you to return. No? Then I must positively leave you. But I must first render you all the little attentions in my power."

73   "The Amontillado!" ejaculated my friend, not yet recovered from his astonishment.

74   "True," I replied; "the Amontillado."

75   As I said these words I busied myself among the pile of bones of which I have before spoken. Throwing them aside, I soon uncovered a quantity of building stone and mortar. With these materials and with the aid of my trowel, I began vigorously to wall up the entrance of the niche.

76   I had scarcely laid the first tier of my masonry when I discovered that the intoxication of Fortunato had in a great measure worn off. The earliest indication I had of this was a low moaning cry from the depth of the recess. It was *not* the cry of a drunken man. There was then a long and obstinate silence. I laid the second tier, and the third, and the fourth; and then I heard the furious vibrations of the chain. The noise lasted for several minutes, during which, that I might hearken to it with the more satisfaction, I ceased my labours and sat down upon the bones. When at last the clanking subsided, I resumed the trowel, and finished without interruption the fifth, the sixth, and the seventh tier. The wall was now nearly upon a level with my breast. I again paused, and holding the flambeaux over the mason-work, threw a few feeble rays upon the figure within.

77   A succession of loud and shrill screams, bursting suddenly from the throat of the chained form, seemed to thrust me violently back. For a brief moment I hesitated—I trembled. Unsheathing my rapier, I began to grope with it about the recess; but the thought of an instant reassured me. I placed my hand upon the solid fabric of the catacombs, and felt satisfied. I reapproached the wall. I replied to the yells of him who clamoured. I reechoed—I aided—I surpassed them in volume and in strength. I did this, and the clamourer grew still.

78   It was now midnight, and my task was drawing to a close. I had completed the eighth, the ninth, and the tenth tier. I had finished a portion of the last and the eleventh; there remained but a single stone to be fitted and plastered in. I struggled with its weight; I placed it partially in its destined position. But now there came from out the niche a low laugh that erected the hairs upon my head. It was succeeded by a sad voice, which I had difficulty in recognising as that of the noble Fortunato. The voice said—

79   "Ha! ha! ha!—he! he! he!—a very good joke indeed—an excellent jest. We will have many a rich laugh about it at the palazzo—he! he! he!—over our wine—he! he! he!"

80   "The Amontillado!" I said.

81   "He! he! he!—he! he! he!—yes, the Amontillado. But is it not getting late? Will not they be awaiting us at the palazzo, the Lady Fortunato and the rest? Let us be gone."

82   "Yes," I said "let us be gone."

83   *"For the love of God, Montresor!"*

84   "Yes," I said, "for the love of God!"

85   But to these words I hearkened in vain for a reply. I grew impatient. I called aloud—

86   "Fortunato!"

87   No answer. I called again—

88   "Fortunato!"

89   No answer still. I thrust a torch through the remaining aperture and let it fall within. There came forth in return only a jingling of the bells. My heart grew sick; it was the dampness of the catacombs that made it so. I hastened

to make an end of my labour. I forced the last stone into its position; I plastered it up. Against the new masonry I re-erected the old rampart of bones. For the half of a century no mortal has disturbed them. *In pace requiescat!*

[Edgar Allan Poe, 1846]

Discussion and Writing Topics

1. Explain how Montresor has gotten away with committing a murder. What precautions has he taken? How is the setting of Carnival important?
2. How does Montresor's knowledge of human behaviour contribute to the success of his crime?
3. Montresor is confessing his crime to his priest, 50 years after committing it. Why? What is the value of confession?
4. Explain how this story works as a successful horror story. What are the elements that it has in common with other stories in the genre?
5. Explain how the first-person narrative point of view makes this telling of the tale effective.
6. Is revenge the same as justice? Is vengeance ever a good motive for murder? Explain your point of view.

Sample Annotated Essays

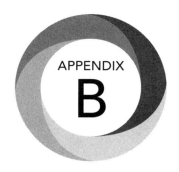

APPENDIX

B

These essays illustrate some of the do's and don'ts discussed in this book. Each essay has two versions—one that is done poorly and another that is well written. The notes point out features that have been explained in this text. MLA style is used for these essays. You can see a sample APA essay on page 138.

Topic Question #1:

Environmentalists exhort people to give up driving their pollution-spewing personal vehicles. However, giving up cars entirely is impractical in Canada. How can Canadians continue to use their cars but be kinder to the environment?

Essay 1A ("Don't" Essay):

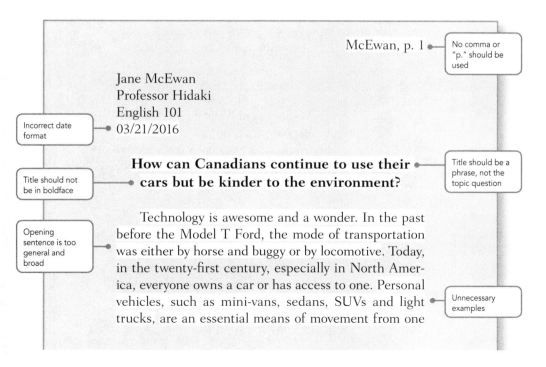

McEwan, p. 1 ← No comma or "p." should be used

Jane McEwan
Professor Hidaki
English 101
03/21/2016 ← Incorrect date format

How can Canadians continue to use their cars but be kinder to the environment?

← Title should be a phrase, not the topic question

← Title should not be in boldface

Technology is awesome and a wonder. In the past before the Model T Ford, the mode of transportation was either by horse and buggy or by locomotive. Today, in the twenty-first century, especially in North America, everyone owns a car or has access to one. Personal vehicles, such as mini-vans, sedans, SUVs and light trucks, are an essential means of movement from one

← Opening sentence is too general and broad

← Unnecessary examples

Wordy

place to another, no matter the distance, whether across the province, across town or from house to the nearest mall in Canada. The distances are vast: from coast to coast Canada is over 8,000 kilometres. Furthermore, the weather is harsh: in winter storms paralyze highways, and the temperature can drop to minus 40 Celsius including wind chill factor and the only places well served by public transit are urban centres. However, motorized vehicles are a huge polluter, spewing toxic exhaust and other pollutants into the air. With all these

Too much unnecessary detail

Statement does not follow logically

Informal usage and switch in pronoun

problems you have to wonder why concerned Canadians would not give up the car. But Canadians do not have to give up the convenience of their vehicles. They can still own cars but cut down on their use. They can also make sure that they drive vehicles that use less gas. Finally, they can make sure that they have responsible driving habits, for both safety and efficiency.

Introduction is too long—it should be shorter than the body paragraphs

Four-sentence thesis should be re-written to make one concise statement

Paragraph is off topic; it's a rant rather than a reasoned argument

Canadians are too lazy. They use their cars to go only a few blocks. They don't like to walk or bike. They think buses are too slow and too crowded. They want everything quick and convenient and don't want to work for anything. That's why the country is in such a mess. We need leaders who tell them what's best for them.

Canadians should buy electric cars to save on gas. Electric cars just have to be plugged in. They don't need gas. Electric cars have come a long way, and they are much better to use now than they used to be.

Paragraph is far too short and undeveloped; the writer should have started with a more general statement and used the electric cars as an example

Topic sentence should focus on the solution, not the problem

Driving a vehicle produces poisonous gas and uses up non-renewable resources. Canadians can also be environmentally conscious by adopting smart driving habits. Drivers have to educate themselves on the environmental impact of what they do behind the wheel.

Points need to be supported—what are smart driving habits?

Conclusion just repeats the main points of the essay—too much summarizing for a short essay

To reduce harm to the environment, people don't have to get rid of their personal vehicles altogether. Instead, they can choose to drive smaller, more fuel-efficient vehicles. They can limit how much they use their cars—using them only when necessary. Finally, they can adopt driving habits which burn less gas.

Essay 1B ("Do" Essay):

McEwan 1

Jane McEwan
Professor Hidaki
English 101
21 March 2016

Using Cars Wisely

Personal vehicles are an essential means of transportation in Canada. The distances are vast, the weather is harsh, and the only places well-served by public transit are urban centres. However, cars are a major polluter, spewing toxic exhaust into the air. Without entirely giving up the convenience of their vehicles, Canadians can use them wisely by limiting trips, using fuel-efficient cars, and driving responsibly.

Canadians should only use their vehicles when absolutely necessary. If they can carpool or commute to work by transit, they should leave their cars at home. When running errands, they can combine trips to reduce the total distance travelled. Instead of driving to the corner store or to visit the neighbour, they can walk or ride a bicycle. Before automatically getting into the car and adding to the pollution, Canadians should think twice and decide whether the trip has to be made by car.

Choosing to drive a more fuel-efficient vehicle is another option. While hybrids, bio-diesel and electric cars are touted as the most environmentally friendly choices, they are expensive vehicles. Canadians can also scale down to smaller cars rather than gas-guzzling SUVs. Four-cylinder compact cars use much less gas. Some drivers can even get by with a Smart car or a Vespa for urban use. Even if they are forced to use a van or truck, drivers can improve fuel efficiency by maintaining their vehicle with frequent tune-ups and by keeping tires properly inflated. Even reducing the amount of junk carried in the trunk can save gas.

Annotations:

- MLA pagination format: student's last name and page number formatted as header in right top corner

- Phrase used as title

- Introduction leads to thesis statement, which comes at the end of the paragraph

- One-sentence thesis statement with parallel structure

- Topic sentence introduces the first idea—when people should drive

- Gives specific examples

- This paragraph does have a concluding sentence, but it is not one that repeats the topic sentence

- Acknowledges that not everyone can go get one of the new environmentally friendly alternatives

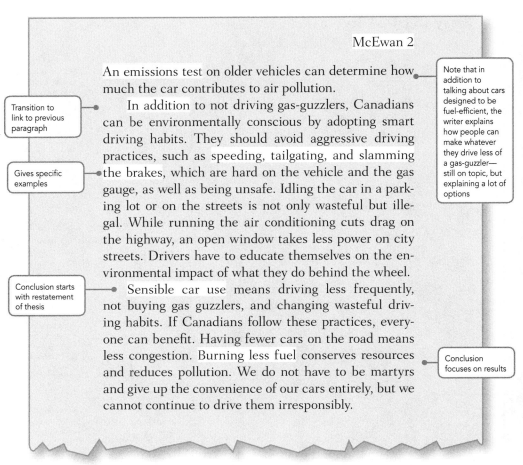

McEwan 2

An emissions test on older vehicles can determine how much the car contributes to air pollution.

In addition to not driving gas-guzzlers, Canadians can be environmentally conscious by adopting smart driving habits. They should avoid aggressive driving practices, such as speeding, tailgating, and slamming the brakes, which are hard on the vehicle and the gas gauge, as well as being unsafe. Idling the car in a parking lot or on the streets is not only wasteful but illegal. While running the air conditioning cuts drag on the highway, an open window takes less power on city streets. Drivers have to educate themselves on the environmental impact of what they do behind the wheel.

Sensible car use means driving less frequently, not buying gas guzzlers, and changing wasteful driving habits. If Canadians follow these practices, everyone can benefit. Having fewer cars on the road means less congestion. Burning less fuel conserves resources and reduces pollution. We do not have to be martyrs and give up the convenience of our cars entirely, but we cannot continue to drive them irresponsibly.

Annotations:
- Transition to link to previous paragraph
- Gives specific examples
- Conclusion starts with restatement of thesis
- Note that in addition to talking about cars designed to be fuel-efficient, the writer explains how people can make whatever they drive less of a gas-guzzler—still on topic, but explaining a lot of options
- Conclusion focuses on results

Topic Question #2

Topic question: Compare the prologue and Act 1, Scene 1, of Shakespeare's *Romeo and Juliet* with Baz Luhrmann's film version.

Essay 2A ("Don't" Essay):

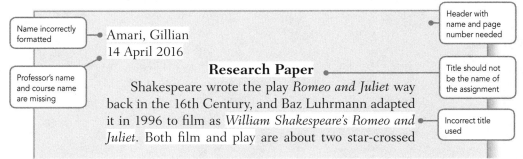

Amari, Gillian
14 April 2016

Research Paper

Shakespeare wrote the play *Romeo and Juliet* way back in the 16th Century, and Baz Luhrmann adapted it in 1996 to film as *William Shakespeare's Romeo and Juliet*. Both film and play are about two star-crossed

Annotations:
- Name incorrectly formatted
- Professor's name and course name are missing
- Header with name and page number needed
- Title should not be the name of the assignment
- Incorrect title used

lovers from different families in the same town, the Capulets and Montagues, who have hated each other for generations and become the cause of the deaths of their favourite children, Romeo and Juliet, who commit suicide tragically. Although both Shakespeare and Luhrmann tell the same story, there are many similarities and differences. However, due to length restrictions for this paper, my professor encouraged me to stop listing and checking off major and minor stuff and concentrate only on the important stuff. And boy has the film director changed Shakespeare's Prologue and Scene 1 of Act 1.

In the play, a chorus comes on the stage and gives a prologue, or a preview of things to come. He sets the scene, which is Verona, Italy, and quickly tells the audience about the two feuding families, the Montagues and the Capulets with their ancient grudge. He gives away the ending by saying that Romeo and Juliet will commit suicide by the end of the play. And their deaths will end the feud forever. Moreover, the chorus says that this tragedy will be a "two hours traffic." (Harrison, 474) Then the story unfolds but not with the main characters but with minor characters, those belonging to the different factions. Sampson and Gregory, both Capulet servants, mock Abraham and Balthasar of the Montague faction with sexual jokes. Benvolio of the Montague clan tries to stop the fight and bring peace, but Tybalt of the Capulets enters the fray and starts swordplay with Benvolio, wanting to kill him then and there. Then the peace officers of Verona appear and try to stop the two sides. Before you know it, the fathers of the Montague and Capulet families show up and want to kill each other, only to be prevented by their wives. The Prince of Verona, Escalus by name, makes the proclamation that since these two feuding families have disturbed the quiet of the streets of Verona at least three times, he will have no more of it: "If ever you disturb our streets again, Your lives

Annotations (left margin):

- Uses a "nothing phrase" as filler ("there are many similarities and differences")
- Inadequate detail for a thesis
- Topic sentence does not set up comparison
- Improper in-text citation—comma not used in MLA, and period should be after the parentheses, not after traffic
- Avoid stretching out a piece of information

Annotations (right margin):

- Conversational expressions used (*way back, stuff, boy*)
- Retelling the action; no analysis or comparison
- Colloquial style
- Improper quoting of verse passages

shall pay the forfeit of the peace" (*Romeo and Juliet*, 475). Then he departs and we are left with the Montagues. It seems that Mr and Mrs Montague are worried that Romeo might have been in the fight, but, learning from Benvolio that he wasn't, now they want to know what the teenager is up to. It seems that Romeo is lost in love with a girl named Rosaline. Benvolio advises him to forget about infatuation and love, but Romeo says he can't. Thus we have the setting and the plot laid out, and finally the introduction of the main character in Act 1, Scene 1.

In the film adaptation, Baz Luhrmann, the director, both follows Shakespeare's script and makes a lot of changes. The scene opens with a black female reporter on TV commenting on the two feuding families, all the while there are images of chaos and destruction caused by members of the two families. "In an explosion of with-it technocontrivance, the play's opening prologue becomes headlines splashed across newspapers, magazines, or words, uttered by a television news anchor. This montage of newspaper clippings and magazine mug shots of the Capulets and Montagues become the available means to contemporise and adapt the old feudal world into a glib, psychedelic one" (http://go.galegroup.com). The verses are the same as Shakespeare's and the accompanying pictures on the TV monitor underscore that the members of the Montague and Capulet families are gangsters and criminal types as both sides are armed to the teeth with automatic pistols.

The opening scene itself gives us a preview of the pastiche created out of the "cinema violence: the Western, the gangster movie, the kung-fu pic, the urban drama, the crime thriller and the action comedy." (Anwar)

Down on the mean streets of fair Verona, we see reckless driving of fancy cars by the Montague members.

Annotations:

- Improper MLA citation
- The qualifying opening "it seems" in both sentences shows that the writer is unsure of the information she is stating
- No comparison; throughout, no mention of the film
- Topic sentence introduces the film alone—no comparison given
- No URL as in-text citation; quotation does not quite fit
- No real comparison; no explanation of changes, only pointing out
- Quotation not relevant to the point made above
- No need to include "we"; colloquial shift in focus

Luhrmann shows which side is which by having focused shots of licence plates with Capulet or Montague on the automobiles and by showing the butt of automatic pistols with family insignias. Moreover, the appearance of the two factions differ: the Capulets wear darker clothing and sport tattoos and ear piercings, whereas the Montague guys are into colourful T-shirts and dyed hair. The rapid cuts from one faction to the other emphasize not only differences between the Montagues and Capulets but also the impending violence. Luhrmann makes some significant changes in that the Capulet hoodlums want violence and the Montague gangsters are more buffoonlike—and seemingly more likable. Benvolio of the Montagues like in the play tries to end the quarrel by quoting mismatched Shakespeare verse. Benvolio tells his men to "put up your swords" when they are pointing pistols. Luhrmann gives a momentary freeze frame of an automatic pistol with the engravure of "Sword 9 mm" to overcome this problem. With the ominous appearance of Tybalt in black clothing and with weapon drawn (Rapier 9 mm), his lines of "What, drawn, and talk of peace! I hate the word As I hate Hell, all Montagues, and thee" (Act 1, Scene 1, lines 77–78). Tybalt shoots the gun from Benvolio's hand and the latter runs away in the midst of a traffic jam of cars. It seems that coincidentally both heads of the two families riding in cars are at this skirmish, and they too wish to participate in the fight. Both men go for their guns/swords but are prevented by their respective wives. Quickly a police helicopter with officers in SWAT uniform and automatic rifles appear to stop the shoot-out. Captain Prince comes forth and lays down the law for the two capos. The feuding families have disturbed the streets of Verona three times and the next time they will have to pay for the "forfeit of the peace" with their lives. This pronouncement is rather curious because the captain of the police in Florida or anywhere in the United States of America does not

Annotations:

Basically retelling the action, no comparison

No comparison, merely pointing out a difference

Does not explain relevance of the colour black, becomes mere minor detail

Too many minor details here

Slang, informal style

Improper citation of verse

Wordy writing

Interesting point but not relevant

Avoid colloquial tone

Informal style

Minor point tossed in, no development or analysis

Criticism too late

There should be a page break before the list of references.

Citations should not be numbered

Improper conclusion; all the similarities finally made, too late—they should have been made in the body of the essay

Weak concluding statement, and in informal English

Incorrect title for Works Cited page

have the right to threaten much less impose such a penalty without due process. This shows that following Shakespeare's lines does not always work in modern adaptations. Anyway, we are left with the Montague family and both parents question Benvolio about their absent son, Romeo. Benvolio assures them that Romeo was not in the fray and that he will find out what is the matter with the boy. He meets the distracted Romeo, who is head over heels in love with a girl named Rosaline. The love-struck lad cares for nothing but the thoughts of love. So ends the first scene of Act one.

As you can see, there are a lot of similarities and differences in Shakespeare's and Luhrmann's versions of the two star-crossed lovers. Both are set in a town named Verona—the playwright's is in Italy and the film's in America. Both have the same words spoken in the Prologue, except that one is done on stage and the other done by an anchor on TV. Both show the length and breadth of the two families' hatred of one another through their servants and associates: they are committed to quarrelling, fighting, and killing. Both show that nothing can stop the feud, not even peace officers of the town, not even the threat of death. And finally both end the scene with the appearance of a young and naively in love Romeo. However, there are also changes. The updating of the times requires alterations. In Shakespeare, the feuding members use swords, whereas in Luhrmann, they have automatic pistols. Instead of unruly servants, the film has rival gang members. Moreover, the parents have given names: Ted and Caroline Montague, and Fulgencio and Gloria Capulet. However, what is most difficult to digest is Shakespearean dialogue in contemporary 1996 United States. Who talks like that!

Bibliography

1. Luhrmann, Baz. (dir.) *William Shakespeare's Romeo + Juliet*. 20th Century Fox. 1996.

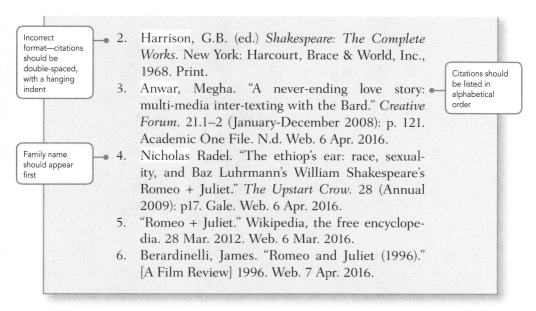

Incorrect format—citations should be double-spaced, with a hanging indent

Citations should be listed in alphabetical order

Family name should appear first

2. Harrison, G.B. (ed.) *Shakespeare: The Complete Works*. New York: Harcourt, Brace & World, Inc., 1968. Print.

3. Anwar, Megha. "A never-ending love story: multi-media inter-texting with the Bard." *Creative Forum*. 21.1–2 (January-December 2008): p. 121. Academic One File. N.d. Web. 6 Apr. 2016.

4. Nicholas Radel. "The ethiop's ear: race, sexuality, and Baz Luhrmann's William Shakespeare's Romeo + Juliet." *The Upstart Crow*. 28 (Annual 2009): p17. Gale. Web. 6 Apr. 2016.

5. "Romeo + Juliet." Wikipedia, the free encyclopedia. 28 Mar. 2012. Web. 6 Mar. 2016.

6. Berardinelli, James. "Romeo and Juliet (1996)." [A Film Review] 1996. Web. 7 Apr. 2016.

Essay 2B ("Do" Essay):

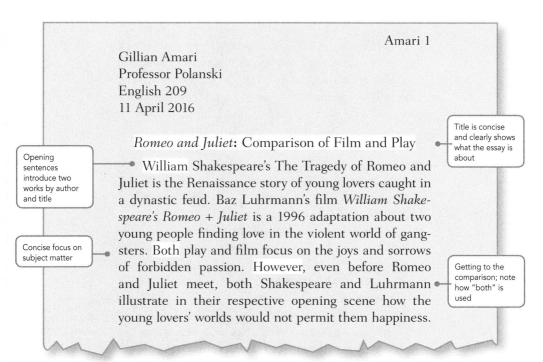

Amari 1

Gillian Amari
Professor Polanski
English 209
11 April 2016

Romeo and Juliet: Comparison of Film and Play

Title is concise and clearly shows what the essay is about

Opening sentences introduce two works by author and title

William Shakespeare's The Tragedy of Romeo and Juliet is the Renaissance story of young lovers caught in a dynastic feud. Baz Luhrmann's film *William Shakespeare's Romeo + Juliet* is a 1996 adaptation about two young people finding love in the violent world of gangsters. Both play and film focus on the joys and sorrows of forbidden passion. However, even before Romeo and Juliet meet, both Shakespeare and Luhrmann illustrate in their respective opening scene how the young lovers' worlds would not permit them happiness.

Concise focus on subject matter

Getting to the comparison; note how "both" is used

Amari 2

[Shows how topic is limited] The Prologue and Act I, Scene 1 then set the stage for the drama and for the changes in presentation: the setting, the violence and the tragic conditions. **[One-sentence thesis statement, showing common elements to be compared]**

[Commonality in play and film] Both play and film set the location of the tragedy in Verona. Shakespeare's setting is fifteenth- or sixteenth-century Verona, Italy, an actual geographical place. Luhrmann's is the late twentieth-century Verona Beach, **[Difference shown]** a made-up city in the United States of America. The city is important because both Prologues address specifically where the action will be played out:

[Cited passage indented: MLA style] Chorus: Two households, both alike in dignity,
In fair Verona, where we lay our scene. (1.1.1–2) **[Proper verse citation following cited passage]**

[Conjunctive adverb signals a change in focus to the differences; followed by explanation] However, the delivery has changed. Because of the times and the stage, Shakespeare has a Chorus coming forth and laying the scene for the star-crossed lovers. Luhrmann drastically alters the male Chorus: he has a female anchor on television speak the lines. Moreover, the anchorwoman is black, and this innovative tweaking helps in the blind casting of actors with Hispanic and African heritage along with those who are Caucasian. (Shakespeare had to do with just white English players.) Whereas the words of the Chorus engage the imagination of the theatre audience, the modern version relies on visual, fast cuts of news items reflecting the discord caused by the two families, the Capulets **[Reminds reader reason for opening scene]** and the Montagues of Verona Beach. In words or visuals, the setting of the town gives an ominous foreboding for the young lovers.

In Verona, the atmosphere of violence is palpable: on the street of the Renaissance town or at a gas station in the modern one, Shakespeare and Luhrmann show how quickly a minor incident may change into a deadly one. Megha Anwar observes: **[Writer of following passage identified]**

The opening scene itself gives us a preview of the pastiche created out of the "cinema violence: the Western, the gangster movie, the kung-fu

Amari 3

pic, the urban drama, the crime thriller and the action comedy." The scene of the "brawl" draws upon all the tropes of the above mentioned genres pistol drawing, car racing, and petrol-pump gutting sequences, sprinkled with humour, suspense and genuine fear.

Inciting insult and violence, the servants of the two families make sexual innuendoes at one another. In the film, at the gas station, the Montague gang members mock their Capulet rivals with a thumb in the teeth (while speaking Shakespearean dialogue). For this insult, the Capulet members respond first in kind but then quickly the mockery turns deadly. In the play, rapiers are drawn; in the movie, sidearms—automatic pistols with the inscription of "Sword 9 mm" or "Rapier 9 mm"—come out of holsters. (Luhrmann ingeniously adds this touch of guns being called swords so that Shakespeare's verse need not be changed drastically.) Cooler heads do not prevail:

> Ben. Part, fools! [*Beating down their weapons.*]
> Put up your swords. You know not what you
> do. (1.1.71–72)

Whether swords or guns are used, the standoff between rival gangs turns lethal. Benvolio of the Montague clan has little chance to diffuse the incident. In later scenes, in both the play and the film, the situations repeat with predictable results.

What starts out as scurrilous humour in which rival members taunt one another becomes deadly. This is especially true when Tybalt from the Capulet household appears. He cannot be appeased; he desires blood, pain and death (1.1.77–78). In both play and film, Benvolio cannot placate Tybalt, and a melee ensues. The disruption is so great that Prince Escalus or Captain Prince and his men must impose the peace.

[Margin annotations:]

Similarity of incident but a contrast of how it is done

Parenthesis explains why

Repeats relevance of the opening scenes to the following tragic sequences

Paraphrased reference rather than quoting the verses

Quick illustration of differences of names

Amari 4

Reminds reader of tragic consequences

Here again the audience is left with the feeling that the young lovers will be also caught in the unending feud. Shakespeare and Luhrmann draw out the tragic conditions. Death and destruction is foreshadowed by law and by the feuding parents. Prince Escalus or Captain Prince is angry and frustrated with the chaos wrought by the Montagues and the Capulets. In play and film, he too adds to the threat of violence and death:

> Three civil brawls, bred of an airy word,
> By thee, old Capulet and Montague,
> Have thrice disturbed the quiet of our streets . . .
> If ever you disturb our streets again,
> Your lives shall pay the forfeit of the peace.
> (1.1. 96–98; 103–104)

Ellipsis to show entire passage not quoted

Moments earlier, in illustrating the fast pace of the fight, Luhrmann has cars careening, guns shooting indiscriminately, and dialogue spoken as rapidly as machine pistols. The citizens of Verona Beach are trapped in a traffic jam as hooligans from both sides either run away or give chase amongst the innocent bystanders.

Longer explanation of Luhrmann's technique

Moreover, Luhrmann's quick cuts and snap frames add to the disorder. Even the old patriarchs are seen grabbing for their "swords" in limousines. In both play and film then, playwright and film director make it clear that the young lovers are "star-crossed": they have little chance for love in a world filled with hate, tinderbox tempers, and impending death.

Citing titles in full signals conclusion

In *The Tragedy of Romeo and Juliet* and *William Shakespeare's Romeo + Juliet,* Shakespeare and Luhrmann respectively demonstrate the difficulty that young lovers will have in a society where feuding families destroy both a chance at peace and at love. Luhrmann takes Shakespeare's sixteenth century into the late twentieth century and retains the violence and

Amari 5

impending tragedy. From swords to guns, from foot to flashy cars, from household livery to gangsta fashion, the film director updates time, place, and atmosphere but still captures the playwright's "death-marked love" in the opening sequence.

> Reminds reader of differences with quick explanation

Amari 6

> Proper MLA format used for references

Works Cited

Anwar, Megha. "A Never-Ending Love Story: Multi-Media Inter-Texting with the Bard." *Creative Forum*, vol. 21, no. 1–2, January–December 2008, p. 121. www.questia.com/read/1G1-258600224/a-never-ending-love-story-multi-media-inter-texting. Accessed 6 Apr. 2016.

Berardinelli, James. "Romeo and Juliet (1996)." www.reelviews.net, 1996. Accessed 7 Apr. 2016.

Harrison, G.B., editor. *Shakespeare: The Complete Works*. Harcourt, Brace & World, Inc., 1968.

Luhrmann, Baz, director. *William Shakespeare's Romeo + Juliet*. Performances by Leonardo DiCaprio and Claire Danes, 20th Century Fox, 1996.

Radel, Nicholas. "The Ethiop's Ear: Race, Sexuality, and Baz Luhrmann's *William Shakespeare's Romeo + Juliet*." *The Upstart Crow*, vol. 28, 2009), p. 17. www.thefreelibrary.com/The+ethiop's+ear%3A+race,+sexuality,+and+Baz+Luhrmann's+William . . . -a 0219520117 Accessed 6 Apr. 2016.

"Romeo + Juliet." *Wikipedia, the Free Encyclopedia*, 28 Mar. 2016, www.wikipedia.org. Accessed 6 Apr. 2016.

Answer Key

Exercise 1.1: Conversational to academic English

1. Colleges focus more on vocational skills than universities do. For example, would-be chefs can learn hands-on skills in a community college. Education in the trades can lead to well-paid jobs.
2. Even though educators insist that attendance is important, students skip classes. They may find the material dull or repetitious. Attendance also depends on class scheduling: students may miss classes if they do not want to get up early, if they want to stretch out their weekend, or if they do not want to come to campus for only one class.
3. Today's children do not know the playground games their parents played. For instance, they do not know traditional skipping chants, so it is a loss of our culture.

Exercise 2.1: Writing thesis statements

1. Essay writing has three main stages—planning, drafting, and editing.
2. Students graduate from high school without adequate reading and writing skills because of the decline of reading, literacy, and practice.
3. Overly strict parenting can lead to dependence, rebellion, and lack of freedom.
4. In *Hamlet*, Shakespeare creates a complicated tragic hero, who cannot make up his mind, pretends to be mad, and has unresolved mother issues.
5. Exercise can be easily incorporated into everyday life—in transportation, household chores, and leisure activities.

Exercise 2.2: Writing titles

1. Essay Writing in Stages
2. Why High-School Graduates Lack Literacy Skills
3. Effects of Over-Protective Parenting
4. Hamlet as Tragic Hero
5. Exercise for Everyday Life

Exercise 2.3: Supporting statements

Here are some ideas that could be found in supporting statements:

1. Finding a job is hard work.
   Explanation: just sending off resumés is not enough.
   Examples: job candidates have to go and talk to people, make connections, call, do work as a volunteer or intern.
2. Video games allow students to develop practical skills.
   Examples: making quick judgments based on observation, hand–eye coordination, strategy.
3. Cooking home-made meals serves more than a nutritional function; it also has social benefits.
   Examples: inviting someone for a home-cooked meal or contributing to a pot-luck shows that the cook cares and has skills; immigrants keep their culture through food and like to share it with others; a person who is dating someone can really impress that person.
4. People can use different techniques to reduce their addiction to their smartphones.
   Examples: they can make a "no phones" rule at mealtime; they can keep their phone on mute; they can reduce the number of times they look at their phones.
5. Extracurricular activities in high school help keep at-risk students from dropping out.
   Explanation: students who are struggling at school will keep going to class if it means they can participate in activities they love, such as sports, drama, art, or music; these activities can often teach them skills which help in their schoolwork (e.g., music requires discipline and paying attention—skills that are important in school).
6. Star professional athletes have various reasons for demanding multi-million dollar contracts.
   Explanation: the amount of money they get has prestige value—the best players receive the highest salaries; their work career is relatively short so they want money for their retirement.
7. People can learn a new language outside the classroom.
   Examples: they can use language-learning software, travel, watch television, move to where they are forced to speak the language, and read books in the language.

Exercise 2.4: Using transition signals

1. The team did not make a plan to divide up the work. Consequently/As a result, they got in each other's way and did not accomplish much.
2. First, gambling addicts must recognize that they have a problem. Then, they must seek help.

3. Schoolyard skipping games have many benefits beyond aerobic exercise. <u>For example</u>, they teach children the rhythm of traditional chants. <u>In addition</u>, children play together cooperatively.

4. The students were supposed to do the project together in their study groups. <u>However</u>, so many students dropped the course that the groups had to be reorganized before the work could proceed. <u>Consequently/Moreover</u>, the instructor had to extend the time allotted for the group presentations.

5. Writing a shopping list helps someone remember the items even if the list is forgotten at home. <u>Similarly/In the same way</u>, taking notes in class helps students remember the information given in the lecture even if they never read them again.

6. People demand lower taxes. <u>On the other hand</u>, they complain about the lack of services and facilities, not seeing the connection between what they pay and what they get for the money. <u>Therefore</u>, politicians find it impossible to satisfy voters.

Exercise 3.1: Personal vs. impersonal essay

1. How have you benefitted from the volunteer work you have done? (personal)
   How do students benefit from doing volunteer work?

2. Why are horror movies so popular among young people? (impersonal)
   Do you enjoy watching horror movies? Explain why or why not.

3. Discuss the popularity of veganism. Is this a legitimate food movement or a bizarre fad? (impersonal)
   Are you a vegan, or would you consider becoming a vegan? Explain why or why not.

4. How could your high-school education have prepared you better for post-secondary studies? (personal)
   How could high-school studies better prepare students for post-secondary studies?

5. Would you eat meat from animals such as dogs, cats, horses, and rabbits? Explain why or why not. (personal)
   Should meat from animals such as dogs, cats, horses, and rabbits be eaten? Explain why or why not.

Exercise 3.2: Good argument or bad?

Most of these examples are weak arguments; only #6 is workable. The reasons and logical fallacies are given below.

1. Contradiction: you cannot have more roads without construction.
2. Appeal to false authority: celebrities are not experts on shoes.
3. Hasty generalization, stereotyping, or overstatement: the assumption is that all women all over the world need male protection, and that is simply not true or valid.

4. Appeal to fear, or faulty cause–effect: the strategy is to frighten the audience into a certain action or belief.
5. False comparison: the writer is misleading by only giving superficial similarities while hiding the many serious differences.
6. A workable argument: each of the points is related to the topic. Note that the statement is about people needing to cook, not about what they actually do.
7. Hasty generalization: text messaging is not the only culprit for problems in essay writing, nor are essay problems only related to basic spelling.
8. Hasty generalization: this does not apply to all children who play video games.
9. Overstatement, or hasty generalization: technology may hasten communication but in the past people could still communicate with one another—it just took longer for messages to arrive.
10. Faulty cause–effect or connection: because the student succeeded in the past, he or she assumes the same outcome in the present.

Exercise 4.1: Paraphrasing

Here are some example paraphrases:

1. Online gambling will be tempting to addicted gamblers and perhaps to some who want to try the games.
2. People should not dismiss privacy concerns by thinking that only people who have done wrong will be exposed.
3. Students often manage to get around whatever measures are used to limit the use of the devices to educational purposes.
4. It seemed that Moose was determined to punish Cecil for his resistance when the other lumberjacks stopped hazing the newcomer.
5. People show only what they choose to on social media.
6. Montresor instructed his servants to remain in his palace while he was away; however, he knew they would all abandon their duties and leave for the festival once he departed.

Exercise 4.2: Editing for conciseness

Reduction to 88 words:
In "We All Should Worry about Cellphone Searches," William Kowalski warns about unwarranted digital invasions by the police. The Supreme Court ruled that the police can go through cellphones. However, cellphones today contain private information that could be misused. Not only do criminals have to worry about this intrusion, but also innocent people are at risk. If the police think someone is suspicious, they can go through that person's phone. People can limit such intrusions into their private lives, but Canada should not allow such invasions of privacy.

Exercise 6.1: Review of parts of speech

1. Richard, noun; see, verb; doctor, noun; sore, adjective; tiredness, noun; told, verb; unhealthy, adjective; advised, verb; quit, verb [infinitive form]; exercise, noun; stressful, adjective
2. band, noun; diligently, adverb; week, noun; were, verb; ceremonies, noun; new, adjective
3. leader, noun; was chosen, verb; charismatic, adjective; hopes, noun; re-election, noun; power, noun; enthusiastically, adverb; endorsed, verb; selection, noun
4. Canada, noun; new, adjective; piece, noun; polymer, noun; clear, adjective; Metallic, adjective; seen, verb; windows, noun; light, noun; make, verb; difficult, adjective; counterfeiters, noun
5. Graphic, adjective; comics, noun; Generally, adverb; themes, noun; tell, verb; complicated, adjective; prefer, verb; images, noun

Exercise 6.2: Find derivatives

	Noun	Verb	Adjective	Adverb
	success	*succeed*	*successful*	*successfully*
1	*beauty*	beautify	beautiful	beautifully
2	caution	*caution*	cautious cautionary	cautiously
3	*danger*	endanger	dangerous endangered	dangerously
4	equalization	equalize	equal	*equally*
5	*falsehood*	falsify	false	falsely
6	height	heighten	*high*	highly
7	infection	*infect*	infectious	infectiously
8	minimum	minimize	*minimal*	minimally
9	person	personalize	*personal*	personally
10	safety	save	safe	*safely*
11	*specialty*	specialize	special	specially
12	stability	stabilize	*stable*	—

Exercise 6.3: Using prefixes to show the opposite meaning

1) illegible; 2) dislike; 3) uncomfortable; 4) atypical; 5) unfriendly; 6) inactive; 7) disagree; 8) ungrateful; 9) impassive; 10) mishandle

Exercise 6.4: Complete the collocations

1. It was a <u>covert</u> operation, carried out with <u>meticulous</u> attention to <u>detail</u>. No one saw it coming.
2. They must have a <u>hidden</u> agenda. They spent a <u>substantial</u> amount of money on a project most of the researchers saw as a complete <u>waste</u> of time.
3. He made an <u>emotional</u> appeal as to why he deserved the <u>break</u>, but I could tell Isabel was not convinced. She wanted to <u>throw</u> the book at him.
4. I was asked to <u>submit</u> a claim with an <u>itemized</u> list of expenses in order to get my refund.
5. I do not know him <u>well</u> enough to ask him to do me a <u>favour</u>. He is just a <u>casual</u> acquaintance.

Exercise 6.5: Find synonyms

Here are some possible word changes:

1. The new proposal puts the <u>supervisor/administrator/boss</u> in a <u>bind/dilemma</u>. She has already <u>earmarked/budgeted/assigned/allotted</u> the <u>assets/funds</u> and <u>employed/engaged</u> the <u>staff/workers</u>. However, the <u>alternate</u> <u>plan/proposition</u> is such a good idea that she is <u>considering/debating</u> adopting it even though it will <u>hold up/impede</u> the start of the <u>work/undertaking/enterprise</u>. Even with the <u>postponement/setback</u>, the company can save money in the long run.
2. City life often <u>means/necessitates</u> getting used to a variety of sounds. From the street come the <u>din</u> of construction, the <u>racket</u> of transit, and the <u>blare/screams</u> of sirens. Those <u>unfortunate</u> enough to have an apartment with thin walls may hear the <u>noises</u> from of their neighbours: the <u>thump</u> of footsteps, the <u>blare</u> of music, and the <u>murmur</u> of voices.

Exercise 6.6: Check your spelling

1. Is the meeting time <u>convenient</u> for you? We could change it to <u>accommodate</u> your <u>schedule</u> if <u>you're</u> going to have trouble <u>making</u> it. The <u>committee</u> will <u>develop</u> the criteria for the evaluation. Once you <u>receive</u> them, you can see <u>whether</u> they <u>fulfill</u> your <u>expectations</u>. I expect we will be able to reach a <u>consensus</u> <u>eventually</u>. [13]
2. The <u>professor</u> told his students that they should <u>have</u> studied more for the exam. He offered extra tutorials for <u>remedial</u> help for those who were struggling with the basic concepts. Some of the students were not <u>grateful</u>. They made the <u>argument</u> that he should just bell <u>curve</u> the marks. Others <u>acknowledged</u> that they needed to <u>improve</u>, and they started <u>studying</u> <u>right</u> away. [10]

3. The <u>writing</u> had <u>a lot</u> of <u>mistakes</u>. It was <u>embarrassing</u> to see that graduates <u>were</u> going to go out in the work world doing work like that. <u>Even though</u> they had talent and skill, <u>their</u> poor writing skills made a bad <u>impression</u>. [8]

Exercise 6.7: Choose the right word

1. I need to order some business <u>stationery</u> for the office. I did not expect to <u>lose</u> a whole box. It should take a <u>week</u> or so.
2. He almost drove <u>past</u> his destination, but he hit the <u>brakes</u> in time. I thought he would go <u>through</u> the red light, <u>too</u>.
3. Camels are the best transportation in the <u>desert</u>, but <u>they're</u> stubborn animals.
4. In a research essay, you have to be careful to <u>cite</u> your references <u>to</u> show exactly <u>where</u> you got the information.
5. She always gives good <u>advice</u>. She does not receive <u>compliments</u> very graciously.
6. Those tours seem to be popular with <u>women</u> travelling alone.

Exercise 6.8: One word or two?

1. He wants to be <u>a part</u> of Howard's project. He does not like working <u>alone</u>. He is <u>all ready</u> to start.
2. It <u>may be</u> time to redo the whole room <u>even though</u> it will cost <u>a lot</u>. They should be able to do most of the work <u>themselves</u>.
3. I only wanted to buy a loaf of bread, but I could not resist the special on brownies at 50 cents <u>apiece</u>. It's not an <u>everyday</u> indulgence.
4. The brothers do not look <u>at all</u> <u>alike</u>.
5. They had to get the rooms <u>all ready</u> for the guests. <u>In spite</u> of the short time they had, they tried to do <u>whatever</u> their mother asked.

Exercise 6.9: Correct word choice

1. She <u>argues</u> that plastic bags are not a huge environmental problem.
2. My car is in the shop because there is a <u>problem</u> with the brakes.
3. In Quebec, I could <u>practise</u> my French.
4. In high school, students are <u>spoon-fed</u> by the teachers.
5. When his passport was <u>stolen</u>, he could not <u>prove</u> his identity.
6. Being able to <u>speak</u> with different <u>people</u> every day, one naturally begins to <u>develop</u> interpersonal skills.

Exercise 7.1: Subjects and predicates

1. <u>Jean</u> <u>changed</u> the ring tone on her phone.
2. The <u>signature</u> on this page <u>looks</u> like a forgery.

3. Watching the game, <u>he</u> again <u>felt</u> the regret of his sports career ending so badly.
4. <u>He</u> <u>has</u> a good poker face.
5. On the back of the painting <u>was</u> a <u>signature</u>.
6. <u>Signing the contract</u> <u>would have meant</u> signing away all his rights to the material.
7. The <u>option</u> with the most leeway <u>would be</u> the best choice.
8. The <u>person</u> who collects the most points <u>wins</u> the game.
9. There <u>are</u> many new <u>features</u> on that phone.
10. <u>Theresa and I</u> <u>went</u> to the concert on Friday.

Exercise 7.2: Verb tense

1. First-year students <u>take</u> a broader range of courses, including English and math, before they <u>specialize</u> in later years. This <u>allows</u> them to have more time before they <u>decide</u> what they <u>want</u> to do and <u>gives</u> them a broader base of knowledge.
2. Last week, we <u>went</u> to see the school production of *Twelfth Night*. As we <u>were watching</u> the play, a drunken spectator <u>started</u> throwing things at the stage. Fortunately, the security guards <u>led</u> him away quickly, and the play <u>continued</u>.
3. In *King Lear*, the father <u>asks</u> his three daughters who <u>loves</u> him the most. Two daughters <u>respond</u> with flattery while the third <u>is</u> reluctant to play the game. The father <u>banishes</u> her because she <u>does</u> not <u>offer</u> empty praise. Later he <u>realizes</u> that she <u>is</u> the most truthful and loving daughter.
   [OR: In *King Lear*, the father <u>asked</u> his three daughters who <u>loved</u> him the most. Two daughters <u>responded</u> with flattery while the third <u>was</u> reluctant to play the game. The father <u>banished</u> her because she <u>did</u> not <u>offer</u> empty praise. Later he <u>realized</u> that she <u>was</u> the most truthful and loving daughter.]

Exercise 7.3: Verb forms

1. The university <u>runs</u> a special intensive language program in the summer. Students <u>come</u> from all over the world to study English and to <u>learn</u> about Canadian culture.
2. They <u>live/are living</u> in the residence where they can <u>meet</u> Canadian students. They are <u>encouraged</u> to eat with the Canadians in the dining hall.
3. Social activities such as movie nights and a weekly soccer game <u>let</u> students <u>mingle</u> and <u>speak</u> English. Students also <u>go</u> on field trips to museums and the theatre.
4. Many students have already <u>benefitted</u> from this program. They have found that learning a second language is not only an important part of education, but it can also <u>be</u> fun.

Exercise 7.4: Passive voice

1. The community centre was torn down and a new one is currently being built.
2. It was designed as a multi-purpose facility serving all members of the community.
3. The centre will be named after the long-time former mayor.
4. The pool will be used by the local swim team for swim meets. The pool is one of the few in the city designed for competitive swimming.
5. The squash team will also be pleased with the new facilities.

Exercise 7.5: Word endings

1. The <u>students'</u> reading <u>assignments</u> were poorly done. The whole class needed an extra <u>class</u>. The instructors had a meeting to <u>schedule</u> the tutorial.
2. The trades <u>offer</u> good jobs. Plumbers can easily make more money than <u>teachers</u> do.
3. The <u>Millers'</u> house is up for sale. It should <u>sell</u> quickly because <u>it's</u> in a good neighbourhood with fine schools and a wide range of recreational <u>facilities</u>.
4. She <u>tries</u> to help the abandoned pets she <u>finds</u> in the <u>fields</u> behind her house.
5. The <u>children's</u> choir is the highlight of this <u>year's</u> Christmas pageant.

Exercise 7.6: Prepositions

1. While he was unemployed, he depended <u>on</u> handouts <u>from</u> his parents. They were happy to help him out because he had helped his nephews <u>with</u> their schooling.
2. <u>In</u> his new book, he describes the customs <u>of</u> the nomads who live <u>in</u> the desert.
3. The students did not participate <u>in</u> the social activities because they were busy playing video games.
4. She expects Jack to finish the project, but she could assign it <u>to</u> someone else.
5. Because he didn't understand financial matters, he depended <u>on</u> John <u>for</u> help.
6. <u>With</u> all the noise, he cannot concentrate <u>on</u> his reading. He went <u>to</u> the library.
7. I applied <u>for</u> the desk job, but James said I wasn't qualified <u>for</u> it and advised me to take some classes <u>at</u> the university.
8. The new bridge will affect the traffic patterns, but we will gain a bike lane.
9. The loss <u>of</u> his bike did not bother him. He always used an old one because the possibility <u>of</u> theft was so high.
10. She never complained <u>about</u> the extra work. She was glad <u>of</u> the opportunity to learn new skills.

Exercise 7.7: Parallel structure

1. To stay healthy, people should eat well, get plenty of exercise, and get enough sleep.
2. In his spare time, he enjoys hiking, watching movies, and doing woodwork.
3. The ingredients of the pasta sauce include Italian sausage, eggplant, red peppers, and canned tomato sauce.
4. The problems of underground economies include the loss of tax revenue, the lack of protection for labour, and the consequent downgrading of the economy.
5. The yoga exercise requires participants to sit with legs crossed, breathe deeply, and think only of their mantra.

Exercise 7.8: Sentence structure

1. Reading the chapter before class helps students understand the lecture better.
2. Although the divorce rate for arranged marriages is low, many couples are unhappy in their relationship.
3. The instructor presented a concept which the students did not understand.
4. Even though the study group worked hard together, only one member passed the bar exams.
5. If it rains tomorrow, the wedding can be moved indoors.

Exercise 7.9: Run-ons and fragments

1. The attack ads offend the viewers and insult their intelligence.
2. Because he drank too much at the wedding, he insulted the hosts.
3. Poseidon wants to avenge the hurt Odysseus caused to his son; he creates a storm to destroy the hero's raft.
4. He writes; she edits. The book that they just finished was nominated for an award.
5. Fewer movies are adult-oriented today. For example, horror films and gross-out comedies are currently running in the theatres.
6. They did not want to get married even though they had lived together for so many years.
7. Wanting to be the first to get the new smartphone, he waited in line all night.
8. Count Dracula first sucks his victims dry of blood, and then he turns them into vampires.

Exercise 8.1: Punctuate and capitalize

1. Parents do not have to feel obliged to pay for their children's university education. If they have the money, they can help their children pay for tuition, but university students are adults and should be responsible for their own schooling. Moreover, they will value their education more if they have

to pay for it themselves, especially if that payment has required sacrifice on their part.

2. I have to change my course schedule. The psychology course I want to take is not offered this semester, but I can finish off my English credits. This course, Introduction to the Canadian Novel, sounds interesting.

3. The students had much more work to do on their oral presentation, so they set up more meeting times. It was difficult to work around everyone's time-tables, but they managed to find some time when everyone was free.

Exercise 8.2: Using apostrophes

1. The children's toys were scattered all over the room.
2. The instructor leaves the last minutes of class for questions.
3. When the going gets tough, the tough get going.
4. The super lets the tenants leave their bikes in the back room.
5. The men's room and the ladies' room needed cleaning.

Exercise 8.3: Correct punctuation

1. The traditional horror tales of vampires, werewolves, and witches are finding new life in popular literature today.
2. Although rain was forecast, the wedding was held outdoors without a problem.
3. Before she could paint the room, she had a lot of prep work to do: emptying the closets, moving the furniture, and cleaning the walls.
4. Elizabeth and Hiro hold the same values even though they were raised in different cultures.
5. I was surprised to hear that she didn't know what the problem was. It's usually a simple case of following the instructions in the manual.

Glossary

abstract Very brief overview of an entire essay or report, usually appearing right after the title page and before the table of contents.

academic style Writing style used for essays; also called formal writing. Different from conversational style in word choice and sentence structure.

active voice Form of the verb in which the grammatical subject does the action of the verb. For example, "Tom <u>took</u> the box" is active; "the box <u>was taken</u>" is passive.

allusion Indirect reference to a person or event.

analogy Comparison. Usually used to explain a complicated or complex idea with a simpler, more understandable one.

antagonist A major character in a story who opposes the hero or heroine. Can be considered the villain.

antecedent The noun that a pronoun refers to. Each use of a pronoun has to have a clear antecedent. For example, "they" must be identifiable as "the students" or whatever noun was used before the pronoun.

anti-hero Main character of a story but one who lacks heroic values or traits. Often used in satire and ironic stories.

antonym Word that means the opposite of another word.

APA style American Psychological Association style. A way to write up references, research source materials, and bibliography for the social sciences.

apostrophe Punctuation mark showing possession or contraction (as in "John's book" or "he can't").

archetype Recognizable character or entity such as a femme fatale or strong man.

auxiliary verb Also known as "helping verb." A verb that is used with the main verb to determine tense or mood. Auxiliary verbs include *be, have, will, do,* and modal verbs (*would, could, can, should, may, might,* etc.).

brainstorm Strategy in essay writing where the writer comes up with ideas for the chosen topic before actually beginning to write the essay.

character Person or entity in a story.

citation Formal reference or acknowledgement of a quotation or idea in a research paper.

clause Sentence (with a subject and verb) that is embedded into another sentence. There are noun, adjective, and adverb clauses.

collocation Group of words that are likely to appear together; words that tend to go together.

colon A punctuation mark (:) that introduces a series, an example, or an explanation.

conjunction A word that joins other words, phrases, or clauses together (such as *and, or, because*).

connotation Idea that is suggested by the meaning of a word. Often used in the expressions "positive connotation" and "negative connotation."

contraction Short form of a word or combination of words in which the omission of a letter or letters is usually shown by an apostrophe. E.g., *can't* is a contraction of *cannot*.

dash Punctuation mark used in a sentence to show a shift in thought or idea.

deductive reasoning Strategy in argumentation where a general observation or conclusion is expressed first and then specific examples or details are given to support it. The opposite of inductive reasoning.

derivative Word that has been made from another word, usually a different part of speech. E.g., the noun *immunization* is a derivative of the verb *immunize*.

ellipsis Omission of words, phrases, or clauses from the original, shown by three consecutive periods (known as ellipsis points).

fiction Made-up story, rather than one relating events that actually happened.

fragment Incomplete sentence; a group of words lacking a subject or a verb or both.

gerund The *–ing* form of a verb that acts as a noun.

hyphen Punctuation mark used to join words or parts of words to make one unit (as in *co-worker* or *French-Canadian*).

idiom Group of words that has a different meaning, often figurative, than the literal meanings of the individual words. E.g., "it's a piece of cake."

indirect speech Reported speech that is a paraphrase of the speaker's words rather than a direct quotation.

inductive reasoning In argumentation, the practice of drawing a general observation, rule, or conclusion from specific cases of the same type. The opposite of deductive reasoning.

infinitive The base form of a verb, usually preceded by *to*.

in-text citation Acknowledgement in the body of an essay and in abbreviated form of ideas or words taken from another author.

irony Literary technique in which the opposite of what is said is meant or done. Often it is used to create humour or show contradiction.

italics Slanted type style used to emphasize or set certain words apart and to identify titles of books or periodicals.

jargon Specialized language, words, and expressions common to a certain trade or profession. Often used negatively to mean language that is incomprehensible to most people.

logical fallacy Flawed reasoning. Error made in structuring an argument.

metaphor Comparison, drawing on similar qualities in unlike things, but without the use of the words *like* or *as*.

MLA style Modern Languages Association style used for citation and bibliographies; style typically used in English courses.

modal verb Type of helping verb that comes before the main verb and shows such ideas as possibility, permission, and polite requests (*may, might, can, could, should, would,* etc.).

non-fiction Type of writing that reports real or actual events in the form of essays, personal narratives, opinion pieces, or biographies. (See also **fiction**.)

parallel structure A kind of sentence structure in which words or phrases with parallel ideas have the same grammatical form. For example, elements joined by a coordinating conjunction (such as *and* or *or*) must be the same part of speech or be in the same grammatical form.

paraphrase Restate someone else's ideas in one's own words.

participle Two forms of a verb that are used in certain tenses and as adjectives. The past participle ends in *–ed* (in regular verbs) and is used in the perfect tenses and the passive voice. The present participle ends in *–ing* and is used as an adjective and in the continuous tenses. (See also **gerund**.)

passive voice Form of the verb where the subject is the receiver of the action rather than the doer. E.g., "The thief was arrested." The opposite of **active voice**.

plagiarism The use of someone else's words or ideas in an essay without acknowledgement; plagiarism is a form of academic dishonesty.

plot The story line in literature—what happens in the story.

possessive Ownership, usually shown by an apostrophe and *s*, or a possessive pronoun (*my, mine, his*, etc.).

predicate One of the required parts of a sentence. It completes the idea by saying something about the grammatical subject. The minimum that a predicate can have is a verb.

prefix Letter or group of letters attached to the beginning of a word to change its meaning and make a new word (e.g., *dys-* in *dysfunctional*).

primary source In literary analysis, the poem, play, novel, or short story that is being analysed. See also **secondary source**.

proper noun Noun that is the name of a person, place, or thing and is therefore capitalized.

protagonist In literary works, the main character, the one who carries the action and events to its conclusion. More commonly called the hero or heroine.

run-on sentence Ungrammatical sentence in which two (or more) sentences have been joined together incorrectly.

satire Literary device in which the subject is mocked either to create humour or to point out something that needs to be corrected.

secondary source Explanation or evaluation of a literary work (the primary source) by someone other than the author of the primary source. Secondary sources can be the notes or introduction to the work or can be an independent text.

semicolon A punctuation mark (;) used mainly to join two independent clauses and to separate items in a list when the items contain commas.

setting The time and place in which a story takes place.

simile Comparison using *like* or *as*. (See also **metaphor**.)

sonnet Poetic form with fourteen lines, a specific rhyme scheme, and a rhythm of iambic pentameter. The two common kinds are Petrarchan and Shakespearean.

stereotype In literature, a character that is not individualistic and developed but that represents an oversimplified idea of some typical kind of person.

subject Noun, pronoun, noun phrase, or noun clause that, along with the verb, is required in a sentence.

suffix Group of letters that is attached to the end of a word to make a new word, usually one that is a different part of speech.

summary Shortened version of a text that gives the main ideas in paraphrase.

symbolism In literature, the use of something, usually concrete, to represent an abstract quality idea. E.g., new growth in spring can symbolize rebirth.

synonym A word that has a very similar meaning to another word.

theme Subject matter of a literary work; the idea that is played out by the characters and the plot.

transition signal Word, phrase, or clause that tells the reader that there is a shift in topic or idea in a sentence or paragraph (e.g., *in addition, for example, in contrast*).

transitive verb Verb that takes a direct object.

uncountable noun Word that has no plural form and cannot be used with words that denote singular or plural such as *a, many,* and *several*. Uncountable nouns include liquids (*milk, water*), objects in fine grains (*salt, sand*), and many abstract nouns (*honesty, courage*).

Index